HEROES
of OLYMPUS

HEROES
of OLYMPUS

By Philip Freeman

Adapted by Laurie Calkhoven

Illustrated by Drew Willis

Simon & Schuster
Books for Young Readers
New York   London   Toronto   Sydney   New Delhi

SIMON & SCHUSTER BOOKS FOR YOUNG READERS
An imprint of Simon & Schuster Children's Publishing Division
1230 Avenue of the Americas, New York, New York 10020

SIMON & SCHUSTER BOOKS FOR YOUNG READERS is a trademark of Simon & Schuster, Inc.
For information about special discounts for bulk purchases, please contact Simon &
Schuster Special Sales at 1-866-506-1949 or business@simonandschuster.com.
The Simon & Schuster Speakers Bureau can bring authors to your live event. For more
information or to book an event, contact the Simon & Schuster Speakers Bureau
at 1-866-248-3049 or visit our website at www.simonspeakers.com.
Also available in a Simon & Schuster Books for Young Readers hardcover edition
Book design by Lizzy Bromley
The text for this book is set in Janson and Yana.
The illustrations for this book are rendered digitally.
Manufactured in the United States of America
First Simon & Schuster Books for Young Readers paperback edition July 2013
0613 MTN
2 4 6 8 10 9 7 5 3 1
The Library of Congress has cataloged the hardcover edition as follows:
Calkhoven, Laurie.
Heroes of Olympus / by Philip Freeman ; adapted by Laurie Calkhoven. – 1st ed.
p. cm.
ISBN 978-1-4424-1729-8 (hardcover)
1. Mythology, Classical–Juvenile literature. I. Freeman, Philip, 1961– Oh my gods.
II. Title.
BL725.C35 2012
398.20938–dc23
2011021078
ISBN 978-1-4424-1730-4 (pbk)
ISBN 978-1-4424-1732-8 (eBook)

Acknowledgments

Many thanks to all who helped this book become a reality, including David Gale, Joëlle Delbourgo, Bob Bender, and Johanna Li. My special thanks to Laurie Calkhoven for her fine adaptation and to Drew Willis for his wonderful illustrations.

Contents

INTRODUCTION..1

CREATION..3

GODS..14

    Zeus..14

    Poseidon..28

    Hades...32

    Apollo..35

    Hephaestus..45

    Ares..46

    Hermes..47

    Pan...50

    Helios..51

    Dionysus..53

    Cupid...59

GODDESSES...65

    Hera..65

Demeter..66

Artemis..71

Aphrodite..73

Hecate..76

Hestia..77

Athena..77

Eos..79

The Muses..80

The Fates..81

Cybele..82

HEROES..84

Perseus..84

Theseus..90

Daedalus and Icarus..99

Bellerophon..102

Melampus..104

Atalanta...107

Procne and Philomela....................................109

LOVERS...114

Narcissus and Echo.......................................114

Pyramus and Thisbe.......................................117

Ceyx and Alcyone..119

Glaucus and Scylla...121

Hero and Leander..124

Hypermnestra and Lynceus...........................126

Baucis and Philemon.....................................128

Alpheus and Arethusa....................................130

Pomona and Vertumnus.................................132

Endymion and Selene.....................................134

Orpheus and Eurydice....................................135

HERCULES..137

OEDIPUS..164

JASON AND THE ARGONAUTS....................178

TROY..203

MYCENAE...232

ODYSSEUS..243

AENEAS...274

ROME..296

   Romulus and Remus...............................296

   The Horatii Brothers................................300

   One-Eyed Horatius..................................301

   Scaevola...302

   Cloelia...303

   Lucretia..304

GREEK AND ROMAN GODS.....................307

DIRECTORY OF GODS, GODDESSES,
MONSTERS, AND MORTALS......................309

GLOSSARY...326

GENEALOGIES..328

INDEX...330

Introduction

I love stories about ancient gods and heroes. Magical stories set in strange and ancient worlds were my favorite bedtime reading when I was young, and they still are today. What could be better than Zeus wielding his mighty thunderbolt or Hercules slaying monsters?

When we use the word "myth" today, we usually mean a story that isn't true. The ancient Greeks used the word "mythos" to mean anything spoken—tales told by great bards and poets in story and song. The Greek and Roman myths were traditional tales that held important meanings, whether they were true or not.

The Greeks had their own stories, but they were also a people of the wine-dark sea. Everywhere Greek colonists settled, the stories of their gods and heroes flourished. They were quick to adopt new tales, and stories flowed into Greece from places like Asia Minor, the Nile valley, and Mesopotamia. When Phoenician traders introduced their alphabet to the area around the Aegean Sea, the Greeks adapted the symbols to their own language and began to write their stories down.

Sometime around the year 750 BC, a poet named Homer recorded the greatest of all the Greek stories: the story of the Trojan War. Others wrote down other tales as well, and throughout Greece, festivals were devoted to tragedies and comedies about the gods, goddesses, heroes, and monsters of ancient times.

Far to the west, a small village on the banks of the Tiber River in Italy had begun to expand beyond its seven hills. The Romans inherited a rich mythology from their own ancestors, but they added many of the Greek stories and made them their own. As Rome grew and its power extended across the Mediterranean and beyond, the Romans spread the ancient myths throughout their empire.

In this book you'll find modern retellings of all the major Greek and Roman myths. These stories are so full of beauty and magic and disturbing twists that today's readers can still find truths in the ancient tales.

May you never lose your love for old stories.

Creation

In the beginning there was Chaos—a great, bottomless pit in a dark universe. Out of Chaos came the green Earth and the black hole of Tartarus below. Eros, or love, also sprang from Chaos, followed by Erebus, the underworld, and his sister, Night.

The family of Chaos bore untold sons and daughters. Some were children of beauty and hope, but most were of darkness and despair.

Earth gave birth to starry Sky who became her husband. Their twelve children were the first gods and goddesses. The youngest, Cronus, was the most stubborn and clever of them all.

Earth also gave birth to creatures like the violent and brutal Cyclopes with a single eye in the middle of their foreheads. Three of Earth's children were huge monsters with a hundred arms and fifty heads each.

Father Sky hated his children. As soon as they were born, he shoved them into a hole in the ground and would not let them see the light of day. Mother Earth groaned in pain. She missed her children, and she wanted revenge on Father Sky. She made a sharp sickle, a curved knife, out of the hardest rock and showed it to her children.

"Who will dare strike back against Sky?" she asked.

Only the youngest of the gods, Cronus, spoke: "Mother, I will do it. I am not afraid of Sky."

Mother Earth gave her son the sickle with its jagged teeth. When night drew near, and Sky stretched himself across the Earth, Cronus sprang from his hiding place. With a single

swing of the sickle, he slashed Sky's flesh. Blood spattered across Earth.

Spiteful Furies, wicked giants, and nymphs rose from the bloody Earth.

Pieces of Sky sailed through the air and landed in the sea. They floated to the island of Cyprus. The pounding waves created a white foam on the beach. Inside the foam, Aphrodite, the goddess of love, was born.

Now it was Father Sky who groaned in pain. He cursed his children and called them Titans. He swore that one day Cronus would pay for his wicked deed.

Now that Cronus had defeated his father, the young Titan ruled all of heaven and earth. He married his sister, Rhea, and fathered five children. Like their parents, the children were immortal, which means they will never die. There was Hestia, goddess of home and hearth, then Demeter who ripens the fruits of the earth, and Hera, goddess of marriage and women. Rhea also gave birth to mighty Hades, ruler of the underworld, and Poseidon, shaker of the Earth.

Cronus had learned from his parents that he would lose his power to one of his children. When each child was born, he snatched it from Rhea and swallowed it whole.

Rhea suffered from losing her children. She went to her parents, Earth and Sky, and asked how she might punish Cronus. They told her what they had told Cronus: that he would one day lose his throne to a son. They also told Rhea to go to the island of Crete to give birth to her sixth child. Alone in a cave high on a mountain, she gave birth to Zeus. Earth took her grandson away to hide in a secret place.

Cronus arrived and demanded his newborn child. Earth had given Rhea a stone wrapped in cloth. Rhea handed the stone to Cronus. He snatched the bundle and shoved it down his throat. He never suspected that he had been fooled.

As the years passed, Earth raised Zeus on Crete, hidden from the eyes of his father. The boy grew wise and strong. One day he left his hiding place and hatched a plan with Metis, the daughter of Ocean. She offered Cronus a potion for his health. It made him vomit up his children. The children banded together with Zeus and challenged their father in the greatest battle the world will ever see.

For ten long years the younger gods battled their elders. It seemed as if Zeus would never be able to defeat his father. Then Zeus's grandmother, Earth, came to him with wise advice. Cronus and the other Titans were afraid of the Cyclopes and the hundred-armed monsters and had left them imprisoned in Tartarus, which was both a place and the god who ruled this black hole. Earth told her grandson that with the help of the Cyclopes and these three monsters, he might be able to defeat his father.

Zeus sped to Tartarus and brought them all back to Mount Olympus, the home of the gods. He fed them nectar and ambrosia, the food and drink of the gods. Then he spoke to them: "Children of Sky and Earth, for ten long years we have been fighting the Titans. Neither side can win. I call on you to help us, to remember who it was who freed you from the darkness of Tartarus."

One of the hundred-armed monsters, Cottus, answered for all of them: "Son of Cronus, we know that you are wiser than your father and his brothers and sisters. We will fight with you and crush the Titans into dust."

The Cyclopes forged lightning bolts for Zeus and joined the young Olympians in war. They fought until the sky roared, the sea rolled, and the earth quaked. Zeus raged with all his might. He threw lightning bolts down on his enemies from the sky. Forests burst into flame and smoke rose to the heavens. At last, the tide of the battle turned. Cronus and the Titans tried to run, but they were captured and sent down into gloomy Tartarus. There they are guarded by the Cyclopes and will never again see the light of day. Except for Atlas. Zeus punished Atlas for siding with the Titans by forcing him to bear the weight of the heavens on his shoulders.

Just when Zeus thought the war was over, Typhon, son of Tartarus, rose against the young immortals. He was a horrible creature with a hundred snake heads. He bellowed like a bull as he climbed Mount Olympus. The young gods panicked. Zeus took his weapons—thunder and lightning— down to face the creature and struck him again and again. Then Zeus picked up Typhon's broken body and cast him down into Tartarus to live forever with the Titans. He rages there still, bellowing typhoons across the sea.

Zeus was now the leader of the immortals from the shining heights of Mount Olympus. He was careful not to be overthrown like his father and grandfather before him. He took the stone Cronus had swallowed and set it up at the holy valley of Delphi beneath Mount Parnassus, in the center of the earth, as a monument to himself.

Zeus was the most powerful of all the gods, but he knew he

could not rule alone. He gambled with his brothers Poseidon and Hades to divide the world between them. Poseidon won the sea. Hades won the underworld, and Zeus, the sky. Earth and Mount Olympus belonged to all three brothers, but all the gods knew that Zeus was their king.

The king of the gods decided he should marry. Earth and Sky had told Zeus that a son born to Metis would be more powerful than Zeus. So, Zeus chose Metis as his first wife. When she was pregnant, Zeus swallowed her whole. He thought he had seen the last of his bride and her child, but he had a terrible headache. He ordered Prometheus, a nephew of Cronus, to split open his head with an ax. Prometheus did, and out came the goddess Athena. She was the wisest of Zeus's children. Her mother remained trapped inside Zeus as a source of good advice.

Zeus's second wife was Themis, goddess of order and justice. Some say she is the mother of the Fates, the rulers of human destiny. Eurynome, daughter of Ocean, was his next bride. She gave birth to the Graces, goddesses of beauty.

When Zeus married Demeter, he fathered Persephone. Zeus's next wife, Leto, gave birth to Apollo, the god of archery, and Artemis, the goddess of the hunt. Finally, he married his sister Hera and became the father of Hebe, Eileithyia, and Ares, the god of war. Some say Hephaestus was also their son.

The earth below Mount Olympus was beautiful but empty except for wild animals and green plants. The gods looked down from Olympus and saw no one who could worship them. A few tales say it was Zeus who solved the problem, but most say it was clever Prometheus who first had the idea of creating mortals to serve the gods.

Prometheus took clay from the earth and mixed it with water and then shaped it into men. They were formed in the image of gods with two legs so that they would walk upright and gaze at the stars. There were no women.

Prometheus taught men to build houses and to track the movements of the stars across the night sky. He taught them mathematics, arts, medicine, how to work with metals, how to tell the future, and even how to write. He showed them how to grow food and tame wild horses. At last he led them to the shore and taught them how to build ships to sail across the seas.

Men lived at peace with the gods and feasted with them. One day Zeus was invited to join a celebration in a seaside town. At such festivals the gods always chose the best portion of meat, leaving the mortal men skin and bones. Prometheus decided to play a trick on Zeus. He killed an ox for the feast. Then he roasted the animal over the fire and put the best meat inside the ox's ugly stomach. He wrapped the bones in rich, juicy fat and laid both choices on the table.

When Zeus took his seat at the head of the table, he was surprised at how Prometheus had divided the portions. "My good friend, great among the immortals, this doesn't seem a fair choice."

Prometheus smiled. "Zeus, greatest of all the gods, please choose whichever part you desire."

Zeus suspected a trick, but the smell of the rich fat was too much to resist. He chose that portion only to discover that he had chosen a bag of bones. He was furious at Prometheus and at man. He stormed away from the feast and decided to take

back the fire that he had given men to roast their food and keep themselves warm. Prometheus stole fire from heaven and, hiding it in the stalk of a fennel plant, brought it back to men.

Zeus was angrier than ever. He punished Prometheus in a most terrible way. He ordered Power and Strength, sons of the goddess Styx, to take Prometheus to a cliff in the Caucasus Mountains and bind him to a pillar of stone. Then he sent an eagle to tear the god open and eat his liver. Because he was immortal, Prometheus could not die. His liver grew again each night, only to be eaten by the same eagle the next day. Prometheus was chained for eternity on a cold mountain at the end of the world.

Zeus was still angry with men and decided to punish them. He told Hephaestus to mix together clay and water in the shape of a goddess and give her life and speech. Zeus ordered Aphrodite and the Graces to give this new creature, a mortal woman, beauty. He also asked that she be given the pain of heartbreak and the sorrow of love. Athena taught her weaving and all the gods gave her gifts to make her irresistible to men.

Her name was Pandora, which means "bearer of all gifts." Zeus told Hermes to take the woman down to earth and give her to Prometheus's brother, Epimetheus. Epimetheus and all mortal men gazed on her in wonder.

Until that time, men had lived free from care, but Zeus gave Pandora a tightly sealed jar. Unable to resist her curiosity, Pandora opened the jar. Out flew every kind of evil, so that from that day forward the earth was full of pain, sickness, and woe. Pandora slammed the lid back on, but it was too late. Only Hope remained in the jar, unable to escape.

Zeus had given the evils of the world to humanity, but he still believed men and women could live lives of honest labor and worship. One day he left Mount Olympus to walk the earth. Everywhere he went, he saw wickedness. He came upon the kingdom of a savage ruler named Lycaon. Zeus appeared before his palace and asked to spend the night. He showed the people of the town that he was no ordinary traveler and they began to worship him. But Lycaon did not believe a god had come to visit, so he tested Zeus.

Lycaon took a hostage from a nearby kingdom and slit his throat. He roasted the body and served it to Zeus for dinner. Zeus knew what Lycaon had done. He destroyed the palace with lighting bolts and killed all the people inside except for the king. The king's skin turned into shaggy gray hair and his arms turned into legs. Then Lycaon began to howl like the wolf he had become.

Lycaon was the last straw for the king of the gods. Zeus told the gods he was going to destroy the human race. Some of the gods wondered who would worship them, but Zeus promised to create a better race of humans. Then he called down all the waters of the heavens on the earth and ordered Poseidon to raise the ocean waves. The river gods flooded the dry ground. No creature, animal or human, was able to survive the flood.

Zeus looked on the waters covering the earth and spotted a chest floating on the waves. Inside were a man and a woman—Deucalion, son of Prometheus, and his wife Pyrrha, daughter of Pandora. Prometheus had warned his son of the coming flood. For nine days and nights the couple floated on the waters until they came to rest on the peaks of Mount Parnassus above Delphi.

Zeus was furious at first, but he knew that Deucalion and Pyrrha honored the gods and treated strangers with kindness. He ordered the waters to return to the seas. When the couple left their chest, they saw that the world was empty. They made their way to a temple of Themis, goddess of order and justice, and fell to their knees. They begged for help.

Themis took pity on the pair. "Leave here with your heads veiled and your robes undone. As you go, throw behind you the bones of your mother," she said.

Deucalion turned the oracle over and over in his mind. At last he realized that the bones Themis spoke of must be the stones of Mother Earth.

Pyrrha and her husband picked up rocks from around the altar and did as they were told. As soon as the stones hit the ground, they began to grow. The stones thrown by Deucalion took the form of men. Those tossed behind Pyrrha became women. From these stones the entire human race is descended, tough and enduring like the rocks our ancestors sprang from.

Gods

ZEUS

Of all the gods on Mount Olympus, Zeus was the most powerful. He shared some of his power, but he warned his fellow gods not to threaten him: "Learn how much stronger I am than the rest of you immortals. Drop a golden cord from the heavens. Grab the end and all you gods and goddesses pull with all your might. It won't budge me an inch. I am Zeus, the highest and the wisest."

No one challenged Zeus after he defeated the Titans and Typhon. The other gods knew they could not win against him.

Zeus was the god of the sky and the raging thunder. He used lightning bolts against anyone, mortal or immortal, who stepped out of line. He was especially concerned with justice and the care of strangers. No human ever knew if the beggar at his door might be Zeus in disguise.

One mortal who tested Zeus was Salmoneus, a king in western Greece. Salmoneus told his subjects that he was Zeus.

He attached bronze kettles to his chariot and claimed he made thunder when they clattered. He threw torches into the sky and called them lightning bolts. Zeus grew tired of the foolish king and destroyed him and his city in a blaze of real lightning.

Another Greek king named Ixion refused to pay his father-in-law, Eioneus, the promised bride price for his daughter. When Eioneus came to collect the money, Ixion threw him into a burning pit. Everyone was horrified at the murder, but Zeus had a soft spot for the king—and for his beautiful bride. He invited Ixion to come to Mount Olympus. While he was there, Ixion behaved badly. Zeus chained the king to a fiery wheel that revolves forever in the sky.

Zeus's anger didn't just fall on kings. He discovered that the physician Asclepius, a son of Apollo, was using drops of the snake-haired Gorgon's blood to bring people back to life. Zeus could not allow mortals to learn the secret of eternal life and become gods. He killed the physician with a lightning bolt.

Zeus was concerned with justice, but he was often wicked himself. He had created women as a punishment for men, but he fell under their spell too. Zeus fathered numerous children with mortal women. Many of them became heroes of Greek mythology. But mortal women often paid for the god's attentions with punishment from Zeus's wife, Hera. She was the god's chief wife and very jealous of the other women in his life.

One of the first unlucky women to catch Zeus's eye was Io, a priestess at the temple of Hera. Every night he came to Io in a vision and tried to charm her. "Most blessed maiden. I am on fire with love for you and would give anything to enjoy your company. Go out to the wild meadows of the river among

the flocks and cattle of your father. I will come to you."

Io was tormented by these visions. She went to her father
for help, and he sent messengers to the oracles at Delphi and
Dodona to learn what he should do. Their advice was confus-
ing. Finally, Zeus's oracle told Io's father to cast his daughter
out of the house to wander the land. If he did not obey, Zeus
would kill his entire family with a thunderbolt.

Io's father had no choice. It didn't take long for Zeus to
find Io. He surrounded her with a mist and forced himself
upon her. Hera noticed the strange cloud and swept down
from Olympus. Zeus quickly turned Io into a white cow and
claimed he had done nothing wrong. Hera didn't believe him.
She demanded the white cow as a gift, and Zeus agreed.

Hera placed Io under the guard of Argus, a monster with a hundred eyes. Argus tied the cow to an olive tree and watched over her. By this time, Zeus was starting to feel guilty. He sent Hermes, the god of thieves, to steal Io away. Hermes had a difficult time. Some of the monster's eyes were always open and awake. At last the god played a lullaby on his flute until all of Argus's eyes closed. The god then cut off the monster's head so that Io, still in the form of a cow, could escape.

Hera was furious. She placed the hundred eyes of Argus onto the tail of the peacock and set off after Io. She found her wandering and sent a gadfly to sting her until she went mad. Io fled across Greece to the sea—named Ionian after her—then beyond the mountains to Macedonia to escape Hera's fury. She trekked to the waters that separated Europe from Asia and swam across them. At last she came to the Caucasus Mountains near the end of the earth. There she found Prometheus chained to a rock.

Io begged Prometheus for news about how long she would have to suffer. In between having his liver eaten by Zeus's eagle, Prometheus told Io of her fate. She had far to go, over mountains and across deserts. She would narrowly avoid the Graeae, three gray-haired hags who lived in darkness and shared one eye and one tooth between them. She would also find their sisters, the snake-haired Gorgons, at the ends of the earth. But at last she would find rest in Egypt.

Prometheus also told Io that she would be the ancestor of a man who would at last free Prometheus from his chains, and that Zeus would be defeated by one of his own sons. The only one who could save Zeus from this was Prometheus, and he had no plans to help.

Io took heart from the punishment that would one day fall on the head of Zeus. She roamed Europe, Asia, and Africa until she collapsed on the banks of the Nile River in Egypt. Zeus found her there and made her pregnant with a touch of his finger. Then he restored Io to human form. Io gave birth to a son she named Epaphus, meaning, "touched by the god."

Hera was still watching. She sent spirits to kidnap the baby and take him to Syria. Io found him there and returned with him to Egypt. She married an Egyptian king and finally settled down to a peaceful life.

It is said that Io brought the worship of Demeter to the Egyptians, who called the Greek goddess of grain Isis. She was worshiped in the form of a woman with the horns of a cow in memory of Io's struggles.

One of Io's great-great-great-granddaughters, Europa, was a princess in Lebanon. She was troubled by dreams just like Io. In a vision she saw two women fighting over her. One was a woman of her own country. The other was from across the sea. The foreigner was trying to steal Europa away and said she was sent by Zeus.

When Europa woke, she went to her friends to ease her mind. They ran to a seaside meadow and chased each other across the grass and gathered flowers.

Europa was every bit as beautiful as Io had been and Zeus's heart was overcome with desire. He transformed himself into a handsome white bull and flew down to the seashore. He walked toward the young women as gentle as a lamb. They had never seen such a lovely animal. The bull inched toward the girls and stood before Europa. He licked her neck. Europa

laughed and kissed the bull's cheek. The bull knelt before her
and urged her with its eyes to mount its back.

   The other maidens were frightened, but Europa climbed
onto the bull. Suddenly the animal began to move toward the
sea. Before Europa could jump off, the bull charged into the
waves. He swam until the shore of Europa's homeland was far
behind. Dolphins swam at their sides like wedding guests as

the bull made its way toward Crete, the island where Zeus had been raised as a child.

"Who are you?" Europa cried.

"I am Zeus, king of the gods, and I can take any form I wish," the bull bellowed.

The girl was too frightened to say anything more. She clung to the bull's horns until they made their way to land. Zeus took on human form and forced himself upon Europa. Then he left her, alone and pregnant, in a foreign land. But he did give her three gifts. The first was a hound that always caught its prey. The second was a spear that never missed its mark, and the third was a giant bronze man who ran around the island throwing rocks at any ship that tried to land. In time, Europa had three sons by Zeus. The king of Crete then married Europa and raised her sons as his own.

Europa's father, Agenor, was heartbroken when his daughter disappeared. He sent his wife and his three sons to search for her in every land and warned them not to come home without her. After endless searching, the brothers settled down to found their own kingdoms. One brother, Cadmus, took his mother all the way to Greece and founded the city of Thebes on a new continent. It was named Europe, after his lost sister.

Zeus's favorite place on earth was Arcadia, a rich land of forests, springs, and mountains in southern Greece. One day Zeus saw a young woman hunting in the woods there. She carried a spear and had a bow and arrows slung over her shoulder. She was Callisto, a virgin dedicated to Artemis, the goddess of the hunt.

Zeus watched Callisto remove her weapons and lie down in the soft grass. He couldn't resist such a beautiful young woman. "Hera will never see me in these thick woods," Zeus said to himself. He took on the form of Artemis and approached Callisto.

The maiden ran to the goddess.

"Callisto, loveliest of all my maidens," Zeus said in his Artemis disguise, "where have you been hunting?"

"Here in these woods, my lady, greatest of all the gods," Callisto said. "I would call you that even if Zeus were here to hear my words."

Zeus laughed and kissed her. Before Callisto knew it, Artemis had become Zeus. Callisto was no match for the god. He forced himself on her and then he left. The young woman struggled to her feet and wandered away in shock, barely remembering to take her weapons.

A few days later, the true Artemis and her band of virgin hunters appeared and called to Callisto to join them. The young woman obeyed, but followed Artemis with downcast eyes. Artemis saw Callisto's sadness, but didn't know the cause. Nine months came and went. One hot day Artemis and her maidens came to a pool in the woods. They undressed to swim in the cool water. Callisto made excuses not to join them, but Artemis insisted. When Callisto removed her robelike garment, Artemis saw that she was pregnant.

"Get out of here," the goddess demanded. "You are no longer one of my followers."

Callisto ran away in disgrace and gave birth alone to a son she named Arcas.

Hera saw this and realized what had happened. She

couldn't take out her anger on Zeus, and so she went after Callisto.

"Did you really think you could get away with this?" Hera asked her. "You think you're so pretty, do you?"

Hera caught Callisto by the hair and threw her to the ground. Callisto stretched out her arms to beg for mercy, but they were already covered with black, shaggy fur. Her fingers were replaced with claws, and her face with rough jaws and a large nose. Hera replaced Callisto's voice with a low growl so that she could not call on Zeus for help. Callisto's human mind was unchanged, but her body had become a bear.

Callisto left her son to be raised by the local king. She wandered the mountains and forests in misery, always fearful of hunters. One day Arcas, who was now a man, was hunting in the forest with his friends. They saw a bear watching them. It moved toward Arcas as if to speak. Arcas was about to plunge a spear into his mother's breast when Zeus snatched Callisto up into the heavens. He made her a constellation of stars.

That was too much for Hera. She asked Tethys, goddess of the sea, and her husband, Ocean, for a favor. "Grant me that she may not bathe in your waters. Let her forever circle the sky without rest."

Tethys and Ocean granted her request. To this day Callisto revolves around the North Star. The great bear never vanishes below the horizon.

After Europa's brother Cadmus founded the city of Thebes, rule of the town passed in time to a Greek named Nycteus. He had a beautiful daughter named Antiope. Antiope caught Zeus's eye as he looked down from the heavens. He came to her in the form of a satyr, a half-man, half-goat creature, and left her pregnant. When Nycteus found out his daughter Antiope was pregnant, he was furious. She fled to the city of Sicyon where she married the king.

Nycteus learned of Antiope's marriage and was angrier than ever. He made his brother Lycus promise to punish Antiope and her king for disgracing the family. Then Nycteus killed himself. Lycus marched on Sicyon and destroyed the city. He killed the king and dragged Antiope out of the town in chains.

Antiope was nine months pregnant. She struggled to walk the rough roads back to Thebes with the army. On the slopes of Mount Cithaeron, she crawled into the bushes to give birth. Lycus left her twin sons, Amphion and Zethus, to die on the mountainside. The army marched on, with Antiope chained behind them. A local shepherd found the babies and raised them secretly as his own sons.

Lycus's wife Dirce punished Antiope every day for many years. Every night, she chained her in a filthy hut.

Meanwhile, Amphion and Zethus grew into fine young men, unaware of who they were or their mother's fate. Zethus became a master herdsman and cattle breeder. Amphion excelled at playing the lyre. The brothers were opposites, but they were devoted to each other.

One night, the chains holding Antiope in her hut mysteriously fell away, perhaps by the power of Zeus. Antiope ran as fast as she could out of Thebes and into the forest below Mount Cithaeron. She found a shepherd's hut and knocked on the door. Two young men answered and invited the poor woman inside to sit by the fireplace. They gave her food and drink and asked how she came to be in such a miserable state. Antiope told the young men her sad story and her sorrow at being forced to abandon her children near the very spot where they sat.

The young men realized they were the sons she spoke of. It was a happy reunion, but Zethus and Amphion wanted revenge. They attacked the city of Thebes, killing the king who had been so cruel to their mother and taking his throne. They tied Dirce to the horns of a bull and dragged her through the streets until she was dead.

The brothers ruled Thebes in peace and harmony. Together they strengthened the city walls. Zethus used his great strength to carry enormous stones. Amphion played his lyre and charmed the stones of the earth to follow him to the walls of Thebes.

Near Sicyon, there is a river that runs from the mountains to the blue waters of the Corinthian Gulf. The god of this river was named Asopus and he had a beautiful daughter named Aegina. Zeus fell in love with her and came to her one night in the form of a flame. Then he carried her to an island near Athens where she gave birth to a son named Aeacus.

Asopus searched everywhere for his daughter. As last he came to Sisyphus, king of Corinth, who said that it was Zeus who had stolen Aegina away. In thanks, Asopus created a stream of fresh water for Sisyphus on the top of a dry fortress overlooking his city. The river god then set out to take back his daughter, but Zeus wounded him with a thunderbolt and he was forced to return home without Aegina.

Zeus punished Sisyphus for betraying his secret. He sent

Sisyphus to Hades to forever roll a boulder up a hill, only to have it roll down again when it reached the top.

Hera was furious at the latest woman to catch her husband's fancy. This time, instead of changing the girl into an animal, she poisoned the water of Aegina's island and killed her. Her son Aeacus named the island after his mother. When he grew to manhood and became king of Aegina, Hera struck again. She killed everyone on the island with a horrible plague except for Aeacus and his son, Telamon.

King Aeacus prayed beneath an oak tree to his father, Zeus. Zeus sent a flash of lightning across the sky with a peal of thunder. Aeacus then saw a column of ants carrying grain, and he prayed again to Zeus: "O most excellent father, grant me as many subjects as there are ants here beneath your sacred oak tree." The branches of the tree swayed even though there was no wind. Aeacus shivered and continued to wait. At last he fell asleep. He dreamed that the ants grew in size and took on human form. When he awoke he found his island full of men and women working to build homes and farms.

Aeacus became known throughout Greece for his fairness. Kings came to him to be judged and cities asked him to help them appeal to Zeus to restore fertility to their lands. After a long life, Zeus appointed him guardian of Hades, where he kept the keys to the kingdom of the dead.

Atlas, one of the Titans, had seven daughters known as the Pleiades. One of them, Electra, lived on the island of Samothrace. Zeus saw her there and took her to Mount Olympus. Electra clung to the Palladium, a sacred statue of Athena next to Zeus's throne, for safety, but Zeus only cast the statue out of Olympus. He forced himself on Electra and then returned her to Samothrace. She gave birth to twin sons, Iasion and Dardanus. Some say that Iasion become a god. Dardanus became the ancestor of the Trojans.

Electra's sister, Taygete, was a nymph living in the mountains to the west of Sparta. Like Callisto, she was devoted to Artemis. Zeus fell in love with Taygete, but Artemis tried to protect her. She turned the nymph into a doe. Zeus wasn't fooled. He found Taygete and fathered a son by her named Lacedaemon, who became the ancestor of the Spartans.

Taygete was still grateful to Artemis. She dedicated a doe with golden horns to the goddess. Hercules searched for the sacred deer in one of his labors.

Zeus placed all seven daughters of Atlas in the sky as the constellation called the Pleiades. Except for the sharpest eyes on the darkest nights, only six stars are visible. Some say that the seventh star, Electra, covered herself in mourning when the city of Troy fell to Sparta.

As the years went by, the descendants of Taygete's son Lacedaemon grew into the powerful kingdom of the Spartans. A son of this royal house named Tyndareus was driven from his home. He traveled to Aetolia near Mount Parnassus and married a beautiful princess named Leda. Then he returned to Sparta with Leda as his queen.

Zeus was taken with Leda's beauty. Hoping that Hera wouldn't notice, he went to Leda one night in the form of a swan and left her pregnant. That same night, Tyndareus shared his wife's bed. Some stories say that Leda then laid two eggs. From one came twins fathered by Zeus, Helen and Pollux. From the other came Clytemnestra and Castor, fathered by Leda's mortal husband.

Castor and Pollux grew into brave men who one day would sail with Jason on the *Argo*. They rescued their sister Helen from King Theseus of Athens long before Paris stole her away to begin the Trojan War. When Castor was killed in a cattle raid, his immortal brother Pollux prayed to Zeus that he might give up half his immortality so that he and Castor could spend alternate days on Olympus and in Hades. In time Zeus made them into the stars that became the twins of the constellation Gemini.

Zeus also fell in love with a young Trojan prince named Ganymede. Ganymede was watching over his flocks on Mount Ida near Troy when Zeus first saw him. Most stories agree that Zeus came down from Olympus in a whirlwind and snatched the boy. Other stories say that the god sent an eagle to grab Ganymede, or that the eagle was Zeus himself.

Ganymede's father, Tros, searched everywhere for his son. Zeus took pity on the father and sent Hermes to Troy to comfort him. Hermes told Tros that he should be happy because Ganymede was now cupbearer to the king of the gods. He would live forever in the halls of Olympus. Zeus gave Tros a pair of the finest horses and a golden grapevine crafted by the god Hephaestus. Tros took comfort in these words and gifts, glad that his son had found such favor with Zeus.

POSEIDON

Poseidon was best known as the god of the wine-dark sea. He also ruled over earthquakes and stallions racing across the plains. An ancient hymn told his story:

> I first sing of the great god Poseidon, shaker of the earth and lord of the deep. The gods gave you two privileges—to be tamer of horses and savior of ships. Hail to you, Poseidon, dark-haired rider of the earth. Be gentle in your heart and protect those who sail the seas.

The ancient Greeks prayed for Poseidon's mercy. As a people of the sea, they knew that a peaceful voyage could suddenly turn deadly. The god who shook the land and whose horses thundered over the fields could also calm the waves and let them live another day.

Poseidon himself cared little for the problems of men. He lived in the depths of the sea, and rose to the surface only to create terrible storms or to turn cities into ruins.

Poseidon was jealous of his little brother, Zeus. In one of the rare uprisings against Zeus, Poseidon joined Hera and Athena and tried to overthrow his brother. The goddess Thetis called upon a hundred-armed creature from Tartarus called Briareus to end the revolt. Some said Briareus was Poseidon's own son, but he stopped the sea god and Zeus remained king.

After Zeus divided the world and Poseidon won control of the sea, Poseidon fought with other gods to be patron, or ruler and protector, of the most important Greek cities.

First there was Corinth, where Poseidon had a contest with the sun god Helios for control of the town. Briareus was again called upon. He gave Poseidon the isthmus and nearby lands, but to Helios he gave the heights of the city.

Next the sea god fought with Hera to rule Argos. Three river gods—Inachus, Cephisus, and Asterion—were called in to judge. They awarded the town to Hera. Poseidon was so angry that he dried up all three rivers.

The most famous story was of the contest between Poseidon and Athena to see who would be in charge of Athens. Zeus told the city's king, a man who had the tail of a snake and was named Cecrops, to judge the contest. To prove his powers to the king, Poseidon struck his trident on the top of the rocky Acropolis above the town and created a spring of salt water. Athena made an olive tree grow from the hill, bringing a new food to the city. Cecrops decided that olives were more useful than seawater, and Athena won. Poseidon was furious and flooded the countryside for revenge.

Poseidon was married to Amphitrite, the daughter of Ocean and Tethys. At first, she wanted nothing to do with the god of the wine-dark sea. She fled to the Titan Atlas to hide. Poseidon sent spies to find her. At last, one of them named Delphinus came upon Amphitrite on an island and convinced her to marry Poseidon. Poseidon was so grateful that he placed Delphinus among the stars as a constellation shaped like a dolphin.

After he married, Poseidon—like his brother Zeus—pursued other goddesses and mortal women. The goddess Demeter changed herself into a mare and hid in a herd of horses to escape him, but Poseidon turned himself into a stallion. Demeter was no match for the sea god. She gave birth to two children. The first was a daughter named Despoina. The second was a famous stallion called Arion.

Poseidon also forced himself on Medusa when she was a young maiden instead of a monstrous Gorgon. The story says that Medusa was the most beautiful girl in the world and had many human suitors. Poseidon came to the girl as she worshipped at the temple of Athena and forced himself upon her. Athena, who had always been jealous of Medusa's beauty, blamed the girl. She turned Medusa's flowing hair into snakes so horrible that they turned anyone who looked at them into stone.

Like Medusa, the beautiful virgin Theophrane had many suitors. Poseidon kidnapped the girl and took her to an island. The suitors tried to rescue her. To confuse them, Poseidon changed Theophrane into an ewe and the rest of the people on the island into goats. The suitors searched the island, but found only goats. They began to kill the animals for food. Poseidon turned them into wolves, and the bloodshed continued. Then Poseidon changed himself into a ram and made Theophrane pregnant. She gave birth to a ram with a golden fleece. Many years later, Jason and the Argonauts would search for the remarkable ram.

One of Poseidon's granddaughters, Iphimedia, was in love with the sea god. She would often sit on the shore and cup the waters in her hands, then pour them into her lap. Poseidon must have been surprised to find a woman who was actually in love with him. Iphimedia bore him two sons who were also his great-grandchildren. Otus and Ephialtes were powerful and handsome. By the time they were nine years old, they were more than fifty feet tall. They ripped mountains from their roots and piled them on top of one another to build a tower to the heavens and attack the gods. They captured Ares, one of Zeus's sons, and stuffed him into a bronze jar.

If the giants had been full-grown, they might have conquered heaven and earth, but the gods used tricks to defeat the boys. The boys were great hunters, so Apollo sent a deer between them. Otus and Ephialtes threw their spears at the same instant and struck each other dead. Zeus punished them in Hades by binding the brothers back to back with snakes. They spent eternity facing away from each other, watched over by an owl.

Zeus never forgot that Poseidon had once joined Hera and Athena in rebelling against him. As punishment, he sent his brother to Troy to serve King Laomedon along with Apollo. The two gods were disguised as mortals, and Laomedon put them to work. Poseidon directed the building of Troy's walls, while Apollo herded the city's cattle.

At the end of a year, Laomedon sent the gods away without pay and threatened to cut off their ears. Apollo sent a plague to destroy the city while Poseidon sent a sea monster to snatch Trojans off the beach. Laomedon agreed to sacrifice his own daughter to satisfy the monster. Hercules rescued the girl and slew the sea monster just in time. Then Laomedon refused to give Hercules his reward—Laomedon's daughter for his wife. So Hercules killed the king and took the girl.

Poseidon swore that one day the walls of Troy would fall.

HADES

The Greeks feared Hades even more than Zeus and Poseidon. They tried never to say his name out loud and draw his attention. They called him "the god below," or "the invisible one." Mortals were frightened of him and of the end of life.

Prayers did not move him. All mortals, good and bad, eventually went down to the house of the dead where Hades ruled.

There are few myths about Hades. Almost all we know about him comes from descriptions of the home that shared his name. It is a dark place of endless sighs and hopeless, hazy

existence. Hades ruled this land, while Death lived there along with his brother Sleep.

Every soul that died was led by Hermes, or sometimes by Hades, to the banks of the River Styx. Souls that had not been buried properly had to stay on the far side of the river for at least a hundred years. Others were ferried across the river by the boatman Charon. Greeks were buried with a coin on their mouths to pay Charon, who charged the dead for their passage. On the other side of the Styx the souls were greeted by the three-headed dog Cerberus, wagging his tail.

The worst of the dead were condemned to torture. A rare few were allowed into the delightful fields of Elysium. Most were left to wander the plains of the underworld for eternity.

Some Greeks believed a soul might be reborn into a new life, or a higher existence in the world of the gods.

A young man named Er died in a war and lay on the battle-field for ten days. His family placed his body on a funeral pyre to be burned. Just before the fire was set, Er rose up, alive.

Er said he returned to tell what happened after death. He said that after he had died, he joined many souls in another world. At a place of judgment, he found four doors. Two lead to and from heaven. The other two lead to and from the underworld. After the judges ruled on their lives, the dead were led to the entrance to heaven or to the land beneath the earth.

At the same time, souls were leaving heaven and the under-world after a journey of a thousand years. Those who had been to heaven had been rewarded for the good they had done in their previous lives. Those who emerged from the underworld told of terrible punishment.

After the souls leaving heaven and the underworld rested on a plain for seven days, they continued to a shining column. This column held together the cosmos. Sirens created the music of the spheres and the Fates spun the lives of those who would be reborn. The gods allowed the souls to choose their own destinies.

One soul wanted to be a powerful king. Others chose the life of animals. Some who were men wanted to be women, and some who were women wanted to be men. The last soul to choose, the hero Odysseus, found the life he wanted in the form of a simple, private man.

When all the souls had chosen, they drank from the River Lethe to forget their past lives. At midnight, there was a great clap of thunder and an earthquake. The souls shot up into the sky like stars and were reborn to their lives. Er awoke on his funeral pyre, ready to tell his tale to all who would listen.

APOLLO

The goddess Leto, daughter of the Titans Coeus and Phoebe, became pregnant by Zeus. Leto wandered the world looking for a quiet place to give birth. Jealous Hera sent a dragon named Python after her, so Leto left the mainland and searched for an island. Then Hera warned all the islands against allowing Leto on their shores, so none welcomed her.

At last, in great misery, Leto came to the island of Delos in the Aegean Sea. Delos was small and barren. It floated about on the waves from place to place, unfixed to the seafloor below.

"Delos, if you would consent to be the birthplace of my children, my son will build a great temple here. Your soil will blossom with the fruits of the earth," Leto said.

Delos replied: "Leto, I would be honored to host you. No one ever comes to my shores. Will you swear that your son will build his temple here?"

Leto swore by the River Styx, the unbreakable vow of the gods, that all would come to pass as she had promised.

Leto was in labor for nine days and nights, attended by many goddesses. Hera stayed on Mount Olympus and kept Eileithyia, the goddess who brought comfort to women in childbirth, at her side. Finally, Iris, the goddess of the rainbow, brought Eileithyia to Delos secretly. The goddess eased Leto's pain, and Leto gave birth to Apollo. The goddesses cried with joy and bathed the child in the purest water. Then, Leto gave birth to Apollo's sister Artemis.

Leto's troubles were not over. Hera chased her and the newborn babies across the sea to Lycia and then to the mountains near Delphi. A giant named Tityus attacked her, and Leto called on her young children to save her. Apollo and Artemis slaughtered the giant.

Apollo was the god of music, medicine, archery, and prophecy. When he was only four days old, he began to look for a place to build an oracle, the temple where the mortals who worshipped him could come for his advice. Beneath Mount

Parnassus at the site of Delphi, Apollo built his oracle, taking over the temple of Themis and his uncle Poseidon.

The dragon Python tried to stop Apollo, but the god of archers was eager to kill the beast that had once threatened his mother. He pierced him with a mighty arrow and killed him. Young Apollo took on the title, Pythian, after the dragon he had slain.

When the temple was finished, Apollo had no priests to serve him. Gazing out to sea from the cliffs of Delphi, he spotted a merchant ship and flew down to it. Apollo turned himself into a dolphin and jumped onto the deck. Suddenly, the ship began to sail against the wind until it reached port. Apollo changed back into his true from and bought the sailors to his temple to be his priests. He also chose a young woman to be the first Pythia, the priestess who would reveal his words to mortals.

He also built a temple on Delos, as Leto had promised.

Apollo often defended his mother. When Niobe, daughter of the king of Lydia, married Amphion of Thebes, the couple had seven handsome sons and seven beautiful daughters. Niobe refused to worship Leto as a goddess: "I too have divine blood in my veins. Aren't I as beautiful as any goddess? And most of all, why should I worship Leto, mother of only two children, when I have seven times that many?"

Leto heard Niobe's words and was very angry. She called Apollo and Artemis to her side and began to tell them of Niobe's insults.

"Stop, Mother," said Apollo. "To continue would only delay her punishment."

Apollo and his sister flew to Thebes, where the sons of Niobe were riding fine horses. Suddenly the eldest fell down dead, then the second, then the third. At last all seven lay on the ground, struck by Apollo's arrows.

When their father heard the news, he plunged his own knife into his heart. Niobe threw herself onto the bodies of her sons and shouted out to heaven: "Feed yourself on your revenge, Leto. Fill your bloodthirsty heart! I have lost my sevens sons, but I still have seven daughters. After so many deaths, I still win!"

The daughters, who stood weeping above the bodies of their brothers, began to fall to Apollo's arrows. Finally only the youngest clung to her mother's knees. Niobe cried out to Leto: "Please, great goddess, leave me the youngest. Spare me just one, I beg you."

As soon as these words left her lips, her youngest daughter fell down dead. Niobe collapsed in grief. A whirlwind caught her up and carried her across the sea and back to Lydia. There on a mountaintop she sits, a weeping woman of marble, mourning for her children.

Apollo was also unforgiving when his own honor was insulted. As the god of music, he was proud of his skill. One day the satyr Marsyas was watching over his flocks when he found a flute that had been cast aside and cursed by Athena. He was enchanted by the sounds it made. He practiced and became so good that he challenged Apollo to a contest. Apollo accepted and asked King Midas of Phrygia to be the judge.

Marsyas and Apollo both played beautifully. The satyr was a better musician than the god and matched every trick that Apollo came up with. At last, Apollo turned his flute upside down and played just as well—a skill that Marsyas could not match. As soon as Apollo was judged the winner, he hung the satyr from a tall pine tree and stripped the skin from his body. No one ever again challenged Apollo to a contest of musical skill.

Apollo did not forget that King Midas favored Marsyas until the end of the contest. He gave Midas the ears of an ass. The king was so ashamed that he always wore a cap. Only his barber knew his secret. The strain of keeping such a secret was too much. The barber dug a hole in the earth, whispered the news into it, and covered the hole again. When spring came, reeds grew from the hole. When anyone passed by, the wind blowing though the reeds gave voice to the secret. Soon everyone knew what Apollo had done.

For a handsome young god, Apollo was often unlucky in love. The nymph Daphne, daughter of a river god, was his first romantic failure. It started when Apollo told Cupid that he should leave the bows and arrows to him.

"My arrows may not be able to pierce everything," Cupid answered, "but they can pierce you."

Cupid then flew down to Arcadia where he spied the beautiful maiden Daphne. He shot her with a special arrow to make her turn away from love. From that moment, Daphne wanted nothing to do with men. She was courted by many suitors.

"Father, dearest, please let me remain a virgin all my life," Daphne pleaded.

Daphne's father said she would never have to marry. Then

Cupid flew to Olympus and shot Apollo with an arrow that made him fall madly in love with Daphne. Nothing Apollo did could win her heart. Finally he came to her in the hills of Arcadia and tried one last time to speak with her. She fled, but Apollo cried out for her to wait and listen to him. Daphne only ran faster.

"Father, help!" she cried. "Let your waters change this beauty of mine into something the god will despise."

In an instant her limbs became numb and her skin began to harden. Her hair sprouted green leaves and her arms turned into branches.

The legs that had run so fast became fixed in the earth and her head became the top of a laurel tree.

Apollo loved Daphne even in this new form. He pressed his lips to her bark and wept. "You will

always be my love. My hair will forevermore be entwined with your laurel."

The god plucked a sprig from her boughs and wove it into a crown that he placed on his head. The tree seemed to agree to this honor and nodded in the breeze.

Another of Apollo's early loves rejected his advances. Sibyl was a young prophetess. Apollo offered her anything she might wish.

Sibyl laughed and pointed to a heap of sand. "Grant me then that I might have as many years of life as there are grains of sand in that pile."

Apollo said the gift was hers even if she did not agree to be his lover. Then he offered her immortality if she would be his. Sibyl saw little need to live forever when she had so many years stretching before her, so she refused.

But Sibyl had forgotten to ask for eternal youth to go along with her long life. She had a thousand years to grow old. Her hair and teeth fell out, her limbs shriveled, and she shrank to the size of a speck. Toward the end of her life she lived in a bottle hanging from the ceiling of her shrine, wanting nothing more than to die.

Apollo's other romantic attempts were just as disappointing. A young woman named Marpessa chose a mortal man named Idas over the god. Apollo wanted to kill the mortal, but Zeus intervened and granted Marpessa the right to choose Idas. A maiden named Sinope tricked Apollo into granting her any request. When Apollo agreed, she asked to remain a virgin all her life. The last maiden to catch Apollo's eye was Cassandra, the daughter of King Priam of Troy. Apollo taught her the art of prophecy, but once Cassandra learned to foresee the future, she rejected Apollo. In revenge, Apollo made sure that no one would believe any prediction she made. Cassandra paid a terrible price for rejecting Apollo's love.

The god was just as unlucky with men. Apollo fell in love with the handsome young man named Hyacinth. The god and the boy spent every day in the woods and fields around Sparta, hunting and playing sports. One day they had a discus-throwing contest. Apollo threw the iron disk so hard it soared through the clouds. Zephyrus, the west wind, was also in love with Hyacinth and jealous of Apollo. As the discus sailed back to earth, Zephyrus directed it toward Hyacinth, crushing his skull. Hyacinth died. Then Apollo made a beautiful flower spring from the drops of blood on the grass. From that day forth the flowering hyacinth was a tribute to Apollo's lost friend.

Another young man named Cyparissus was also lost to Apollo. Cyparissus loved a sacred stag. He led it to water and made sure it had the finest grass to eat. One hot summer day the deer lay down to rest in the cool forest while Cyparissus was out hunting. The boy had no idea when he threw his spear that the stag was nearby. The weapon pierced the animal's heart and it died in the boy's arms. Apollo tried to comfort him, but Cyparissus asked that he might be allowed to be sad forever. Apollo granted his wish and turned him into a cypress tree with dark limbs and drooping branches, forever mourning for his lost friend.

Apollo was usually kind to the objects of his love, but he could be brutal and violent, too. When Princess Creusa refused him, he dragged her to a cave and forced himself upon her. The young woman hid her pregnancy and bore a child, named Ion, in secret. She brought the baby in a cradle to the deserted cave and left him there to die.

Apollo sent Hermes to bring the infant to his shrine at Delphi. Ion grew up in Apollo's temple, not knowing who his parents were. Creusa meanwhile married a man named Xuthus who became king of Athens, but they were childless.

One day Creusa came to Delphi to discover if she would have another child. She met Ion, now a young man, and the two were drawn to each other. She told Ion that, years before, a friend of hers had left her baby to die. She wanted to ask the oracle about the child, but was afraid.

Xuthus also came to Delphi to ask if he would ever be a father. The Pythia told him that the first person he met as he left the temple would be his son. As soon as he stepped out of the door, Xuthus saw Ion and convinced him to return to Athens as his heir. Creusa suspected a trick and decided to poison Ion with a drop of Gorgon's blood, but Apollo stepped in and saved the boy.

Ion accused Creusa of attempted murder, and she fled to Apollo's sacred temple. The Pythia entered carrying the very cradle in which Creusa had abandoned her son. She confessed that she had left her child to die in that cradle, and Ion realized that Creusa was his mother.

Mother and son happily returned to Athens. Ion became the ancestor of the Ionian tribe of the Greeks.

There was no happy ending for a young maiden named Chione when both Apollo and Hermes fell in love with her. She had just turned fourteen, the age when Greek girls married. Hermes put her to sleep with a magic spell and forced himself upon her. That very night, Apollo disguised himself as an old woman to gain her trust, and then did the same. The young woman became pregnant with the sons of two gods. Hermes's son was named Autolycus. He became a thief and the father of Odysseus. Apollo was the father of her son Philammon, a famous musician.

Chione began to boast of her good fortune in being the mother of the sons of two gods. She even mocked Artemis, saying that she must be more beautiful than the goddess. Artemis shot an arrow through her head, piercing her tongue and killing Chione instantly. When her father came to look for her, he found Chione's body burning on a funeral pyre. He ran to the top of Mount Parnassus and threw himself off the summit. Apollo, in an act of mercy, changed him into a hawk to soar among the clouds.

HEPHAESTUS

No one was sure where Hephaestus, the god of the forge, came from. Some say he was a child of Zeus and Hera. Others that he was born of Hera alone. The rest of the gods at Mount Olympus laughed at him because he was crippled. But Hephaestus was respected for his magical ability to bend metal into any shape he chose. When the other gods needed a new shield or sword, Hephaestus was the one they turned to.

Some stories say that when Hera saw that her baby, Hephaestus, was lame, she threw him from Mount Olympus in disgust. The goddesses Thetis and Eurynome rescued the child and raised him in a cave by the sea. For nine years he learned the art of forging metal. Then he sent magnificent golden thrones to the gods on Olympus. He didn't forget his mother's cruel treatment. Hera's throne held her fast when she sat in it. Zeus commanded Hephaestus to free the goddess who gave birth to him, but Hephaestus said he didn't have a mother. Dionysus got Hephaestus drunk and finally talked him into setting Hera free.

Another story tells us that Hephaestus was the healthy child of Zeus and Hera. One day when the couple was having one of their quarrels, Hephaestus tried to protect his mother from Zeus. Zeus was so angry that he grabbed his son by the ankle and hurled him from Mount Olympus. Hephaestus fell for a whole day and crashed onto the island of Lemnos. The natives could not mend his crippled leg.

One of the few myths about Hephaestus tells us that he married the beautiful Aphrodite. The god suspected that his wife was unfaithful, so he forged a net and fixed it to the top of their bed. As soon as he left to visit the mortals on Lemnos, Aphrodite welcomed Ares, the god of war, into her bedroom. Hephaestus's net came down and trapped the pair in an embrace.

Warned by the sun god, Helios, Hephaestus came home and caught them. Then he went to Zeus to complain. Zeus and all the other gods rushed to Hephaestus's house to laugh at the couple. Poseidon talked Hephaestus into letting the lovers go, and they fled away to hide in shame.

ARES

Aside from sneaking into Aphrodite's bedroom, there are few stories about Ares, the god of war. The Greeks hated Ares almost as much as Hades. To the citizens of Greece, Ares was the spirit of war for its own sake. He was a bully and a coward who cried to Zeus whenever he lost a fight. Even during the Trojan War, Zeus wanted nothing to do with his own son: "Don't come complaining to me you lying, wretched creature. I hate you more than any of the gods on Olympus. Conflict and fighting are all you care about. You're as heartless as your mother, Hera!"

The Greeks turned to Athena, the goddess of wisdom, as the divine being to rule over military matters. With Athena, war was a sad but necessary means of settling conflicts between cities.

Ares had no wife of his own, but he fathered four children with Aphrodite. These were Deimos and Phobus—also known as Fear and Panic—a daughter Harmonia, and, according to some authors, Cupid. Ares also had children with mortal women, including several of the Argonauts who would one day sail with Jason, as well as the Amazon queen Penthesileia and the beautiful maiden Alcippe. When Poseidon's son Halirrhothius forced himself on Alcippe, Ares killed him and was brought to trial for murder in Athens. At a hill just below the Acropolis, he was tried by the gods and set free. Thereafter the site was known as the Areopagus or "Hill of Ares."

HERMES

One of Zeus's loves was the nymph Maia, daughter of Atlas, who lived in a cave in Arcadia. When Hera was asleep, Zeus would secretly visit Maia. In time, she gave birth to Hermes.

On the morning of his birth, Hermes sprang from his cradle and left the cave to explore. The first thing he saw was a tortoise. The baby laughed. "Where did you get that pretty shell? I think you could be useful to me. It's dangerous here in the wild mountains. Let me carry you inside my cave where it's safe. We could make wonderful music together."

Hermes picked up his new toy and carried it home. Then he took a sharp knife and cut off its legs and hollowed out its flesh until only the shell remained. He stretched seven strings across the back and plucked them with his fingers. He sang songs and rejoiced in the beautiful sound of the instrument he invented.

Soon he grew bored and placed the lyre in his cradle. Hermes left the cave again and wandered north until he came to fertile land below Olympus. He spotted Apollo's sacred herd of cattle. With a wicked grin, Hermes led fifty of the beasts away. He saw the animals' tracks would be easy to follow, so he made the cattle walk backward and padded his own feet with leafy sandals.

Along the way, he met an old shepherd tending his vineyard. Hermes said the man's vines would always bear sweet wine if he told no one what he saw. Back in Arcadia, Hermes placed the cattle in a hidden stable. Then he slipped back into the cave and crawled into his cradle.

To the world he looked like an innocent babe, but his mother knew the truth: "I know what you've been up to. Leto's son Apollo is going to be pounding down our door looking for his cattle. Oh, your father is to blame! He begot you to be a nuisance and a trickster to men and gods alike."

Baby Hermes told his mother that he would handle Apollo.

At that moment, the sun was rising on a new day. Apollo searched for his missing cattle. The tracks seemed to lead in the wrong direction and he lost the trail. The old shepherd confessed that he had seen a baby with feet wrapped in leaves and a herd of cattle walking backward. Apollo followed the strange trail over the mountain to Maia's cave. He saw a baby sleeping peacefully in his cradle, but he wasn't fooled. "Get up you cunning thief! I know you stole my cattle. Tell me what you have done with them or I will hurl you down to Tartarus."

Hermes replied: "Son of Leto, what are you saying? I'm just a little baby. I have no idea where your cattle are."

Apollo carried Hermes off to a council of gods on Mount Olympus. Zeus asked the child what had happened. The young god swore he had never seen the cattle.

Zeus laughed, but he knew little Hermes was lying. Hermes was forced to lead Apollo to his secret stable and return the animals. Apollo was ready to throw Hermes into Tartarus, but the baby began to pluck his tortoise-shell lyre. Apollo was enchanted. He agreed to set aside his anger if Hermes would give him the lyre and teach him to play. The young god agreed, and from that day forth, Apollo became the god of music.

Hermes grew up to become the trusted messenger of Zeus as well as the god of travelers and thieves. He fathered many children, including the god Pan. The Greeks looked for Hermes at their final breath to guide them down to Hades.

PAN

Hermes fell in love with a nymph named Dryope, and she became pregnant. When it was time for her to give birth, no one was prepared for the newborn babe they saw. The laughing child had the feet of a goat and two horns, along with a full beard. The nurse screamed and ran away, but the proud father took the boy in his arms. He carried him to the halls of Mount Olympus and presented him to the other gods. They named him Pan because he brought joy to everyone.

Pan grew up to have a goatish nature. One day he saw the nymph Syrinx in the forest of Arcadia and chased her. She was used to being chased by satyrs, but Pan was faster. She ran as fast as she could until she came to a river she could not cross. Pan was closing in and she prayed to the nymphs of the river to transform her. Pan grabbed her from behind, but all he found in his hands were water reeds. Disappointed but curious, Pan cut the reeds to different lengths and sealed them with wax to make a musical instrument.

When he wasn't chasing nymphs, Pan was the god of goat-herds and shepherds. He could also bring terror to the hearts of anyone who offended him. Among such unlucky souls he inspired uncontrollable fear—better known as *pan*ic.

HELIOS

Helios, the god of the sun, was born of the Titans Theia and Hyperion when the world was still young. Each morning he drove his chariot across the sky. Each evening he journeyed back across the ocean to his palace in the east.

Without him all plants, animals, and humans would die, ice would cover the lands, and darkness would descend upon the world forever. Helios was so busy that when Zeus gave portions of the earth to all the gods, Helios missed out. So, Zeus raised the island of Rhodes from the Aegean Sea to be the sacred land for Helios.

Aphrodite was angry with Helios for telling Hephaestus about her and Ares. She made the sun god fall hopelessly in love with Leucothoe, a daughter of the Persian king. Every day as he soared across the sky, Helios watched her. One night as Leuco-thoe was weaving, Helios took the form of the girl's mother and dismissed her attendants. Then he revealed himself and told the princess he loved her. Leucothoe fell into his arms.

Clytie, a nymph who loved Helios, burned with jealousy. She sent word to the king that his daughter had taken a lover. The king had Leucothoe buried alive. Helios couldn't do anything until he had finished his journey across the sky. That night he tried to revive her, but it was too late. He sprinkled Leucothoe with divine nectar until her body smelled sweet and she turned into a shrub of frankincense, the finest perfume in all the world.

Clytie continued to love the sun, but he scorned her. She sat beneath the open air, neither eating nor drinking, watching Helios sail across the heavens. Her limbs became fixed to the ground and her face burned away until she was nothing but a small flower, the heliotrope, forever following the sun across the sky.

Clymene, a daughter of Ocean and the wife of an Egyptian king, was another of Helios's lovers. She bore Helios a son named Phaethon. Phaethon told his best friend who his father was, but the friend called him a fool. Clymene swore that her words were true and urged Phaethon to journey to the palace of his father.

Phaethon traveled east to the farthest borders of the world. He found the palace of the sun and climbed the stairs to the throne room, but he could not bear to gaze at the bright god.

"Welcome, Phaethon, a son no father would deny," said Helios.

"If you are really my father," said the boy, "swear to me by the river Styx that you will grant me whatever I wish."

"Gladly, I swear," replied the sun god.

"Let me drive your chariot across the sky," Phaethon demanded.

Helios urged the boy to ask for some other wish, but Phaethon would not change his mind. So Helios gave Phaethon the reins of his chariot.

Phaethon was unable to control the horses from the

moment they leaped into the sky. He dropped the reins and the chariot tore across the sky. Mountains burst into flames and seas boiled. Cities and forests went up in smoke. The fields of Africa became the Sahara Desert. Gods and men prayed to Zeus to do something before the world was destroyed.

Zeus cast a lightning bolt at the chariot, tearing it into pieces. Phaethon's burned body fell into a river. The daughters of Helios wept for Phaethon until their tears became amber. They left behind these words so that he would always be remembered:

> *Here lies the body of Phaethon,*
> *who drove the chariot of the sun. He failed*
> *greatly, but greatly did he dare.*

DIONYSUS

In the city of Thebes, there once lived a beautiful young woman named Semele, daughter of Cadmus. Zeus fell in love with her and came to her in mortal form to woo her. Eventually he revealed his true identity to her, and Semele became pregnant with his child.

When Hera heard of this, she began to plot revenge. She came to Semele disguised as an old woman. The two talked of many things and Semele shared the secret of her baby's father. The old woman shook her head. "My dear, I do hope it is Zeus, but you never really know, do you? A man will say anything. Next time he shows up, I would ask him to reveal himself as a god in all his glory."

Semele considered the old woman's words. How did she know for certain that the man was Zeus? She decided to find out the next time Zeus came to her.

"If you are really a god," she said, "grant me a wish."

"Anything you want," Zeus answered. "I swear to you by the River Styx you shall have it."

"Show yourself to me as a god, just as you appear to Hera," Semele said.

Zeus groaned in despair. He had sworn by the Styx and could not break his vow, so he put aside his mortal disguise and appeared as himself. In an instant, Semele was reduced to ashes. Before she burned away, Zeus snatched the unborn child and sewed it into his thigh to grow until it was ready to be born.

A few months later, Zeus removed the stitches and took out the baby, whom he named Dionysus. He gave the infant to Hermes, who took him to Semele's sister Ino to be raised in secret. The boy's aunt dressed him like a girl to keep him safe from Hera, but Hera knew. She drove Ino mad. Ino leaped into the sea with her son and they became sea gods. Zeus found baby Dionysus and turned him into a goat for his own protection. He was raised by the kindly nymphs of Nysa in distant Asia.

After Dionysus put aside his goat form and grew into a young god, he set off to see the world. He had discovered the secret of making wine during his time in Nysa and wanted to spread the knowledge along with his religious cult throughout the world. He wandered far and wide until he came to the shores of the Aegean Sea. He hailed a pirate ship to take him to the Island of Naxos. The pirates took one look at his rich purple robes and sturdy shoulders and decided to sell him into slavery in some distant land. They forced him onto the ship and tried to tie him up, but the bonds kept slipping off his hands and feet.

The helmsman Acoetes understood what was happening: "You fools, don't you see that you've taken a powerful god on board? No chains can hold him. We must set him free at once or he will surely send a raging tempest to destroy us all."

The captain of the ship sneered: "Acoetes, you are an idiot.

Pay attention to your sails, and leave this boy to real men."

When Acoetes hoisted the sails, the mast sprouted grape-vines and the sails turned to ivy. Sweet wine flowed over the decks and wild animals appeared. Dionysus turned into a lion and roared. The pirates leaped into the water, and Dionysus turned them all into dolphins, except for Acoetes. From that day forward, dolphins have been kindly to humans.

Hera continued to search for Dionysus. She drove the young god crazy, and he wandered through Egypt, Syria, and Asia Minor until he came to the temple of the Great Mother goddess Cybele in Phrygia. The priests and priestesses cured Dionysus with music and dancing and sent him on his way. A band of women known as the Bacchae (after Bacchus, another name for Dionysus) followed him, each carrying a wooden wand wrapped in ivy and crowned with a pinecone.

Before he left the land of Cybele, Dionysus offered to grant King Midas his heart's desire because he had been kind to him. The king was more kind than wise. He asked his divine visitor to make whatever he touched turn into gold. Dionysus agreed. King Midas eagerly touched an oak branch and watched it turn into a golden twig. Then he touched a stone and the pillars of his palace, all of which turned to gold. The king touched everything he could find.

At last Midas grew weary and called for food and drink. Platters of delicious food and goblets of sweet wine turned to gold when they touched his lips. The king was starving. He realized how foolish he had been and prayed to Dionysus to lift the dreaded power. The god heard his prayer and told Midas to go and wash in a nearby stream. The king plunged into the river. The rocks in the streambed turned to gold, but the gift—or curse—of the golden touch left Midas forever.

Not every king welcomed Dionysus as Midas had. When Dionysus crossed into Thrace, King Lygurgus chased the young god into the sea and seized his followers. Dionysus freed his Bacchae and drove Lygurgus mad. The king struck his own son with an ax thinking he was a grapevine. His subjects were so horrified that they bound the king and tied him to horses to be torn apart.

When Dionysus moved south into Greece, the daughters of King Minyas wanted nothing to do with his wild, new religion. They scorned those who followed the god into the mountains to dance wearing animal skins. Dionysus appeared before the daughters as a young girl and tried to tell them that his rites were not indecent. Wine was not evil, he explained, but necessary to achieve balance in life.

The daughters would not listen. Then Dionysus filled the room with the sound of beating drums and tambourines. Milk and nectar dripped from the ceiling and the women were overcome with madness. They tore one of their own children to pieces and ate him. Then they ran off to the mountains where Dionysus changed them into bats.

When Dionysus returned at last to his hometown of Thebes, he expected to be welcomed. His grandfather Cadmus and the oracle Tiresias embraced Dionysus's new religion, but the women of the city and his cousin, King Pentheus, scorned him. Dionysus drove the women mad and sent them into the hills with his followers.

To Pentheus, the worship of Dionysus was still a silly excuse to behave badly in the forest. "It's Aphrodite they're devoted to, not Bacchus! I've captured some and put them under guard at the jail, but I'll hunt down the rest in the mountains and throw them into iron cages. I'll put a stop to this worship of the so-called god Dionysus."

Tiresias tried to explain that the proper worship of Dionysus was to find balance in life. A spy sent into the woods said that the women were drinking only moderate amounts of wine and dancing to the flute. But the king refused to listen.

Dionysus then appeared to Pentheus dressed as one of his own priests and offered to take him to the mountains to see the worship for himself. First Pentheus would have to dress as a woman and watch quietly from a tree. Pentheus agreed and followed Dionysus into the woods. As soon as they arrived, Dionysus revealed the king's true identity. The women, driven mad by Dionysus, pulled Pentheus out of the tree and tore off his limbs. His own mother Agave was the first to attack.

The women marched back to Thebes, Agave carrying her son's head in her arms. She believed she had killed a lion. As the spell wore off, she realized the horrible truth. Dionysus blamed the people of Thebes for rejecting him. "If you had only known how to keep your minds balanced, I, the son of Zeus, would have brought good fortune to you—but you would not welcome me."

Dionysus then transformed his faithful grandfather Cadmus into a snake and his grandmother Harmonia into a wild beast.

As cruel as Dionysus was to his grandparents, he loved his mother very much. He complained that she was confined to

Hades while he lived as a god. He decided to journey to the underworld to rescue Semele and bring her back to the land of the living. He searched high and low for an entrance to Hades, until at last he came to an elderly man who offered to show him a secret door. After a long journey, the god found Semele and brought her back. Then at last he led his mother to Mount Olympus where Zeus and the other gods welcomed her and her son ever after as immortals.

CUPID

In some stories Eros was one of the first gods, born from Chaos. In later stories, Eros was the son of Aphrodite who flew about the world shooting arrows of love into unwilling victims. This Eros was known as Cupid. One of the best-loved myths of ancient times was told of Cupid.

Once upon a time a king and queen in a distant land had three daughters. The oldest two were pretty and had many suitors. They were married, but the youngest sister, Psyche, was so lovely that no man thought himself worthy of her. Her beauty was so astonishing that visitors from many lands came just for a glimpse of her. Pilgrims threw garlands at her feet. Soon the temples of Aphrodite were neglected.

When Aphrodite found out she was being ignored for a mortal woman, she was furious. The goddess told her son Cupid to shoot Psyche and make her fall madly in love with the meanest, most disgusting man on the face of the earth. She wanted Psyche to have a terrible life.

The girl's father worried that such beauty might be a curse from the gods. He asked a sacred oracle what he should do about Psyche: "King, put the girl on a mountain cliff dressed in her finest gown for a wedding—or a funeral. Your son-in-law will come to her there, but he won't be a mortal. He will be a savage, wild beast that flies through the air on wings and troubles the world with fire and sword. He is so terrible that Zeus and the gods shake at his approach."

The poor father could not bear to abandon his daughter to such a fate, but Psyche herself led the way to the cliff dressed as a bride of death. She knew that the oracle's words were Aphrodite's revenge, and it was no use to resist.

Psyche waited for something terrible to happen. Suddenly a gentle wind carried her down to the valley far below. She saw a beautiful palace with walls made of gold and floors covered with jewels. A voice told her that all she saw was hers. Invisible servants prepared a fine dinner, and then showed her the way to her bedchamber.

Alone in her room, Psyche began to fear what would happen next. The sun slowly set and the room grew dark. Suddenly, a man took her in his arms. He was gone before the first rays of sun entered the windows of the chamber. The same thing happened the next night and the next.

One night, Psyche's husband warned her that she could never see his face. He told her she was pregnant and that her child would be a god, but only if she didn't try to discover who he was. Psyche agreed but begged her husband to bring her sisters for a visit to show them she was safe.

The next day when the two sisters arrived at the cliff where Psyche had waited for her doom, the wind carried them to the castle. Psyche showed them the palace and fed them a glorious feast. As the sun began to set, the wind carried them back to the top of the cliff.

Envy seized the sisters.

"Our little sister enjoys the life of a goddess while I'm married to a fat old husband as bald as a pumpkin," said the elder.

"I don't care if she is our sister," replied the other. "It's not fair that Psyche should have a handsome young god in a glorious palace. If it's the last thing I do, I'll see that she loses everything!"

The next day the wind carried the sisters to Psyche again. They told her stories of farmers who had seen a giant snake slithering through the forest on the way to the castle. They told Psyche that her husband would eat her alive as a plump, tasty meal. Psyche denied it was true, but she began to wonder.

That night, after her husband fell asleep, Psyche gathered an oil lamp and a sharp knife. She held the lamp up to her husband's face, ready to cut off the monster's head. Instead she saw the loveliest man she could ever imagine. His cheeks were rosy and his hair flowed down in perfect ringlets. She pricked her finger on the bow and arrows at his feet and fell deeply in love with her husband, who she now knew was Cupid.

As she drew near to kiss him, a drop of hot oil fell onto his shoulder and woke Cupid with a start.

"Psyche, why didn't you listen to me?" Cupid asked. "I can never see you again—never. All that we had is lost."

With that the god disappeared. Psyche fled into the woods to drown herself in a river, but the waters would not receive her. She lay on the grass weeping until Pan saw her and led her to the home of one of her sisters. Psyche collapsed in tears and told her sister everything. Instead of comforting her, the wicked woman ran to the cliff and launched herself into the air, crying, "Take me, Cupid! I will be a worthy wife to you." But instead of a gentle wind, the sister felt the rush of cold air as she fell down on the jagged rocks below. Psyche told her other sister the story of losing her husband forever. The other sister did the same, and also fell to her death.

Psyche wandered in the forest. A bird saw her and told Aphrodite. The goddess was furious: "Instead of doing his job, my precious son took up with that girl and got her pregnant! I'm too young to be a grandmother!"

Aphrodite brought Psyche to her palace, but instead of servants and fine meals, Psyche received beatings. At last the goddess, weary of tormenting the girl, told her she would be freed if she could complete a few tasks. Psyche was placed in a granary full of mixed wheat, barley, millet, poppy seeds, chickpeas, lentils, and beans and told to sort each grain into a separate pile by morning—or die. Psyche knew Aphrodite was looking for an excuse to kill her, so she sat on the floor and waited for death. A little ant took pity on the girl. He brought all his friends and they began to sort the seeds. By morning, the grains were separated.

The goddess was even more furious at Psyche's

success. She ordered the girl to go among a flock of sheep whose fleece shined with gold and gather some of the wool—or die. The only problem was that the sheep were vicious killers. Once again, Psyche sat down and waited for death, but a slender reed told her a secret. The sheep were ferocious during the day, but if she waited until evening, she could gather some of the wool from branches they had brushed against in passing. Psyche did this and brought the wool to Aphrodite.

"You think you're so clever, do you?" asked the goddess. "For your next task you must draw a cup of water from a spring of the River Styx. It's at the bottom of an impassible gorge in the mountains, but I'm sure that won't be any trouble for you." Aphrodite laughed in wicked delight and handed Psyche a silver cup.

Psyche knew she could never do what Aphrodite asked. She climbed to the top of a cliff to throw herself off. Just then, the eagle that served Zeus was flying by. Cupid had once done him a favor, so the eagle swooped down, took the cup from Psyche, and filled it in the spring. Psyche presented the goblet to Aphrodite.

The goddess couldn't believe that a young girl could complete these deadly tasks. She decided on a final test that Psyche would never finish alive. She was to go down into the land of the dead and bring back some of Persephone's perfume. Aphrodite gave the girl a jar and sent her on her way, confident that she would never see her again.

No mortal could journey to Hades and come back alive. Psyche climbed to the top of a tall tower to throw herself off, but the tower told her that the journey was not impossible. It told her to go to a remote grove near Sparta where she would find an entrance to the land of Hades. She was to carry two barley cakes in her hands and two coins in her mouth. She was to ignore all requests made to her by anyone she met on her journey and to speak only when she arrived at the house of Persephone. She must not open the jar for any reason.

Psyche thanked the tower for its kindness. She found the entrance to Hades and entered into the dark world. A crippled man asked for her help, but she passed him by. Charon poled her across the River Styx for one of the coins in her mouth. A dead man in the water begged her to pull him into the boat, but Psyche closed her eyes and ignored him. Some old women urged her to stop and weave with them, but Psyche walked on. She tossed one of the barley cakes to the three-headed dog Cerberus and came at last to the palace of Persephone. Smiling, the goddess of the underworld granted Psyche's request and filled the jar, sealing it tightly.

Returning the way she had come, Psyche gave the other cake to Cerberus and her final coin to Charon. She labored up the long, dark path and emerged at last into the land of the living. Then she began to wonder. If the perfume was so powerful, could it help her win back Cupid's love? She opened the jar, and immediately fell into a sleep like death.

Cupid found Psyche in the forest and woke her with a prick from his arrow. After giving the perfume to his mother, he asked Zeus and the rest of the gods to make Psyche a goddess. Even Aphrodite was impressed by Psyche's bravery. With a nod from Zeus, Hermes brought forward a cup of divine ambrosia. Psyche drank deeply and the fire of immortality ran through her veins. Everyone cheered the new goddess. Satyrs played flutes, the Muses sang wedding songs, and Aphrodite herself danced to the music. In due time, the child of Cupid and Psyche was born, a daughter named Happiness.

Goddesses

HERA

Hera, the queen of heaven, was the goddess of marriage and childbirth. She was also the goddess troubled women turned to whether they were young girls, brides, or old women. She was sympathetic to their pain and sorrow, and a goddess of comfort and hope throughout a woman's life.

In spite of her sympathy for women, Hera's revenge was terrible when it came to women who were involved with her husband, Zeus. Io, Callisto, and Leto were just of a few of Zeus's innocent lovers tormented by his wife.

Hera was never shy about standing up to her husband, either. One day when the sea goddess Thetis came to seek a favor for her son, Hera burst in and screamed at Zeus:

"Which of the gods is plotting with you now? You and all your secret plans. Why don't you have the guts to let me know what you're up to?"

Zeus yelled back: "Woman, I've had just about enough of you! If you keep on nagging me, you're going to regret it. I'm the ruler of the gods, not you. I'm going to do what I think is right whether you like it or not."

Stories of arguments between Hera and Zeus are many. Once they even argued about who enjoyed love more, men or women. They asked the oracle Tiresias to settle the matter because he had been both a male and a female. He told them that women enjoyed love more—ten times more. Hera struck Tiresias blind for revealing the secret, but Zeus gave him the power to predict the future and he became a great prophet.

Like all goddesses, Hera enjoyed her famous beauty. When Side, the wife of the hunter Orion, boasted that she was fairer than the wife of Zeus, Hera cast her into Hades forever. Likewise, after the queen of the Pygmies claimed her own beauty was beyond compare, Hera turned her into a crane.

DEMETER

Like her sister Hera, Demeter was a child of Cronus and Rhea. Unlike Hera, Demeter cared little for love or for contests of beauty. She ruled over the fertile green earth and life-giving grain.

Demeter wasn't completely against love. At the wedding of King Cadmus of Thebes and his bride Harmonia, she fell in love with a mortal named Iasion. The couple had two sons: Plutus, a god of riches under the earth, and Philomelus, a mortal farmer who invented the wagon.

Demeter could be terrible in her anger. A man named Erysichthon was cutting firewood when he came upon a sacred grove of Demeter. The wood nymphs in the trees cried as he chopped their limbs. Blood dripped from their leaves. The trees prayed to Demeter for revenge. She heard their prayer and struck Erysichthon with an uncontrollable hunger. Soon Erysichthon ate himself alive.

The best-known tale of Demeter is the story of what happened when Hades kidnapped her daughter Persephone. One day the maiden was gathering violets and roses in a meadow. Suddenly, a giant chasm opened. Hades flew out in a golden chariot and grabbed Persephone. She called to Zeus for help, but Hades flew back to the underworld with her and closed the ground above him.

Persephone sat weeping in the dark palace of the underworld, longing to see the light of day. Her sobs echoed throughout the land of the dead, but could not reach the land of the living.

Demeter flew down from Mount Olympus and searched the world for her daughter. She looked everywhere and asked everyone if they had seen her. No one could tell her where Persephone was. She raced across the Earth seeking her child. At last she came upon the goddess Hecate, who told her an amazing tale: "Demeter, goddess of the fruits of the earth, you wish to know who carried off Persephone and brought pain to your heart? I heard her cry out. I did not see who stole her away."

Demeter then sought out the sun god Helios who sees all

from his chariot. Helios finally told her the truth: "Daughter of Rhea, I am moved by your sorrow. It is Zeus who allowed Hades to seize the maiden. The lord of the dead holds her in his underworld kingdom and will not let her go. She is there by the will of Zeus and there is nothing you can do."

Demeter swore she would never return to Olympus. She took on the form of an old woman and wandered the earth, weeping for the daughter she would never see again.

One day she came to the town of Eleusis, north of Athens, and sat by a well. It wasn't long before the four daughters of King Celeus came to fill their brass pitchers. They greeted the old woman and asked her what brought her to the town. Demeter said that she had been kidnapped from Crete by pirates, but that she had escaped. She wanted a quiet place to live out her days. Perhaps the girls knew a household that needed a nurse for a child?

The daughters' own mother had recently given birth to a son. They led Demeter to the palace to meet their mother, who welcomed the old woman and offered her the job of caring for her son. Demeter loved the child at once and promised to care for him as if he were her own.

Every night while the palace slept, the goddess nursed the baby on ambrosia and buried him in the hearth fire to burn away his mortality. One night, his mother walked in and screamed. The goddess pulled the baby out of the fire and addressed the mother: "I am Demeter, you foolish woman! I would have made your son free from old age and death. Now he will know the pain of life as a mortal."

The goddess then ordered the people of Eleusis to build

her a temple so that she could establish her religion in their city. The boy may have lost his chance to live forever, but she would show her followers how to escape the gloomy land of Hades after death.

The king and citizens of Eleusis built Demeter a wondrous temple. When it was finished, the goddess entered and closed the doors. She stayed there weeping for Persephone and stopped caring about the earth's harvests. No seeds ripened. Hunger spread across the world. Starving people called on the gods for help, but only Demeter had the power to make grain grow.

Zeus sent golden-winged Iris to urge Demeter to return to Mount Olympus, but Demeter was unmoved. All the gods made their way to the temple to beg her to make the earth bloom again. Without grain the people of the earth would die and no one would worship the gods.

Demeter refused. She would never set foot on Olympus or send forth the fruits of the earth until she saw her daughter.

Zeus then sent Hermes to Hades to plead for Persephone's release. The ruler of the underworld was surprisingly agreeable and drove Persephone back to her mother in his golden chariot. Demeter threw her arms around her daughter and held her as if she would never let her go. Then she asked Persephone if she had eaten anything when she was with Hades. Persephone had eaten one small pomegranate seed because Hades had insisted. Demeter groaned and explained that since Persephone had tasted the food of the underworld, they could not be together always. She would have to spend a third of each year with Hades, then she could return to the land of the living.

Demeter was not happy, but she agreed to restore the earth to its fruitfulness. She declared that each winter she would mourn for her daughter. Thus, when Persephone journeys to the underworld in the autumn, the land turns brown and the sky grows cold and dark until spring, when Demeter and Persephone are together again.

ARTEMIS

Daughter of Zeus and Leto, and sister of Apollo, Artemis was the goddess of the hunt. She honored those who devoted themselves to her, but was harsh with followers like Callisto who lost their virginity. Artemis was even more harsh with men who wanted her.

A young man named Actaeon discovered this one day when he was hunting with his dogs. The grandson of King Cadmus of Thebes, Actaeon had the finest hounds in all of Greece. Artemis was hunting in the same forest and stopped to swim in a cool spring. She was splashing with her nymphs when she saw a man's face staring at them from behind a tree.

Actaeon was enchanted by Artemis's beauty. The nymphs gathered around her to shield her from his eyes, but the goddess rose up before him: "Take a good look, my young friend. You can tell all your friends that you saw the goddess of the hunt naked—if you can."

She splashed Actaeon with spring water, and he suddenly began to sprout antlers. His ears became pointed, and his arms and legs turned into those of a deer. He tried to cry out for mercy, but his human voice was gone. He ran from the spring in terror and found his hounds in a nearby glade. The dogs sank their teeth into his hide. He tried to tell them who he was, but he could not. The dogs ripped the life from the deer, wondering where their master was. Artemis stood on the edge of the glade, watching and smiling.

One foolish hunter named Burphagus tried to force himself on Artemis when he found her in the woods of Arcadia, but she killed him with an arrow from her quiver. Another great hunter, the giant Orion, met the same fate when he insulted the goddess.

There are different stories about Orion's death. Some say he tried to force himself on Artemis. Others say she loved him and killed him in a fit of jealousy when he went to live with Eos, the goddess of the dawn. Still other stories say that the goddess was angry after he beat her in a contest. Most stories agree that Artemis killed Orion by forcing a scorpion to sting him. She later placed him in the sky as a constellation along with his faithful dog Sirius and the scorpion that caused his death.

APHRODITE

Aphrodite was the goddess of love. But for a mortal to love a goddess was a dangerous business. A young Trojan named Anchises learned this when he tended cattle alone on Mount Ida, far above Troy.

The gods had grown tired of Aphrodite's tricks, so Zeus struck her with a longing for a mortal man. One look at Anchises was all it took for Aphrodite to fall in love. She raced to her temple on the island of Cyprus where her attendants bathed her and anointed her with sweet perfume. They dressed her in a beautiful gown, and then she flew down to Mount Ida.

Aphrodite put aside her divine glory and appeared before Anchises as a young maiden wearing a silky robe and beautiful jewels.

Anchises jumped to his feet: "Welcome, goddess on earth. Whether you are Artemis, Athena, or even Aphrodite, I will build you an altar and worship you forever."

Aphrodite smiled: "Dear Anchises, I am no goddess. I'm a mortal girl, daughter of King Otreus of Phrygia. I was dancing with my friends when Hermes whisked me away and brought me here. He said I was to be the wife of King Anchises. I hope you will take me to meet your parents, but first, perhaps, we could spend the night here."

Anchises was very much in love: "If you are truly a mortal woman, gladly I will take you for my wife."

The goddess smiled like a shy young girl. Anchises took her into his bed where they made love. When dawn came, the longing sent by Zeus had passed. Aphrodite rose and put on the shining form of a goddess. "Get up, Anchises! Aphrodite, goddess of love, now stands before you."

Anchises bowed down before Aphrodite in terror: "I knew when I first saw you that you had to be a goddess. Please have mercy on me!"

Aphrodite answered: "Calm down. You are loved by the gods, as are your people. No harm will come to you. But if you ever tell anyone about your night with me, you will suffer. I am disgraced. Worse still, I am pregnant! I will bring the boy to you to raise. Tell him his mother was a mountain nymph. If you say my name, you are a dead man."

Aphrodite flew back to Cyprus but returned nine months later with the boy, whom his father named Aeneas and raised as a prince of Troy. In time, Aphrodite forgot her anger and claimed Aeneas as her son.

Aphrodite was sympathetic to true love, even among mortals. Pygmalion was a king on her island of Cyprus. The young ruler could not find a woman to live up to his high standards. He lived in his palace without a queen.

Pygmalion sculpted a life-size maiden in precious ivory. She was more perfect than any woman ever born and he fell deeply in love with the statue. He kissed the statue and brought her gifts of pretty shells, sweet flowers, and amber jewelry. He dressed her in fine robes, and pretended that she loved him, too.

One day during a festival of Aphrodite, Pygmalion approached the altar. He prayed to Aphrodite to give him a woman like his ivory maiden. The goddess heard his prayer. When the king returned to his palace, he kissed the statue on the cheek. She seemed warm to his lips, but surely this was his imagination. He kissed her again, and her skin felt soft. At last he placed a hand on her chest and felt her heart beating. The goddess had granted his wish.

The ivory maiden opened her eyes and beheld Pygmalion. She smiled and hugged him, and then agreed to be his wife.

Some stories say that Pygmalion and his bride had a daughter named Metharme who became the mother of a boy named Adonis. Most say the child was a son of Cinyras, king of Assyria, by his daughter Myrrha.

Adonis was so beautiful that Aphrodite placed him in a chest and gave it to the underworld goddess Persephone to hide him from the world. Persephone also loved the child and wanted to keep him. Zeus asked the muse Calliope to judge the case. Calliope said that Adonis would spend one third of the year with Persephone, one third with Aphrodite, and one third as he chose. The boy so loved Aphrodite that he spent his own time with the goddess.

When Adonis was a young man, he and Aphrodite spent their days hunting. He wanted to chase larger game, but the goddess warned him to stick with smaller animals like rabbits. One day he saw a wild boar running through the woods and chased it with his spear. The boar turned and charged Adonis, sinking his razor-sharp tusks deep into the young man. Aphrodite arrived and took Adonis in her arms, but it was too late. From his blood she made a bright red blossom, the anemone, rise from the earth. It lives only a short time, but while it blooms it is the most beautiful flower in the world.

HECATE

If there was a goddess of mystery in the ancient world, it was Hecate. According to one early story she was the daughter of the Titans Perses and Asteria. When most of the other Titans were overthrown by Zeus and cast down into Tartarus, Hecate was spared and was honored by the ruler of the gods. She was praised as protector of horsemen, sailors, and fishermen, as well as herdsmen and hunters.

There are few stories about Hecate. She appears briefly to help Demeter find Persephone, but then quickly disappears. Still, she was worshipped throughout the ancient world as a goddess of the underworld. She ruled over crossroads and was a goddess of dark magic. She was said to keep the keys that controlled the three-headed dog, Cerberus, and to wear the sandals of the goddess who ruled Tartarus.

Ancient Greeks made sacrifices for the gods. Hecate's favorites were red mullet fish, little cakes with candles, and fresh young puppies. At the time of the full moon, meals of garbage were offered to the goddess made up of old bread, rotten eggs, spoiled cheese, and dog meat. Those who wished to curse their enemies or make magic spells stronger invoked the name of Hecate. She was, like Hades, a god best worshipped with respect but otherwise treated with devoted silence.

HESTIA

Another goddess mentioned in only a few myths is Hestia, although this goddess of the hearth was welcomed in every household. She was a daughter of Cronos and Rhea, like Zeus and Hera. Hestia's only task was to guard the life-giving fire at the center of every home. She refused to marry both Poseidon and Apollo, and remained a virgin. The lack of myths about her might be a result of her chosen job. As guardian of the hearth, she was never able to leave the sacred fire unguarded.

But Hestia was still greatly admired. As one early hymn sings:

> *Hestia, you who dwell in the lofty halls with undying gods and with men who walk the earth, you have gained an everlasting home and highest honor. Your portion among the gods is precious and everlasting. Without you, there would be no feasts for mortals. To you, the first and last drops of sweet wine are poured in sacrifice.*

ATHENA

Most stories say that Athena was the daughter of the goddess Metis whom Zeus swallowed after getting her pregnant. Athena leaped from the head of Zeus months later, fully grown and wearing armor. She was a goddess of both warfare and the feminine arts. As the goddess of

Athens, she was honored with the grand temple of the Parthenon on the Acropolis.

Most of Athena's myths involve battles, warriors, and helping heroes in their quests. In some stories Athena is a patroness of crafts. The most famous of these begins with a young woman named Arachne. This maiden was so skilled at weaving that nymphs gathered to watch her work. Her graceful fingers flew across the loom. Everyone thought she must have been taught by Athena, but Arachne was insulted: "I taught myself. If the goddess thinks she is better than me, let her come to a contest."

Athena heard the girl's boasting and paid her a visit. She took on the form of an old woman and went to Arachne's cottage. "You're good, no doubt, but you are only a mortal," she said. "Pray to Athena for forgiveness for your pride and I'm sure she will grant it."

Arachne was displeased. "Mind your own business, old woman. If Athena is so great at weaving, let her come and challenge me."

The goddess then revealed herself. The nymphs fell to their knees, but the girl insisted on a contest. Two looms were set up, and Arachne and Athena began to weave. Athena moved with lightning speed as she wove stories in cloth of foolish mortals who had dared to challenge the gods. Arachne answered with pictures of cruel gods tricking men and women. Athena could not find even the smallest mistake in Arachne's weaving. She was furious and injured the girl. Arachne was in such pain that she hung herself.

Athena was sorry. She sprinkled the dead girl with herbs and watched her hair fall away. The maiden's body shrank, leaving a tiny head, a large belly, and eight long legs. Arachne was restored to life as a spider. Her offspring weave beautiful patterns in their webs to this day.

EOS

The goddess of dawn was rosy-fingered Eos, daughter of the Titans Hyperion and Theia. She was an unusually romantic goddess who delighted in kidnapping mortal men to love her. One of these was Orion, Artemis's hunting companion. Eos once transported him to the island of Ortygia before he died of a scorpion bite.

Cephalus was a prince who was deeply in love with his wife, Procris. The couple had exchanged a vow that they would always be faithful to each other. One morning when Cephalus was out hunting, Eos offered herself to him. He told the goddess of his promise. Eos assured the prince that she didn't want him to break his vow—unless Procris broke hers first. Cephalus swore this would never happen, so Eos proposed a test. She changed his appearance and gave him many fine gifts. Then she dared him to try, as a stranger, to seduce his wife.

Cephalus went to his palace and charmed Procris with words of love and wonderful presents. At last, to his surprise, his wife was won over.

The next morning Eos returned Cephalus to his own

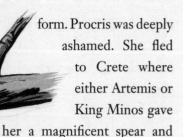

form. Procris was deeply ashamed. She fled to Crete where either Artemis or King Minos gave her a magnificent spear and hunting dog and sent her back to her husband dressed in the clothes of a man. There, she challenged Cephalus to a hunting contest and defeated him. The prince offered to buy the spear and the dog from the stranger, but Procris refused. Cephalus agreed to do anything to obtain the prizes. Then Procris revealed herself to be a woman and his wife. Cephalus realized he was no better than his wayward bride. They forgave each other and found love again.

Eos's most famous lover was Tithonus, a young prince of Troy. Eos so loved Tithonus that she asked Zeus to give him eternal life, which the god granted. But like Sibyl, she forgot to request eternal youth for her love. When Tithonus's hair began to turn gray, Eos grew tired of him. As the years passed, the man became crippled and senile. All he could do was babble endlessly. The goddess wearied of his chattering and turned him into a cicada, an insect that never stops making noise.

THE MUSES

The nine sisters who inspired poets, artists, musicians, scientists, and writers were the Muses. They were Calliope (epic poetry), Erato (lyric poetry), Polyhymnia (hymns), Clio (history), Euterpe (flute playing), Terpsichore (dancing), Melpomene (tragedy), Thalia (comedy), and Urania (astronomy). They were the daughters of Zeus and Mnemosyne, the goddess of memory. They appear in just a handful of myths and had few places of worship. One temple below their home on Mount Helicon housed historical objects and records, and came to be known as the first museum.

Like all gods, the Muses were jealous of their reputations. When the celebrated bard Thamyris challenged them to a singing contest, they easily won and took away both his poetic gift and—more devastating for a bard—his memory. The nine foolish daughters of Pierus thought themselves equal to the Muses and also challenged them to a contest of song. They were beaten and turned into magpies for their lack of respect.

The nine sisters had several famous sons. Clio bore Hyacinth, and Calliope was the mother of the famous singer Orpheus. Melpomene gave birth to the dreaded Sirens who would one day sing so sweetly to Odysseus.

THE FATES

The three daughters of Night who spun, wove, and cut the thread of life for each person on earth were known as the Fates. Their names were Clotho, Lachesis, and Atropos, and even the gods feared them. No one could outwit them, not even Zeus. When every child was born, the sisters determined how long it would live and when it would die.

The Fates were not cruel, but did their job to keep order

in the cosmos. At times they left their dark lair to come to the aid of the gods as they did when the monster Typhon threatened to overthrow Zeus. The sisters pretended to be on Typhon's side and offered him human food to eat, claiming it would make him stronger. It really made him easier to defeat.

The Fates did not usually reveal a person's destiny. But when the prince Meleager was born, they told his mother Althaea that he would die when the log burning in her hearth was consumed. The mother grabbed the wood from the fire and put it away in a chest. There it remained for many years, but the Fates made sure Meleager's destiny would be fulfilled. Meleager went on a hunt for the Calydonian boar. He killed the beast and gave its hide to his female companion Atalanta, but one of Althaea's brothers tried to steal the skin. Meleager killed him in anger. When Althaea found out that her son had killed her brother, she threw the log into the fire. Meleager died in agony, proving that no one could cheat the Fates.

CYBELE

One day when Zeus was visiting the land of Phrygia, he fell asleep in a grassy field. Later, a creature named Agdistis who was both male and female arose from that spot. The gods were fearful of what might happen if such a child grew up, so they cut off the male parts of Agdistis and turned the being into a woman. As a female, she became the goddess Cybele.

An almond tree grew from the male parts of Agdistis.

The daughter of a local river god was walking past the tree one afternoon when she stopped to rest. This young woman, named Nana, took a nut from the tree and put it in her lap, but it disappeared. Soon afterward, she became pregnant and gave birth to a boy named Attis. Attis grew up to be a handsome young man.

Cybele saw Attis one day and fell in love, but he was already promised in marriage to a princess. Just as the wedding was about to begin, Cybele drove Attis mad. He cut himself and bled so much that he died.

Cybele was never a member of the family of gods on Olympus, but was an outsider from the lands of the east. Still, she was worshipped throughout the ancient world:

> *Mother of the gods and all humanity, who delights in the sound of drums and tambourines, the playing of flutes and the howling of wolves, and in the roar of the mighty lion.*

Young men danced in her honor, dressed in full armor, clashing their spears. The most loyal of her followers were priests called the Galli. On warm spring days, these men would cut themselves, just as Attis had done. Such was the price of devotion to the great goddess.

Heroes

PERSEUS

The plains of Argos were once the home of Io, who was forced to flee as a cow from Hera's wrath. Io had many heirs. The most famous of these heirs was Perseus, grandson of King Acrisius.

Acrisius asked an oracle if he would ever have a son. "Not only will you not have a son," the oracle said, "but if your daughter Danae does, he will kill you."

Not wishing to be cursed for killing his own daughter, Acrisius locked Danae in an underground room with only a small window used to bring her food and drink. There Danae passed her days. One night a shower of golden coins fell gently into her lap through the window. Not long afterward she was pregnant. The shower of gold was in fact Zeus.

Danae was terrified, and with good cause. Her father was furious. As soon as Danae gave birth, he placed both mother and child in a chest and cast it into the sea.

The pair were tossed about by storms while Danae held little Perseus in her arms. She prayed for help: "Dear gods, save us from our great peril. Father Zeus, with a humble heart I implore you! But you, little one, warm and well fed, sleep on as we sail through the night in our prison."

Zeus must have heard her, for Danae and Perseus washed up safely on the island of Seriphus. A kindly fisherman named Dictys found them and took them in. He treated Danae as a father would, and he proudly watched Perseus grow into a strong young man.

Danae caught the eye of Polydectes, ruler of Seriphus. He tried to win her as his bride, but she had no interest in him. Polydectes was too afraid of Perseus to seize Danae by force. Instead, he announced that he was planning to court a princess named Hippodamia and required all his subjects to give wedding gifts. Polydectes had no chance of winning the princess's hand, but he wanted to get Perseus out of the way. Perseus was poor and had nothing to give. But he was also brave and had once bragged that he could fetch the head of the dreaded Gorgon Medusa. Polydectes told him to do so, if he dared.

Perseus set off on a quest to kill the most dangerous monster in all the world. Not only were Medusa and her two sisters vicious creatures with hair made of snakes, but one glance at their faces would turn anyone to stone. They could fly, so even if Perseus killed Medusa, the other two would catch and kill him. Fortunately, Athena hated Medusa. She told Perseus how he might slay the Gorgon.

Perseus first went to Africa to find the cave of the Graeae, old sisters of the Gorgons who shared a single eye between them. As one sister passed the eye to another, Perseus grabbed it and made them blind. The sisters cursed the young thief, but asked what he wanted in return for their eye. Perseus needed directions to the home of nymphs Athena had told him about. These nymphs had three magical objects he would need to slay Medusa. The Graeae revealed the secret, and Perseus returned their eye.

The nymphs gave Perseus the objects he needed—a pouch in which to carry Medusa's head, a pair of sandals with wings, and a cap that made the wearer invisible. Then the god Hermes gave Perseus a powerful sword to cut off Medusa's head.

Even with magical tools to help him, it would be hard for Perseus to defeat Medusa and her sisters. They had scales like dragons and tusks like wild boars. No sword or shoes could protect Perseus from their power to turn men into stone. But Athena had more advice: "Go at night while they are sleeping, and take with you a polished bronze shield."

Wearing his invisibility cap, Perseus crept up on the sleeping Gorgons. He walked backward, looking at Medusa's reflection in his shield so that he wouldn't be turned to stone. With one slash of the sword, he sliced off her head and threw it into his pouch. The two Gorgon sisters were awake in an instant. There was no trace of Medusa's murderer. The invisible Perseus flew away on his magical sandals.

Some say the young hero stopped at the house of Atlas who carried the heavens on his shoulders. The Titan had been warned that a son of Zeus would one day steal the tree that bore golden apples. He threw Perseus against a wall.

Perseus said: "Even though you are rude to me, great Atlas, I have a gift for you." He closed his eyes and pulled the head of Medusa from his pouch. The Titan slowly turned to stone. At last he was nothing but rock, the African peak we know today as Mount Atlas.

As Perseus flew over Ethiopia, he saw a beautiful girl tied to a rock. This was Andromeda. Her mother, Queen Cassiopeia, had boasted to the sea nymph daughters of

Poseidon that she was more beautiful than them. Poseidon sent a flood and a monster to destroy the coast. An oracle told King Cepheus that Poseidon would stop only if the king gave his own daughter to the monster. The grieving father ordered Andromeda tied to the rock. He and Cassiopeia then stood by weeping and waiting for their daughter to die.

Perseus offered to kill the sea monster if Cepheus would promise him Andromeda's hand in marriage. The king agreed. When the monster burst through the waves, Perseus saw that it was huge and fast with fangs like a snake. Invisible under his magic cap and flying with his winged sandals, Perseus plunged his sword deep into the monster's neck until it died.

Andromeda's mother and father were overjoyed. They held a feast for the hero, but the king had forgotten to mention that his daughter was already engaged to her uncle, Phineus. Phineus burst into the dinner and Perseus was surrounded by an angry mob. Perseus battled Phineus and his men, but he was outnumbered. He shouted that any friends of his in the hall should close their eyes. He then pulled out Medusa's head and turned Phineus and two hundred men into stone.

Perseus stayed in Ethiopia only long enough to father a child with Andromeda. The boy, Perses, was left to inherit the throne from Cepheus, but Perseus wanted to return to his mother. He and Andromeda sailed to Seriphus. Some stories say that Polydectes had forced Danae to marry him while Perseus was away. Others say she and Dictys had hidden from him. In any case, Perseus turned Polydectes to stone and made Dictys ruler of Seriphus.

Now that his tasks were done, Perseus gave his magical tools to Hermes and the head of Medusa to Athena. Then he sailed back to Argos with his mother and his wife. Acrisius, who had thrown Danae and Perseus into the sea so many years before, feared for his life. He fled to the town of Larissa, and Perseus followed. He arrived just as the local king was holding games. The young hero competed in throwing the discus. Perseus launched his discus farther than anyone, but the wind caught it and turned it back toward the crowd. It flew at terrific speed and struck an old man who had been secretly watching—none other than Acrisius himself.

With his grandfather dead, Perseus was free to return to Argos and claim the throne. He felt guilty because he had accidentally killed his grandfather. So, he asked his cousin, Megapenthes, who ruled in the nearby town of Tiryns, to trade kingdoms. Perseus became king of Tiryns while Megapenthes ruled over Argos. In the years to come, Perseus built the great palace of Mycenae on the hills overlooking the Argive plain. He and Andromeda lived a long and happy life with many children, and then Athena placed them among the stars along with Cepheus and Cassiopeia.

THESEUS

Perseus was known and loved by the people of Argos, but Athens had its own brave hero, Theseus. Unlike Perseus, he did his deeds with only a little magical help.

The story begins when Aegeus, king of Athens, went to the oracle at Delphi to ask if he would have a child. The priestess of Apollo went into a trance and said: "Open not the swollen mouth of the wineskin, O king of the people, until you come once more to the city of Athens."

Aegeus left the temple scratching his head. He journeyed home by way of the city of Troezen to ask its wise king Pittheus if he understood the riddle. Pittheus realized that Apollo was telling Aegeus that his next child would be a mighty hero, and he should wait until he returned to Athens to be with a woman. Pittheus lied and said he didn't understand the oracle. He got Aegeus drunk and led him to the room of his own daughter, Aethra.

When Aegeus woke the next morning, he had a terrible headache. He had a hunch that Aethra might be pregnant and gave her secret instructions before leaving. "If you have a son," he whispered, "send him to me in Athens when he grows up—if he can retrieve these." Aegeus then took a sword and a pair of sandals and placed them underneath an enormous boulder. If the boy was able to lift the stone, he was to bring the sword and the sandals to Athens and claim his throne.

Aethra gave birth to a baby boy and named him Theseus. Some stories say that the princess was never sure if her baby's father was Aegeus or the sea god Poseidon. She raised Theseus to believe he was Poseidon's son.

Theseus was strong and clever. When he reached manhood, his mother led him to the rock. She confessed that she didn't know for certain who Theseus's real father was, but she told him to try to claim his place in Athens. Theseus put his shoulder to the giant rock and rolled it over, revealing the sword and sandals.

Theseus wanted to build his reputation as a hero, so he decided to make the trip to Athens by land, even though the sea route was safer. A series of outlaws kept watch on the road that led from Troezen to Athens. Travelers who took that route seldom lived to tell the tale. But Theseus wanted to prove himself a true hero. So the boy took the sword and sandals, and set off down the dangerous road.

It wasn't long until Theseus came to Epidaurus, where he met a crippled man named Periphetes. This outlaw was nicknamed Clubman because of the giant iron club he used as a cane. When anyone passed by, Periphetes beat him or her to death. This villain was strong but slow. Theseus was smart and fast. He dodged the first blow, came up behind Periphetes, and grabbed the club. He then pounded Periphetes with his own club.

Not far down the road was another outlaw named Sinis, the Pine Bender. He grabbed careless travelers and tied their legs to a pine tree bent to the ground. Then he tied their arms to another tree bent from the opposite direction. He cut the cord holding the trees together and tore his victims apart. Theseus took hold of the outlaw before he could be captured himself. He tied Sinis between two pine trees and cut the cord.

Theseus then detoured along the coast to seek out the Crommyonian sow. Some say she was a wicked woman, but most agree that she was a fierce pig. This beast was a deadly threat to anyone who crossed her path. After a brief struggle, the young hero killed the sow and continued on his way.

Next Theseus came across the outlaw Sciron who lived on a cliff above the sea. Sciron captured travelers and forced them to wash his feet. In the middle of this task, he kicked them over the edge of the cliff into the sea where a giant turtle waited to eat them. Theseus pretended to begin to wash Sciron's feet, but instead he grabbed the outlaw and threw him over the cliff to be eaten.

Theseus had almost reached Athens when darkness fell. He was at the village of Erineus and met a kindly man named Procrustes who offered him a room for the night. This villager frequently took visitors into his home. After feeding his guests a meal, he would lead them to a comfortable bed. Before they knew it, they were tied up while their host pulled out a saw and ropes. He said that his guests must fit the bed exactly. Those who were too tall were cut to size. Those who were too short were stretched with ropes. Theseus turned the tables on Procrustes, and fatally made him fit into his own bed.

When Theseus walked through the gates of Athens, everyone knew that the young hero had cleared the road of outlaws. But they did not know who he was. His appearance was strange to the Athenians. He wore a long, loose garment and had his hair neatly braided. Workmen finishing the roof of Apollo's temple mocked him. They asked why such a beautiful maiden was walking around by herself. Theseus unyoked a pair of oxen from a nearby cart and threw both of them onto the roof with his bare hands. No one in Athens ever teased him again.

Medea, a sorceress who had gone to Athens for protection, was suspicious of Theseus. She was King Aegeus's advisor, and they had a son together named Medus. Medus would inherit his father's throne if there were no other son. Medea realized who Theseus was. She whispered to Aegeus that this celebrated hero was a danger to the city. Aegeus was already on his guard against anyone who might try to steal his throne because he had a brother, Pallas, the father of fifty grown sons, who was eager do just that. It was easy for Medea to talk the distrustful Aegeus into getting rid of Theseus.

Aegeus sent Theseus to slay a dangerous bull. The king expected the young man to be killed, but it was the bull that died. Surprised, the king invited Theseus to a feast and placed him on the seat of honor. Medea mixed deadly poison in a goblet of wine and offered it to Theseus. The young hero was just about to drink when Aegeus saw the sword hanging from his belt. He recognized it as his own and knocked the cup from Theseus's hands. Aegeus proclaimed that the visitor was his own son, the heir to the throne of Athens.

Medea was driven into exile with her son. Theseus's uncle Pallas and his fifty sons tried to slay the hero, but were defeated. Theseus was now sure to be the next king.

Every nine years the king of Athens was forced to send seven young men and seven maidens to Crete as victims for the monstrous, man-eating Minotaur. Many years before, Minos, king of Crete and son of Europa and Zeus, had attacked Athens. Athens was forced to surrender and to agree to send fourteen young people to a terrible death every nine years.

The Minotaur was born because Minos disobeyed Poseidon. After the old king of Crete died, Minos drove away his brothers and took the throne. He asked Poseidon to prove that he was best suited to rule by sending a magnificent bull as a sign. Minos promised to sacrifice the beast to Poseidon. The bull was so splendid that Minos couldn't bear to kill it, so he substituted another beast. Poseidon was not pleased. He made Pasiphae, Minos's wife, fall madly in love with the bull. Pasiphae asked a builder named Daedalus to help her win the bull's love. This craftsman built a lifelike wooden cow big enough for the queen to crawl inside. The queen then became pregnant by the bull and gave birth to a terrible creature with the head of a bull and the body of a man.

Minos was afraid to kill the monster. He ordered Daedalus to build a maze called the Labyrinth to hide the Minotaur. Prisoners were punished by being forced into the Labyrinth's twists and turns. Not one found their way out before the Minotaur ate them.

All the people of Athens prayed that their children would not be chosen as food for the Minotaur, but Theseus volunteered to be one of the victims. His father begged him to change his mind, but the young man wanted to kill the monster. King Minos laughed and encouraged the boy in his hopeless quest. Theseus boarded a ship with Minos and the rest of the young men and women. Aegeus made the ship's captain promise, on his return to Athens, to raise a white sail if his son lived, and a black sail if Theseus died.

Minos and Theseus quarreled on the voyage. The king grew so angry that he threw his ring into the sea and demanded that Theseus find it. Theseus dove in and met a group of sea nymphs who gave him the ring, along with a crown that Aphrodite had given to Thetis at her wedding to Peleus. Minos was even angrier when Theseus returned with both prizes.

When the ship reached Crete, Theseus begged to join some contests. Minos hoped Theseus would defeat his own general Taurus, who always won every event. Theseus then defeated Taurus in wrestling, and the king's daughter Ariadne fell in love with Theseus on the spot.

Ariadne couldn't bear the thought of Theseus being eaten by the Minotaur. She went to Daedalus to see if he knew a way out of the maze. The architect told the girl to have Theseus tie a ball of thread to the entrance and unroll it as he worked his way deep into the Labyrinth. If he was able to kill the Minotaur, he could follow the thread back out. Theseus made his way into the depths of the maze in front of the rest of the victims. He killed the Minotaur and then led the youths and maidens out of the twisting Labyrinth by following the thread. With Ariadne at his side, he sailed away from Crete.

Some stories say Theseus stopped at the island of Naxos on his way home. By then Ariadne was pregnant, but he either forgot her or abandoned her on the beach. He left behind the young woman who had given up everything to save him.

Theseus was so anxious to get home to his father and tell him the good news that he forgot to raise the white sail. Aegeus waited on the heights of the Acropolis for his son to return. When he saw the black-sailed ship, he thought Theseus was dead and threw himself onto the rocks below. When the prince rushed from the port to the city, he heard the sad news that Aegeus was dead. Theseus was now king of Athens.

Up to that time, the countryside around the city, known as Attica, was made up of dozens of quarreling villages. The villages didn't cooperate with Athens. As a result, the city was weak. Theseus took control of the villages, made them part of Athens, and created a democratic government.

Government didn't interest Theseus for long. As soon as he had control of Attica, he looked for a new adventure. The young king had heard of women warriors who lived on the distant shores of the Black Sea. These females spent their spare time practicing war rather than weaving. If they had boy babies, they killed them. Healthy girls were raised to be warriors. When a daughter came of age, she would cut off her right breast so that she might better draw a bow. They were called Amazons from the words *a* (no) and *mazos* (breast).

After a long sea voyage, Theseus arrived at the land of the Amazons and was welcomed by their queen, Antiope. At the end of his visit, he seized Antiope and sailed away. Soon after he arrived back in Athens, he saw thousands of Amazon warriors galloping toward the city. A brutal war followed. Theseus and his men defended their city bravely, but they were no match for the women. The Amazons forced their way into the very heart of Athens.

Everything depended on a final battle. Theseus called his men together and made sacrifices to the god Fear, praying that they might not falter. When the Amazons attacked, the Athenians fought until the temples and marketplace were covered with blood. The female warriors were at last defeated. As the Amazons made their way back home, Antiope bore Theseus a son, Hippolytus, and died.

Theseus could be reckless in his adventures. He asked his friend Peirithous, king of the Lapith tribe in Thessaly, to help him kidnap the young princess Helen. The friends went to Sparta and saw the maiden dancing in the temple of Aphrodite. They grabbed her and took her back to Athens. Theseus left Helen with his mother Aethra until she reached marriageable age.

As soon as Helen was settled, Peirithous asked Theseus to join him on a quest. He was determined to journey to the underworld, kidnap Persephone, and make her his own. Theseus thought Peirithous was mad, but he could not resist the challenge. They journeyed down to the land of the dead and came to the palace of Hades. The overconfident young men told the god why they were there, then sat down in two fine chairs near his throne. As soon as they were seated, snakes wrapped around their limbs, holding them tightly in place. Hercules came down to the underworld soon afterward. He freed his cousin Theseus but was unable to free Peirithous. Hercules returned Theseus to the surface while Peirithous remained seated forever in the land of the dead.

Theseus returned to Athens and found the city in chaos after a war with the Spartans. Helen's brothers, Castor and Pollux, destroyed Attica and took their sister back. They also took Theseus's mother to be Helen's slave. The people of Athens knew that their king had been engaged in heroic nonsense instead of defending his city, so they banished him. Theseus cursed the people and sailed to the island of Scyros, where he was welcomed by the local king, Lycomedes. After a good dinner, his host invited Theseus to take a walk along the beautiful cliffs to help forget his troubles. Lycomedes was secretly jealous of Theseus, so he pushed his guest over the cliff and ended the hero's life.

For many years Theseus was forgotten by the Athenians until his ghost led them to victory against the Persians at the battle of Marathon. The citizens brought his bones home and honored him as a divine hero, founder of democracy, and savior of Athens.

DAEDALUS and ICARUS

When Theseus fled from Crete with Ariadne, Minos was angry that Daedalus had helped the hero. He threw Daedalus into prison along with his son Icarus. While he was in prison, Daedalus thought about the twists and turns of his own life.

Daedalus had been born in Athens. He became a master sculptor and inventor, and the best young men were eager to study under him. One of these was his nephew, Perdix. The boy showed such skill that he threatened to outshine his master. Daedalus could not bear that, so he tossed Perdix off the Acropolis. He was put on trial for murder, but fled to Crete.

Now, years later, Daedalus was desperate to flee from Crete. Minos patrolled the coast with his ships, but he did not rule the sky. Daedalus built wings of feathers and wax for both himself and his son. When the wings were ready, he warned Icarus to be careful. If he flew too low, the waves would make the wings useless. If he flew too high, the sun would melt the wax. One clear night they set out from the prison roof.

No mortal had ever sailed through the sky like a bird, save for Perseus on his winged sandals. Icarus loved flying. He swooped up and down like an eagle, ignoring the warnings of his father. Daedalus shouted at him to set a steady course, but the boy flew higher and higher. It wasn't long before the heat of the sun melted the wax of his wings. Icarus plunged to his death.

Daedalus was heartbroken, but he continued until he arrived at the court of Cocalus in Sicily. The king was pleased to greet the famous builder and kept Daedalus carefully hidden. Minos sailed the Mediterranean in search of him. He cleverly gave each ruler he visited a spiral shell and promised a reward if the king could pass a thread all the way through it. No one had been able to accomplish this task, but Cocalus was eager to win the treasure. He gave the puzzle to his secret guest. Minos knew only Daedalus had the skill required, so whichever king claimed the reward would surely be hiding him.

Daedalus tied a thread to a tiny ant and coaxed the insect to crawl all the way through the shell. When Cocalus went to collect his prize, Minos knew he had found Daedalus. He demanded the king surrender the builder or go to war. Cocalus quickly agreed, but asked Minos if he couldn't first prepare a grand feast for him. He also promised to have his beautiful daughters give Minos a bath he would never forget.

After a fine banquet, the girls led Minos to the tub. The young women brought large jars of water to fill the tub and poured them over Minos. The screams of the king echoed through the town. The daughters had filled the jars with boiling water. The king who had caused the death and misery of so many met his own painful end in a bathtub at the hands of beautiful young maidens.

BELLEROPHON

Like Argos and Athens, the city of Corinth also had heroes. One of the most famous was Bellerophon, grandson of Sisyphus. Like many heroes, Bellerophon often acted foolishly. In one violent outburst, he murdered his own brother. He fled to the town of Tiryns in Argos. Proetus ruled there in those days before his daughters were driven mad by Dionysus. Bellerophon pleaded with the king to purify him. Proetus carried out the ceremony so that Bellerophon would not be cursed by the gods.

Stheneboea, the wife of Proetus, fell in love with Bellerophon and was rejected by him. She made up a story and demanded that Proetus kill Bellerophon. Proetus feared the curse of Zeus if he killed a guest in his home, so he asked Bellerophon to deliver a letter to his father-in-law, King Iobates of Lycia, across the Aegean Sea. The young man was eager for a journey, so gladly agreed.

Bellerophon traveled to the court of Iobates. Good manners meant hosts couldn't question guests until they had been wined and dined, so the king did not ask his visitor his business

until nine days had passed. When Bellerophon handed over the letter, the king read: "King Iobates, please kill the man who brought you this letter."

The ruler was now in the same position that Proetus had avoided. He had to honor the wishes of a relative, but he also feared the curse of Zeus.

Iobates came up with the perfect solution. He asked Bellerophon to kill the monster known as the Chimaera. This fearsome creature was a lion in front, a fire-breathing goat in the middle, and a serpent behind. The king knew Bellerophon could not survive. But the young hero, with the help of Athena, tamed the winged horse Pegasus and flew against the Chimaera. He slew the monster and returned to the king ready for his next adventure.

Iobates sent Bellerophon against a powerful enemy, the Solymi. These fierce people were always at war with the Lycians on their borders. Bellerophon and Pegasus swept down on them from above and killed them all. Next, Iobates sent Bellerophon against the Amazons, but he defeated them too. Finally, the king picked the best and bravest of all his warriors and set a trap for the hero. Bellerophon fought ferociously and cut down all the soldiers set against him.

At last Iobates showed him the letter from Proetus and offered Bellerophon his daughter Philonoe in marriage along with half his kingdom.

The couple lived happily in Lycia and had many children, but Bellerophon could not forget that Proetus and Stheneboea had wronged him. He flew to Tiryns on Pegasus and offered to give the queen a ride on his magic horse. Just as Stheneboea was enjoying the ride, Bellerophon pushed her off the horse.

Some stories say that Bellerophon wanted to live among the gods. He flew on Pegasus to Mount Olympus, but Zeus sent a gadfly to sting the horse and Bellerophon was thrown to the ground and crippled by the fall. Ever after, no one would welcome this mortal who had challenged the gods. Bellerophon was doomed to wander the earth alone.

MELAMPUS

Not all heroes had superhuman strength and flying horses. Some, like the seer Melampus from the town of Pylos, used magic to accomplish great deeds.

Melampus and his brother Bias grew up the best of friends.

Melampus longed for the country life, so he left his brother in the city and went to live in a rural part of the kingdom. In front of his quiet house was a large oak tree in which a family of snakes had built their lair. Melampus killed the older snakes, but took their young and raised them as pets. The snakes became so tame that they slept on his bed.

One night Melampus awoke to discover the snakes licking his ears. The next morning, he was amazed to find that he could understand the singing of the birds. He understood the chattering of mice in the barn and the braying of his goats. The language of every animal was revealed to him, but it was the birds that interested him the most. Flying between heaven and earth, they heard the gods and shared the secrets of what was to come. By listening, Melampus could discover the future.

Melampus's brother Bias was deeply in love with Pero, the daughter of Neleus, king of Pylos. Neleus told Bias he could have his daughter's hand in marriage if he brought to him the cattle of Thessaly's King Phylacus. These animals were guarded by a fierce dog that never slept. Melampus knew from the birds that he would be imprisoned for a year if he tried to steal the cattle, but he loved his brother so much that he tried to help. Of course he was captured.

Melampus spent the next year in a dark hut. One evening he heard one worm tell another that he had finished chewing through the roof beam. Melampus asked to be moved as some worms had revealed his roof was about to fall in. The guards laughed but did as he asked. The next day the roof of the hut collapsed. King Phylacus heard about this strange event and called Melampus to his court. He offered to let Melampus go free if the seer could reveal how Iphiclus, the king's son, could have a child. The young man was a great athlete and so fast he could run over the top of a wheat field without crushing the grain, but he was unable to have children. Melampus offered to help if Phylacus would give him his cattle as a wedding gift for Bias. The king agreed.

Melampus sacrificed two bulls and the birds of the air feasted on the meat. Last to arrive was a vulture. The soothsayer asked the vulture if he knew why Iphiclus was unable to father a child. The old bird said that Phylacus had once stuck a bloody knife into a sacred oak. As the years passed, the bark of the tree grew over the knife. The gods were displeased. To make things right, Phylacus needed to dig the knife out of the tree and feed the rust from the blade to Iphiclus. Phylacus did as he was told. Nine months later, Iphiclus's wife gave birth to a boy.

Melampus returned to Pylos with the cattle, and Bias married the princess. Melampus lived a happy life and had many children. Kings called on him for his skills in prophecy and magic. After the daughters of Proetus were driven mad by Dionysus, Melampus returned sanity to the girls. He did so only after he made Proetus swear to give him a large part of his kingdom. He shared this land with his brother Bias so that both grew old as lords of Argos.

ATALANTA

Most women in Greek myths spent their days weaving and raising children. But a few accomplished more amazing deeds. One of the most famous of these was Atalanta. Her father, Iasus, wanted only sons and so left his newborn daughter to die in a dark forest. A she-bear nursed Atalanta with her own cubs. Then a band of hunters found the girl and raised her in their village. She grew into a beautiful young woman.

Atalanta lived a carefree life roaming the mountains and hunting with male friends. She dedicated herself to the goddess Artemis, swearing she would never marry. Most of her friends accepted this. One day when she was hunting with the centaurs Rhoecus and Hylaeus, they tried to force themselves on her. Atalanta killed them with her swift arrows.

Atalanta was the only woman allowed to take part in the Calydonian boar hunt along with Meleager and Theseus. Some stories say it was she who killed this dangerous beast. Not long after, Atalanta defeated the great king Peleus, father of Achilles, in a wrestling contest. Some stories even claim that she sailed with Jason and the Argonauts.

Atalanta made a name for herself, and her father realized she was the girl he left to die. He welcomed his daughter home and tried to take up his fatherly duties. First among these was to arrange a marriage. Atalanta convinced Iasus to ask the men who wanted her hand to compete against her in a race. If a man won, she would marry him. If he lost, she would kill him on the spot.

Atalanta knew that no man could beat her, but she was so beautiful that many men tried. At the end of each race, Atalanta waited for them at the finish line with a sword in her hand.

One young man from the mountains of Arcadia loved Atalanta. Melanion knew he could not beat her in a fair race, so he went to the temple of Aphrodite and prayed for help. The goddess gave Melanion three golden apples and a plan to win.

The young man arrived at the palace and asked for Atalanta's hand. Iasus urged him to change his mind, but Melanion was determined to try. Atalanta took her place at the starting line and flashed Melanion a charming smile, knowing he would soon be dead.

The race began and Melanion took off. Atalanta let the boy get ahead for a short stretch. Then she began to fly down the course. Just as she was passing Melanion, he threw a golden apple

on the ground. Atalanta had never seen anything so beautiful. She stopped and picked it up, letting Melanion pull ahead of her.

Atalanta caught up again, but just as she did Melanion dropped another apple. The young woman couldn't help but stop and pick it up.

They were nearing the end of the race and Atalanta was coming from behind. Melanion took his final apple and threw it far to the side of the track. Atalanta could not resist the golden fruit. She ran to the edge of the path, swooped up the apple, and flew to the finish line. It was too late—Melanion crossed just ahead of her.

Iasus gave the couple his blessing and they married. Melanion could not believe his good luck, but on the way back to Arcadia with his wife, he insulted Zeus in his own temple. Such an insult did not escape the ruler of the gods. Zeus turned both Melanion and Atalanta into lions. The couple lived out their days roaming the mountains and hunting their prey. It was a cruel fate for Melanion, but for Atalanta it was a wonderful life.

PROCNE and PHILOMELA

There was once a king of Athens named Pandion who had two beautiful daughters, Procne and Philomela. Although his family life was peaceful and happy, Athens was threatened by raids from outside the city. When the bloodthirsty brutes were almost inside Pandion's gates, King Tereus from Thrace arrived and drove away the invaders. Tereus, a son of Ares, was a great warrior. Pandion was so grateful that he promised his friend the hand of his eldest daughter in marriage.

Procne said farewell to her father and sister with many tears, then boarded Tereus's ship to sail to her new home in Thrace. They had a son named Itys who was his father's pride and joy.

When Itys was five years old, Procne asked Tereus if she might make the journey back to Athens for a short visit: "If I have found any favor in your eyes, allow me to travel to my home. Or, if you prefer, let my sister come here to visit me. It would mean so much to me, dear Tereus, if you allowed her to come."

Tereus agreed to fetch Philomela himself. The journey to Athens was swift and soon he was sailing into port. Pandion greeted his son-in-law warmly. The kings talked late into the evening. Then Philomela walked into the room. She had been an awkward girl on Tereus's previous trip, but now she was a beautiful young woman.

Tereus wanted Philomela more than anything in the world. He hid his feelings and greeted her as if he were the most proper of brothers-in-law. He then told of how Procne longed to have her sister visit. He swore he would protect Philomela from all harm. Everyone was deeply touched by Tereus's love for his wife. Philomela begged that she might be allowed to return with dear Tereus.

Pandion hesitated, but his daughter's pleas and Tereus's earnest vows convinced him. Pandion agreed to let Philomela go. The king of Athens waved good-bye. He felt a terrible worry in his heart.

As soon as the ship landed in Thrace, Tereus dragged

Philomela to a hut hidden deep in the woods. The maiden begged to see her sister. The king laughed, then forced himself on her.

Afterward, Philomela stood before Tereus, unbroken: "You monster! Do you care nothing for your friendship with my father? Does my sister's love mean nothing to you? I will shout out your foul deed until the very trees and rocks cry out your shame."

Tereus pulled out his razor-sharp sword. Philomela offered him her throat. But the king didn't kill her. He sliced off her tongue so she could not tell what he had done.

Tereus placed guards outside the hut and returned to his palace. He told Procne between sobs that her dear sister had died on the voyage. Procne was deeply sad. She built a memorial to Philomela and offered sacrifices so that her spirit might find rest.

A year passed. The guards outside Philomela's wretched hut were ever watchful and the woods beyond were dark and deep. Even if she could escape, how could she explain what had happened without words? But pain brings with it sharp wits. There was an old loom in her hut, so Philomela made the guards understand that she would like to weave upon it. She was given the materials needed and began her work.

On the tapestry she wove the story of her voyage from Athens, the vicious attack by Tereus, and her lonely prison. She showed how she had suffered. When she finished, she rolled up the weaving and gave it to an old woman to deliver to the queen. Procne read the story it told. Then, without a word, she withdrew to her room.

Normally, Procne was not allowed beyond the palace

grounds alone, but that night was the celebration of Dionysus when women worshipped the god in the nearby woods. Procne joined in the festivities dressed as one of the god's followers. Then she slipped away and came to the small hut. In her disguise, the guards did not recognize her. She slipped inside.

Philomela was overjoyed to see Procne. Procne told Philomela to ready herself for vengeance: "This is no time for tears. I will burn Tereus alive in his palace or cut out his own tongue and eyes. I will do anything to punish him for what he did to you."

Procne then snuck her sister into the palace. When Philomela was safely hidden, Procne's young son Itys ran to his mother. She hugged him and said: "How like your father you are." A terrible plan began to form in her mind.

Later that evening, Procne invited her husband to a banquet. This was a special feast of her homeland, she said, in which only the lord of the house dined, served by his wife. Once he was seated, she brought him platters of meat cooked with tasty herbs. The king was hungry, so he enjoyed every bite. He praised his wife for the delicious meal and asked her to call their son Itys to join him. But she said: "That won't be necessary, my lord, for the one you seek is now inside you."

Tereus didn't understand what she meant, but then Philomela walked into the room covered in blood and holding the knife that mother and aunt had used to butcher the boy. She then hurled the head of Itys into the lap of Tereus.

When he realized what had happened, he screamed in agony, asking the Furies to witness the sisters' monstrous deed.

Procne and Philomela fled from the castle, running into the forest as fast as birds in flight. Tereus raced after them, anxious to slay them both. The gods took pity on the sisters and transformed Tereus into a hoopoe—a small bird with a stiff crest like a war helmet. They changed Procne into a swallow and, at last, Philomela became a nightingale that sings sweetly for all to hear.

Lovers

NARCISSUS and ECHO

Tiresias of Thebes became the most famous soothsayer in all of Greece. People from far and wide, including the nymph Liriope, asked him what the future held. She gave birth to the most beautiful baby anyone had ever seen and named him Narcissus. Liriope asked Tiresias if her son would live a long and happy life. "Only if he never knows himself," was the seer's mysterious reply.

By the time Narcissus was sixteen, he was famous for his good looks. He wanted nothing to do with love and claimed that no one would ever touch his heart.

The nymph Echo had once been an attendant of Hera. No one could talk as much as Echo. Whenever Zeus saw the nymph in Hera's company, he knew he could sneak away without notice. Hera grew so angry at Echo for distracting her that she made it so Echo could only repeat the last few words spoken to her.

Banished from Mount Olympus, Echo wandered the fields and forests. One day she came upon Narcissus while he was hunting with his friends, and fell in love. How could she tell him if she could only repeat the words he spoke? She followed him until he became separated from his friends. Narcissus called out:

"Is anyone here?"

"Here," said Echo.

Narcissus was surprised by the sound of a woman's voice.

"Please, come to me," he urged.

"Come to me," replied Echo.

The youth could find no one.

"I'm here, let's meet together," Narcissus pleaded.

"Let's meet together," answered Echo.

The nymph ran to Narcissus and covered him with kisses.

Narcissus pushed her away and ran. Still hopelessly in love, Echo stayed hidden in the forest longing for a glimpse of Narcissus as he hunted. She lost all interest in eating and sleeping. Soon she was nothing but bones, then even these turned to dust and she was just a voice haunting the forest.

Narcissus scorned everyone who tried to win his love. One bitter young man rejected by Narcissus prayed to the goddess Nemesis. From the dark places of the earth the goddess of revenge heard his cry.

There was a crystal-clear pool in the woods. One day Narcissus came to it and cupped his hands to bring water to his lips. He saw his reflection. The young man had never seen anyone so beautiful. He tried to take the figure in his arms, but

every time his fingers touched the water, the reflection disappeared in the ripples.

Narcissus sat by the pool unable to tear his eyes away. Night came and the bright moon rose, but the young man took no notice. Food and drink meant nothing. He wasted away day after day.

"You are so near, but I cannot touch you, alas," he moaned to his reflection.

"Alas," Echo sighed.

Even when Narcissus was only skin and bones, he could only gaze at his image. With his last breath he looked into the pond and whispered: "Farewell."

"Farewell," cried Echo.

The youth died at the edge of the pool, his weary head drooping over the water. The gods transformed his broken body into a beautiful flower that bends ever downward. Even in Hades, Narcissus spends eternity gazing at his own image in the River Styx.

PYRAMUS
and THISBE

In the great city of Babylon lived two young lovers side by side but far apart. They were Pyramus, the most handsome youth in the land, and Thisbe, the most beautiful maiden. Although their houses shared a common wall, their families hated each other and the two were never allowed to speak to each other. But love always finds a way.

There was a small crack in their shared wall that no one

had ever noticed. Pyramus and Thisbe found this opening and whispered through it when both houses were asleep. Each time they parted, they promised to meet again the next night. Soon the two could no longer bear to be apart. They made plans to meet at an ancient tomb outside the city beside a cool spring with a tall mulberry tree.

Thisbe carefully opened her door the next evening and walked quietly through the streets of Babylon. Once outside the gates, she came to the tree and sat down to wait for Pyramus. But suddenly she saw a lion in the darkness. It had just killed a cow and its face was covered in blood. As it approached the spring to quench its thirst, Thisbe ran away in terror. She dropped her cloak on the ground as she fled. The lion found the cloak and tore it with its bloody jaws, though it left the cloak on the ground beside the tree.

Pyramus arrived at the pool just as the lion left and saw its tracks along with the bloody cloak of his dear Thisbe. He recognized the garment and thought that a lion had slain the maiden. He collapsed in grief, believing that it was his fault she had died. He then pulled out his sword and plunged it into his side. As he fell on the ground, his blood shot into the air, turning the white berries of the tree bright red.

It was then that Thisbe came back to the pool. She saw a body lying there and was frightened, but realized it was her own Pyramus. She ran to him and held him in hers arms, crying out his name. At the sound of her voice, Pyramus used the last of his strength to open his eyes. He gazed at her one last time, then closed his eyes forever. Thisbe wept over his body long into the night. Then she took his sword and stabbed herself in the heart.

The gods took pity on the two lovers. From that day forward the fruit of the mulberry turned crimson when it was ripe in their memory. Even their parents were touched by the love their children had shown each other and placed their ashes in a common urn.

CEYX and ALCYONE

Over the mountains, north of the sacred site of Delphi, was the small kingdom of Trachis, ruled over by Ceyx. Ceyx was the son of Lucifer, the morning star. He was a good king who loved peace and welcomed refugees to his land. He took in Peleus, father of Achilles, after he had killed his brother. He gave shelter to Hercules when Hercules was weary. Both guests repaid their host. Peleus helped slay a monstrous wolf, and Hercules drove away hostile invaders from Ceyx's borders.

Ceyx was troubled by all his kingdom had suffered and wanted to seek the council of Apollo at Delphi. The king decided to travel there by sea. His beautiful wife, Alcyone, daughter of the god of the winds, begged him to reconsider. Like all Greeks, she knew the sea was dangerous and could crush a ship in a moment.

Ceyx loved his wife, but he felt he had to consult with the god: "I swear to you by the bright fire of my father, I will return to you—if the Fates allow."

Alcyone could not change her husband's mind. She watched him sail away. He waved to her for as long as he could see her.

A few days later, a terrible storm began to blow. Rain fell, lightning lit the sky, and waves rose like mountains over the little ship. Every man, King Ceyx included, tried to hold the ship together. They prayed and wept and cursed until an enormous wave crashed over the ship and broke it into pieces.

A few men, including Ceyx, clung to timbers hoping to outlast the storm. The force of the waves was too strong. One by one they slipped beneath the raging water until only Ceyx remained, clinging to a plank. He thought only of Alcyone. He prayed that his body might wash onto his own shore so that her hands might bury him. Finally, the waves closed over him.

Alcyone prayed to Hera every day for her husband's safe return. The wife of Zeus could not bear to hear Alcyone's prayers. She asked the god Sleep to send a vision to Alcyone, revealing the fate of her husband. Sleep ordered his son Morpheus to enter Alcyone's dreams and reveal the truth. Morpheus appeared before her wearing the form of her husband, with water dripping from his hair: "Sweet Alcyone, cease your prayers for my safe return. I was caught in a raging storm and dragged to my death by the cruel sea. Good-bye, my love."

Alcyone awoke crying, "Wait, I will come with you!," but the vision was gone. Her attendants told her that it was just a dream, but she knew the truth. "My husband is dead," she cried. "The gods have sent me a message."

She made her way to the shore and knelt in the sand, weeping and looking out to sea. Suddenly she saw the body of her husband drifting on the waves. Alcyone leaped into the sea. By the will of the gods, her arms became wings. She flew to Ceyx and kissed him. He felt her touch and opened his eyes.

The gods had revived Ceyx. They changed both husband and wife into birds, named halcyons or kingfishers. It was said that Alcyone's father, Aeolus, caused the winds to cease for a week each winter. During these seven halcyon days, the pair floated peacefully in their nest on the waves of the sea.

GLAUCUS and SCYLLA

The sea was home to a god named Glaucus who fell deeply in love with a young maiden named Scylla. Glaucus was once a fisherman on a quiet shore. One day he took his catch and laid it in a meadow. As soon as the dead fish touched the grass they began to stir; then they jumped back into the water. Glaucus wondered if the grass had magical powers. He nibbled a blade. Suddenly he ran to the shore and jumped into the waves, leaving the land behind forever.

The sea nymphs brought him to the ancient gods Oceanus and Tethys. They instructed the nymphs to sing a magic song nine times and bathe Glaucus in the waters of a hundred streams.

When this was done, Glaucus was a god. He awoke to find his beard was green, his arms blue, and he had the long tail of a fish in place of his legs.

Glaucus enjoyed his life in the sea, swimming with the nymphs. One day his travels took him to a secluded cove where he spied a mortal woman of extraordinary beauty. This was Scylla who was swimming in a hidden inlet. Glaucus greeted her.

Scylla sprang from the water and sprinted up the side of a nearby cliff overhanging the sea. Hiding behind a rock, she looked down at this strange creature. Glaucus pleaded: "Dear maiden, please don't run away. I am no wild creature of the sea, but a god. I was once human like you, but was changed to what you see. I thought I was happy, but what good is it to be divine if you are frightened of me? Please come down."

Scylla ran away before he had even finished speaking. Glaucus did not know how to win her love, but then he remembered Circe.

The famous sea witch was the daughter of Helios, the sun, and granddaughter of Oceanus himself. She lived on an island where she used her magic to turn men into beasts. Glaucus begged her for a love potion, but Circe wanted him for herself: "Why seek after some mortal woman when you can have a goddess? Forget this girl and be mine."

Glaucus answered: "Trees will grow upon the waves before I abandon my love for Scylla."

Circe flew into a rage. She knew she could not harm Glaucus, but she could destroy his dreams. So she mixed dreadful herbs and roots, then sung over them the charms of Hecate. When all was ready, she made her way to Scylla's cove.

The maiden didn't see Circe pour her poison into the peaceful water, then fly away. Glaucus arrived just as the witch

left and watched his love from a hiding place, not wishing to frighten her again.

Scylla waded into the cove. The water was cool and wonderful. Then monstrous heads suddenly sprang from her body. Six snarling beasts like wolves with horrid teeth and long snakelike necks shot forth from her. She screamed in terror and ran to the overhanging cliff hoping to leave the beasts behind. Soon she was rooted to the rock and couldn't move. The maiden had become the ugliest monster anyone could imagine. Scylla screamed until she lost her mind. She struck out at anyone who sailed near, tearing them to pieces. She became a legend among sailors who avoided her. Only Glaucus wept for her, knowing what she had once been and what she had become, all because of his love.

HERO and LEANDER

On the shores of the narrow straits of the Hellespont that separated Europe from Asia lived a young priestess of Aphrodite named Hero. She was from a rich and noble family in the city of Sestus and there she served the goddess in her temple. Hero was so beautiful that all the men from the surrounding towns prayed to be with her: "I've been to Sparta and seen Helen herself, but I've never beheld a girl as lovely as her. Oh Aphrodite, send me a woman like that!"

There was one young man who longed for Hero more than any other. His name was Leander and he lived just across the Hellespont in Asia. He was from a humble family. When he first saw Hero, a fire kindled inside him. He dreamed of her day and night. But what did he have to offer to someone as beautiful as a goddess?

One day at the temple he knew he had to talk to Hero or die of longing. He stood trembling before her, but had no words to express his love. Hero was moved by this shy young man. She took his hand. Then she smiled and began to tease him: "Stranger, I'm just a girl. Is there something you want to tell me? I can't say my father would be pleased that such a handsome young man is trying to charm me. The goddess I serve would be none too happy either."

Leander found his voice: "Most excellent maiden, fairest flower that ever bloomed on these shores, I swear that my intentions are honorable. I love you with all my heart. The goddess you serve is dear to me and I have the highest regard for your father and mother. I know I am only a poor boy, but my love is pure."

Hero saw that Leander meant every word. She knew that he was the man for her. Her father would never permit her to take this poor lad as her husband, so they made a secret plan.

All that summer and autumn, every night when the sky was clear, Hero placed a lamp in her window. Leander would see the light shining across the narrow Hellespont from Europe to Asia and dive into the

waves. He followed the light to the home of his true love. They vowed to live in their hearts as husband and wife forever. Just as the dawn broke, Leander would swim back to his home in Asia. They told no one of their secret marriage.

When winter came, gales stirred the frosty seas. Hero begged Leander to wait until spring to return to her, but he would not allow wind and waves to separate them. One stormy night, the lamp blew out while he was midway across the straits. The waves crashed against him and the wind blew him back. Without the light to guide him, Leander became lost. The bitter wind blinded him and the water poured down his throat, yet he struggled on.

Day finally came and Hero looked desperately from her window, hoping to catch a glimpse of Leander. Her worst fear came true when she saw, on the rocks below, the lifeless body of her love. Unable to live without him, she threw herself from the window to her death. The townspeople found the couple together, gently tossed by the waves of the sea.

HYPERMNESTRA and LYNCEUS

One of the many descendants of Io, who was turned into a cow by Hera, was Danaus. Danaus had a twin brother named Egyptus who had fifty sons. Danaus had only had daughters, also fifty in number. Egyptus ruled over Egypt while Danaus was king of the smaller land of Libya. Both brothers were suspicious of each other.

One day Egyptus sent a message to Danaus offering to make peace. He offered to seal the bargain with the marriage of all fifty of his sons to all fifty of his brother's daughters. Danaus suspected a trick. With the advice of Athena he fled with his daughters and settled in Greece near Argos, where he became king of the region.

Egyptus sent his sons to try to convince his brother to allow the wedding to take place. Danaus decided to remove any future threat from his brother and his nephews. First he agreed to the wedding. Then he gave a sharp dagger to each of his daughters. At the end of the marriage feast, each of the sons led his new bride back to his quarters. The daughters pulled daggers from beneath their pillows and slit their husbands' throats.

All except one. The eldest daughter, Hypermnestra, had been given to her cousin Lynceus. She was touched by how kind and caring her new husband was and could not go through with the plan: "Get up! Go, flee from this place before you sleep forever. Don't let my father or wicked sisters catch you. They have pounced on their new husbands like lionesses and slaughtered each one. My father can do what he wants with me, but I cannot kill someone so gentle and kind. Go, don't look back! We will find each other again someday."

Hypermnestra then helped Lynceus escape to a nearby village. There, he lit a beacon to show he was safe, then fled the country.

The other forty-nine daughters brought the heads of

their husbands to their father, but Hypermnestra arrived empty-handed. Her father put her in chains as a punishment. In time he forgave her and allowed his daughter to join her husband who became king of Argos.

The sisters of Hypermnestra had difficulty finding good men. Their father searched for new husbands for them, but men were afraid to marry women with such bloody pasts. Finally, with a great deal of bribery, Danaus found husbands for his daughters. Their wicked deed did catch up with them eventually. When they died and went down to Hades, they were forced to spend eternity pouring water into leaky jars that had to be constantly refilled.

BAUCIS and PHILEMON

Once in the hills of Phrygia there was a remarkable tree. From a single trunk grew both a sturdy oak and a broad linden. How it came to be is a story of true love and a reminder to show kindness to strangers.

Zeus was concerned with the care of strangers. He would disguise himself as a beggar to test how the people of a land would treat him. Once he took Hermes with him and visited Phrygia. The pair went from house to house. They asked for a cup of water or a crust of bread, but were sent away empty-handed.

At last they came to a hut on a hill that was smaller than the rest. The cracks in the wall were so big, the fierce winter wind blew through the shack. Zeus knocked on the door and was welcomed by an old couple. Baucis and Philemon were poor but happy.

Philemon set out a bench for his visitors. Baucis fed the fire to heat water in her single pot. She collected cabbage leaves from her garden and placed them in the water. Philemon added strips of bacon cut from a precious side of pork.

When the broth was ready, Baucis wiped the table with mint leaves and placed all the food they had before the strangers— olives, eggs, wild nuts, figs, radishes, and a small piece of cheese. She put the soup before them along with cups of sour wine. The old couple were proud to be able to lay out what for them was a grand feast.

The wine cups never became empty. Baucis and Philemon suspected their visitors were more than beggars. They asked their guests to wait while they roasted a goose. This bird was the source of their eggs and the guardian of their home, but they were willing to sacrifice it. Zeus and Hermes watched as Philemon and Baucis chased the goose. At last Zeus spoke: "Please forget about the goose, dear friends. We are gods and have no need of such food. None of your wicked neighbors welcomed us, even though they had far more to give. They have been punished—come and see for yourselves."

The couple were amazed. The entire countryside of fields and houses was covered with a great flood. They wept for their neighbors, and then looked at their hut. It was now a grand palace.

Zeus told them to ask any favor. Baucis and Philemon wanted to be priests of the gods in their new home. They also asked that neither one would have to live without the other.

Zeus granted their wishes. The couple lived into extreme old age. One evening, Baucis saw Philemon sprout leaves. Philemon watched Baucis shoot forth green limbs. The change was so fast that all they had time to say was, "Farewell, my dear love!"

The tree long stood, an oak and a linden woven together. Peasants came to lay boughs beneath the tree as an offering to the gods and as a memorial to the loving couple.

ALPHEUS and ARETHUSA

Few love affairs have happy endings like that of Baucis and Philemon. Often, as in the case of Echo and Narcissus, the feelings were not shared. Such was the love of the river god Alpheus for the beautiful nymph Arethusa.

Arethusa lived in the hills of southern Greece where she was devoted to Artemis. Even for a nymph, Arethusa was extraordinarily lovely and had many suitors. She took no joy

from her beauty. All she wanted was to roam the hills and valleys serving the goddess.

One hot summer's day when she was alone, she came to a
cool stream with crystal-clear water. Willows lined the banks
and gave pleasing shade to a pool in the stream. Arethusa came
to the water's edge and dipped her toe in. Then the nymph
removed her clothes, laid them on a branch, and waded naked
into the water. She swam with joy, until suddenly she thought
she heard a voice coming from deep in the pool. She jumped
out on the far bank and stood in terror: "Where are you going,
Arethusa? Why in such a hurry? I so enjoyed having you swim
through my waters."

The voice called out twice, frightening the maiden, but
she was reluctant to run since her clothes were on the opposite
side of the stream. Then the river god Alpheus rose in human
form from the pool.

Arethusa set off across the forest at a speed no man could
equal, but she was not being chased by a man. As fast as the
nymph was, the god was even faster. Alpheus chased her across
the forest and over mountains, then down through valleys and
up towering cliffs. Arethusa managed to keep just ahead him,
but she was getting tired. At last she called out to Artemis:
"Great goddess, hear me! If ever I have served you faithfully
or carried your bow and quiver on the hunt, help me escape
this god."

Arethusa could run no more. Exhausted she stood with
sweat dripping from her body as Alpheus drew near. Then
she felt the sweat begin to flow so fast that she seemed to be
melting. Her entire body turned to a stream of water and sank
into the ground. Artemis then transported her to safety on an

island off the coast of Sicily where the nymph became a spring.

Such was the love of Alpheus that he would not be discouraged. He turned back into his watery form and followed the maiden through a passage deep under the sea until he reached her island. There he mingled his waters with her own so that the two became one—whether Arethusa wanted it or not.

POMONA and VERTUMNUS

In ancient Italy there lived a beautiful nymph who cared nothing for fields and forests. She spent her time tending the fruit trees of her orchard. Her name was

Pomona and instead of a hunting spear, she carried a pruning hook to trim the branches of her trees. She cared nothing for gods who tried to woo her. She built high the walls of her garden so that no one would interrupt her work with foolish talk of love.

Vertumnus, a god of the countryside, loved Pomona more than all the others. Pomona had scorned him so many times that he disguised himself so that he could catch glimpses of her. One day he was a farmer hauling a basket of barley, the next he was a reaper fresh from cutting hay. Sometimes he dressed as a gardener so that he could help her care for her trees.

One day the god transformed himself into an old woman and entered the orchard. Pomona invited her guest to sit in the cool shade of an apple tree. The white-haired visitor talked of how beautiful Pomona's trees were, but said the maiden herself was even fairer. The old woman dared to kiss the nymph as a grandmother would. Then she began to speak: "Look at that tree holding up the vine that grows next to it. Such a vine is not ashamed to seek the support of a sturdy elm. Is it so different for a maiden such as you? You should not try to live your life standing on your own. I know young Vertumnus loves you. He would gladly help you care for your beautiful orchard."

The old woman then told Pomona a story of a stubborn princess named Anaxarete. She was loved by men throughout her kingdom and beyond, but rejected them all. A poor youth named Iphis loved her more than anyone, but she scorned him. The lad was crushed. He took a rope to the palace and hung himself. His own mother wept on his still-warm body as Anaxarete happened to glance out the window. Not even this tragic scene could touch her heart. She then tried to turn away, but found she was fixed to the spot where she stood. Her limbs turned to marble, then her heart to stone, until she was nothing but a cold statue, feeling nothing forever more.

The old woman cautioned Pomona not to be like the foolish princess. Then the god took his true form and stood before the nymph as Vertumnus. Pomona felt love stirring in her heart at last, then reached out and took his hand.

ENDYMION and SELENE

Selene, the goddess of the moon, traveled across the sky at night looking down on the people of the earth as they slept. One evening her eyes fell upon Endymion, the handsome king of Elis in southern Greece. Although the king was married, Selene came to him many times and bore him fifty daughters.

The love of the moon goddess for Endymion was so strong that she persuaded Zeus to grant Endymion anything he wished. The king considered the generous offer and finally asked that he be allowed to sleep forever, never aging. The ruler of the gods agreed. Endymion went to a mountain cave in Caria across the Aegean Sea and he laid his head on a pillow. He closed his eyes for the last time. There he rested in peace, always young, always fair. On moonless nights, Selene came to him and kissed her mortal lover gently in his endless sleep.

ORPHEUS and EURYDICE

The greatest of all ancient bards was Orpheus. Whenever he played his lyre, wild animals stopped to listen and the rocks of the earth followed him. He was the son of Apollo, who taught him to play, and Calliope, the leader of the Muses. Orpheus had many adventures, including a journey with the Argonauts to seek the Golden Fleece, but his greatest quest was because of love.

Orpheus fell in love with a nymph named Eurydice, and the two planned a grand wedding. As the bride walked to the marriage ceremony, she was bitten by a poisonous serpent and died. The wedding turned into a funeral.

Orpheus could not bear the thought of living without Eurydice, so he decided to journey to the underworld to bring her back. He found an entrance to the realm of Hades and followed the long path downward. Charon was so moved by Orpheus's music that he rowed him across the River Styx without payment. The three-headed dog, Cerberus, became quiet.

135

The Furies stopped shrieking. Sisyphus even stopped rolling his stone up the hill. All the shades of Hades wept with joy at the magical sound.

Hades and Persephone, the king and queen of the underworld, were deeply touched by Orpheus's song. He asked to bring his bride back to the world of the living. If this were not possible, then he wished to remain in the underworld rather than live without her. Hades granted the request. There was one condition. As he journeyed back to the world of light, Orpheus had to trust Eurydice was behind him. He must not turn around.

Orpheus agreed and started up the steep path. He climbed with nothing but silence behind him. The thought that Eurydice was not following weighed heavily on his mind. What if Hades had tricked him? At last, the urge to see his bride overpowered him. He turned, only to see the ghost of Eurydice fading away. His sad bride spoke a single word, "Farewell."

Orpheus ran back down the path, but no one may enter Hades twice while living. Charon refused him passage and Hades himself barred the gates. For seven days Orpheus sat on the banks of the Styx and wept. Then he made his way back to the land of the living. He avoided men and women to play sad songs alone in the forest. A group of women came upon him there, worshippers of Dionysus. They fought over Orpheus and tore his body to pieces. His head fell into a stream and floated to the sea. His tongue found breath one final time to whisper the name of his beloved Eurydice.

Hercules

The hero Perseus had many children with Andromeda after he rescued her from the sea monster. One of their sons, Alcaeus, had a son of his own named Amphitryon. Another son, Electryon, had nine sons and a daughter named Alcmene. A third son was named Sthenelus.

When Perseus died, Electryon became king of Argos. The nearby coast was plagued by pirates who killed Electryon's sons. The king asked his nephew Amphitryon to look after Mycenae, the chief city of Argos, and his daughter Alcmene while he went after the pirates. He warned Amphitryon not to marry his daughter before he returned. Amphitryon quarreled with his uncle, drew his sword, and killed him.

Electryon's brother Sthenelus took the throne and banished Amphitryon from the kingdom. Amphitryon and Alcmene made their way to the city of Thebes where King Creon cleansed Amphitryon of the blood-guilt from slaying his uncle.

Now Amphitryon was ready to marry. Alcmene first wanted him to hunt down the pirates who had killed her brothers. Amphitryon collected a band of warriors and set off to destroy them.

On the night of Amphitryon's victorious return, Zeus entered Alcmene's chamber disguised as her husband. The god said it was time for a honeymoon and shared Alcmene's bed. As soon as Zeus left, the real Amphitryon entered the palace. He ran to his wife and embraced her. When dawn came, Alcmene asked her husband why he had come home twice in a single night. Amphitryon was furious, but he learned from the prophet Tiresias that it was Zeus himself who had been with his wife.

Hera said she would make Alcmene pay for being with her husband, along with the child Alcmene would have. The goddess was even more eager to do this when, after nine months, Zeus swore that his offspring born that day would rule over the fertile plain of Argos. She sped down to Mycenae where the wife of Sthenelus was seven months pregnant. The goddess made sure that the son of Sthenelus would be born early. His son, not Alcmene's, would rule over Argos.

Meanwhile, Hera sent Eileithyia, the goddess of childbirth, to Alcmene. Eileithyia crossed her legs and fingers to make sure that Alcmene's son would be born second. Alcmene's screams went on and on. At last one of her servants noticed Eileithyia in the shadows and understood what the goddess was doing. She shouted, "Rejoice, a child is born! Alcmene has given birth!"

"Impossible," cried out Eileithyia. That was enough to break her spell. Alcmene gave birth to not one but two sons. One was Iphicles, fathered by Amphitryon. The other was the son of Zeus. His name was Hercules.

Despite the trick played on Eileithyia, Sthenelus's son,

Eurystheus, was born before Hercules and would one day rule the plain of Argos.

After Hercules was born, Alcmene was afraid that Hera would kill her. She left the baby to die in a deserted field, hoping that this would satisfy the goddess. Athena took the infant to Mount Olympus and asked Hera to nurse the baby. Hera didn't know who the boy was, and she agreed. All went well until Hercules bit his nursemaid. Hera screamed in pain and jumped, spurting milk across the heavens. This came to be known as the Milky Way.

Athena then took Hercules back to Alcmene and talked her into raising him.

Hercules was just a few months old when Hera first tried to kill him. He was in his crib with his brother Iphicles. The goddess sent two poisonous serpents to their home. They slithered across the floor and climbed into the crib. Iphicles awoke and screamed, but Hercules grabbed a serpent in each of his chubby hands. Alcmene and Amphitryon rushed in to find baby Hercules laughing and holding two dead snakes.

Hercules's teachers were the best Greece had to offer. His mortal father taught him to drive a chariot, while a king named Eurytus instructed him in the use of the bow. Helen's brother Castor taught him to fight with a sword, and Hermes's son Harpalycus showed him how to wrestle.

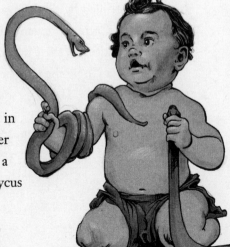

139

Linus, the brother of Orpheus, tried to teach Hercules to sing and play the lyre, but Hercules wasn't good at music. Linus boxed the boy's ears and Hercules smashed the lyre on top of his teacher's head, killing him. Young Hercules was put on trial for murder but argued that a man was allowed to kill anyone who struck him first. The judges set Hercules free.

Amphitryon then sent Hercules into the country to use his energy doing farm chores. The boy outdid all of his friends in farming and hunting. By the time he was a young man, Hercules was a head taller than all his friends. No one could beat him in contests, whether shooting arrows or throwing the javelin.

When Hercules was eighteen, word reached him that an enormous lion was eating the flocks of King Thespius on nearby Mount Cithaeron. The beast was hard to track, so Hercules spent fifty nights in the palace while he hunted. Finally, he killed the lion.

In the days when young Hercules lived in Thebes, the city was controlled by the Minyans to the north. The king of the Minyans, Erginus, demanded that each year the Thebans send him a hundred of their best cattle. As Hercules was returning home after killing the lion, he met the Minyan heralds on their way to Thebes. Hercules was angry about this shame on his town. He cut off the ears, noses, and hands of the heralds and sent them back to King Erginus. The king gathered his army to march against Thebes. When he reached the walls of the city he demanded that King Creon send out Hercules to be punished.

The Thebans had long ago dedicated their weapons to the gods and hung them on a temple wall. Hercules gathered the young men of the town and broke into the temple. They took up the ancient arms and marched against the Minyans. They not only killed Erginus and almost everyone in the Minyan army, but they also burned the Minyan capital to the ground. Thanks to Hercules, the people of Thebes were free.

King Creon was so grateful to Hercules that he gave him his daughter, Megara, to be his bride. The young couple lived happily together and had three sons, but Hera had not forgotten her anger. She whispered in Hercules's ear that he was a nobody and a disappointment to his father. A true son of Zeus would have done more than kill a lion and defeat the Minyans. She told Hercules he was no hero.

Hercules longed for danger and adventure. The conflict between his dreams and the duties of family life confused him. Hera encouraged this confusion until at last Hercules lost his mind.

One day he was performing a sacrifice to the gods. His wife and children looked up at him as he carried the sacred basket of barley around the altar. Hercules was ready to drown the flame of the altar torch and sprinkle the holy water on his family when he froze. His eyes rolled wildly and drool dribbled into his beard. Then he screamed: "Why should I sacrifice before I slay Eurystheus, son of Sthenelus, king of Mycenae? Throw away the basket, pour out the water, and someone get my bow! I'm off to Mycenae. I'll knock down those mighty walls with my bare hands."

Hercules grabbed his bow and club and climbed into an

imaginary chariot. He whipped invisible horses to a gallop. He cried out that he was nearing his goal, and then jumped to the ground to look for his enemies. His children were terrified. Hercules drew his bow on his eldest son, thinking he was a child of Eurystheus.

Megara threw herself in front of her son. "You gave this child life. Will you now take it away?"

Hercules could not hear her. He chased the boy around the yard and then stabbed him through the heart. The blood of the young child spurted from his body as he collapsed into his mother's arms.

"That's one of your family, Eurystheus," cried Hercules. "Now for the rest!"

His second son tried to hide behind the altar, but his father found him and dragged him away. The boy grasped his father's knees and begged: "Daddy, please, don't hit me! I'm your own little boy."

Hercules brought down his club and crushed the boy's skull.

Megara grabbed her last child and ran into their house. But Hercules burst through the door and drew his bow on mother and child. Without a word, he shot them both with a single arrow.

Athena suddenly appeared before him and tossed a huge stone at his chest. The stone knocked the breath from his body and drove away the madness Hera had brought on him. Hercules gazed in horror at what he had done.

Hercules could not forgive himself. As the months passed, he realized he would have to move on or die. He left Thebes to seek the counsel of the oracle at Delphi. When he came to the temple of Apollo beneath Mount Parnassus, he asked the priestess what he must do to find forgiveness. The message she gave him was not pleasing. He must return to his home in Argos and serve his uncle Eurystheus. Hercules would have to perform whatever twelve labors this hated king would ask of him.

This was a bitter pill for Hercules to swallow. Not only would he be a slave, but his master would be the very man who had stolen the throne of Argos from him. Still, he had to follow the will of the god. Hercules left the slopes of Parnassus and walked slowly down the road to Argos.

Eurystheus was terrified when he heard that Hercules was coming. He thought that his nephew was planning to kill him and steal the throne. As Hercules entered the massive gates of the palace with stone lions on each side, Eurystheus hid in a large bronze jar buried in the ground. Hercules marched in and tore the lid off the jar. The king begged for mercy but calmed down when Hercules explained his mission. The ruler of Argos gave his nephew the most dangerous task he could think of. He hoped that Hercules would be killed and never enter Mycenae again.

Eurystheus commanded Hercules to slay a lion that was destroying the country around Nemea to the north. Hercules had already killed a fierce lion on Mount Cithaeron and thought this task would be easy. He strolled toward Nemea and found the lair of the beast. The lion made its home in a cave stretching through the rock to the other side of the mountain. He found the lion outside the cave and notched his arrow for an easy kill. The arrow flew straight at the animal but only bounced off his hide. This lion was a child of the ancient monsters Typhon and Echidna. Its skin could not be pierced.

Hercules came up with a plan. He went to the far side of the mountain and blocked the cave's exit. Then he returned to the entrance where the lion slept. Hercules cut a huge club from a tree and rushed at the animal. The lion made its way into the cave and Hercules followed. He grabbed the lion around the throat and choked it to death with his bare hands. Since no knife could cut its hide, he used one of the lion's razor-sharp claws to skin the animal. He wore the lion's skin as a cloak, and its head as a helmet. This skin and the club he used became his symbols.

Hercules returned to Mycenae where the foolish Eurystheus was once again hiding in his jar. He was even more terrified of Hercules now and told him he couldn't enter the city gates. The king would give the hero his orders through a herald named Copreus. This was an insult because Copreus meant "manure man."

Eurystheus quickly sent Hercules away on his second labor. He had to kill the enormous monster that lived in the swamps south of Mycenae. This monster, the Hydra, had a hundred heads and a wicked temper. Hercules, along with his nephew Iolaus, made his way to the swamp where the Hydra lived along with a giant crab. Hercules used burning arrows to drive the monster from its hiding place and sliced off one of its heads in a single stroke of his sword.

Suddenly two new heads burst from the wound. Hercules attacked the Hydra again and cut off more heads, but from each cut two more heads grew. He finally discovered that the Hydra's

central head was immortal
and could not be destroyed.
To make things worse,
the giant crab
began biting
Hercules's foot.

Hercules ran
from the swamp
and found Iolaus.
He ordered the
young man to
grab a torch
and follow him.
The pair made
their way back to
the Hydra and its angry

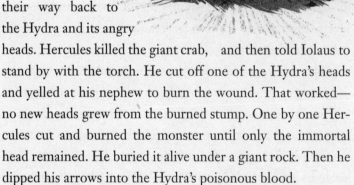

heads. Hercules killed the giant crab, and then told Iolaus to
stand by with the torch. He cut off one of the Hydra's heads
and yelled at his nephew to burn the wound. That worked—
no new heads grew from the burned stump. One by one Hercules cut and burned the monster until only the immortal
head remained. He buried it alive under a giant rock. Then he
dipped his arrows into the Hydra's poisonous blood.

Hercules's third labor was to track down and bring back alive
the deer with golden horns. This deer was sacred to Artemis.
Hercules spent a whole year chasing the deer over the mountains. At last he crept up on it while it slept near a stream and
threw it over his shoulders for the journey back to Mycenae.

Artemis was furious that Hercules had caught her deer.

Hercules explained that he was acting under orders of the king. Artemis let him continue on his way with a warning that he was to free her deer as soon as he reached Mycenae. Hercules agreed. As soon as he showed the deer to Copreus, he let it go.

For his fourth labor, Eurystheus ordered Hercules to return to Arcadia and bring back another live animal. The terrible boar of Mount Erymanthus was destroying the countryside, and killing anyone who came near.

Hercules followed mountain paths until he came to the cave of the centaur Pholus. The centaur cooked a fine meal for his guest, and Hercules asked for wine. The only wine available was in a jar that belonged to all the centaurs. If Pholus opened it, the other centaurs would smell it and go wild. Hercules promised Pholus everything would be fine, so the centaur broke the seal on the jar.

The smell spread throughout the countryside. Centaurs came from all directions ready to kill anyone who stood between them and the wine. Hercules shot all who dared to enter the cave, then ran out to chase the rest away. The centaurs tore whole trees from their roots to use as clubs. The battle lasted for hours until Hercules finally killed the last of the wine-crazed centaurs and returned to the cave.

Hercules found Pholus burying the bodies of the centaurs. Pholus pulled an arrow from one of the creatures and marveled at how such a small thing could have killed his companions. Then he accidentally let the point, poisoned by the Hydra's blood, fall on his foot. Pholus died in agony, after which Hercules buried him beside his kinsmen and continued his hunt for the boar.

He found the huge beast in its mountain hideout and chased it until it got stuck in a deep snow bank. Hercules wrestled the boar and carried it back to Eurystheus alive. The king could not believe Hercules had survived another dangerous mission. He tried to think of a labor that would be both impossible and embarrassing. If Hercules were too embarrassed to do the job, Eurystheus would be rid of him forever.

No job in ancient Greece was more shameful than cleaning up after farm animals. Only slaves and the poorest workers shoveled dung. So, Eurystheus ordered Hercules to clean the stables of King Augeas. Augeas, son of the god Helios, had vast herds of cattle. He let the animal dung build up for years in his barn. The piles were deeper than a man's knees and the smell was terrible. Eurystheus insisted that Hercules accomplish this fifth labor alone.

Hercules knew it was impossible for him to clean the stables of Augeas alone just by shoveling. He didn't dare offend the oracle at Delphi by refusing to try. So, he made his way to the palace of Augeas. As he passed the swift Alpheus River along the way, Hercules had a marvelous idea.

When he reached the palace, Hercules told Augeas he would clean his stables in one day in exchange for a tenth of his cattle. The king knew this was impossible, but he decided to let the young fool try. Phyleus, son of Augeas, witnessed the agreement. Hercules conveniently forgot to tell them that he was acting under the orders of Eurystheus.

The next morning Hercules knocked a large hole in one of the stable walls. Then he strolled through the muck to the other end and made another opening. After this, he went to the banks of the Alpheus and changed the course of the river into a channel he had dug. Fresh water poured through the stables and washed away years of dung in a matter of minutes. Hercules then closed the channel, patched up the holes in the barn, and demanded his payment.

Meanwhile, Augeas had discovered that Hercules was under orders of Eurystheus. The king said Hercules had tricked him and refused to give him a single cow. Hercules called on Phyleus as witness, and the king's son agreed that his father should pay. Augeas ordered both Hercules and Phyleus to leave his kingdom.

Hercules made his way back to Mycenae without any cattle. He stopped at the home of a local king named Dexamenus. This ruler had been bullied into promising his daughter in marriage to a centaur, named Eurytion, who was coming that very day to claim her. Hercules had no use for centaurs after his battle with them during the hunt for the boar. He killed the centaur and then made his way back to Mycenae.

The sixth labor of Hercules was not dangerous, but Eurystheus thought it was impossible. In Arcadia there was a lake in a forest near the town of Stymphalus. A huge flock of birds had settled on this lake and dirtied it beyond use. The people had tried many times to drive them away, but nothing worked. The king ordered Hercules to clear the lake, believing he would fail.

Hercules made his way to the lake and gazed at the number of birds. He could never kill them all, so he sat down on the shore and came up with a plan. He fashioned a pair of bronze rattles that made a horrible sound. Then he ran around the lake creating such a noise that the birds took to the sky and never came back.

By now Eurystheus must have thought he would never get rid of Hercules. The king decided to send him on a mission across the sea to Crete for his seventh labor. Hercules was to capture the bull that had once risen from the sea when Minos prayed to Poseidon. Minos refused to sacrifice the bull, and the god made Queen Pasiphae fall in love with it. She then gave birth to the murderous Minotaur. The bull had escaped the fields of Minos and was now terrorizing the island.

Hercules found the bull and wrestled it to the ground. Then he borrowed a trick that his father Zeus had used with Europa. He rode the bull across the sea and back to the mainland. Once he had shown it to Copreus, he released it to wander around Greece. At last it settled on the plain of Marathon and was slain by Theseus.

Eurystheus was sorry Hercules wasn't killed in Crete. For his eighth labor, he sent the hero to the wild land of Thrace. This time Hercules had to bring back the man-eating mares of King Diomedes. These horses had been raised on human flesh. They were so fierce that their feeding troughs were made of bronze and so strong that they were held in their stables by iron chains. Eurystheus hoped that Hercules would be their next meal.

On his way to Thrace, Hercules passed through the kingdom of Admetus who ruled over Thessaly. He noticed that the palace was in mourning. When he asked why, he was told that a woman had died. Hercules couldn't understand why there should be such a fuss over someone who was not a family member. He spent the evening laughing and joking with the tearful king.

Finally Admetus explained that his wife, Alcestis, had died that day, but he had tried to hide his sorrow because he did not want to be a poor host. Hercules was sorry and asked how such a young woman had died. Admetus told him the story.

Zeus had been angry with Apollo for killing some of the Cyclopes, so the ruler of the gods made Apollo a slave of Admetus for a whole year. The king had been kind to the god, so Apollo granted him a special favor. He didn't have to die at his rightful time if he could find someone to take his place.

Admetus searched for a person to die for him. He went to wealthy nobles and to poor beggars, but no one would take his place. His brothers and sisters, uncles and aunts, and nephews and nieces all refused to journey to Hades. He hoped that his parents, nearing the end of their lives, would be willing. His father said: "Admetus, the light of the sun is all the more sweet to us because it is fading fast. We gave you life, but we will not die for you."

The king had finally given up when his wife Alcestis came to him: "My husband, you have searched high and low for someone to take your place in Hades, but you did not ask the one who loves you most. Admetus, I will die for you."

The king sadly agreed, then sat beside her as she breathed her last.

Hercules swore to help the sad king. He rushed to the tomb and found Death, who had come to claim the queen's spirit. He wrestled Death to the ground and reunited the soul of Alcestis with her body. He then presented the living queen to Admetus. Both the king and his queen had escaped death.

After a good night's sleep in the joyful palace, Hercules

continued on his way to Thrace with a few of his companions. He found the horses and fed them their own master to calm them. Then he led them to the beach to take them by ship back to Argos, but the Thracians launched an attack. Hercules left the horses with his friend Abderus and went into battle. By the time he won, the horses had eaten his friend. Hercules founded a town named Abdera in his friend's memory and created an athletic festival with every sort of game and contest—except for horse races.

Hercules returned to Eurystheus with the mares. The frightened king of Mycenae let the savage animals go. They ran to the forests below Mount Olympus where they were eaten by wolves.

King Eurystheus had a daughter named Admete. This princess demanded that Hercules bring back the belt of the Amazon warrior-queen, Hippolyte.

Soon Hercules was on his way across the Aegean and into the Black Sea with a band of volunteers. Along the way he battled new enemies and killed two sons of King Minos. At last he arrived in the distant kingdom of the Amazons.

Hippolyte was impressed by her guest and offered to give him her belt. Hera, still angry, told the other Amazons that Hercules was there to kidnap their queen. The Amazons attacked Hercules's ship. Hercules thought Hippolyte had set a trap for him and killed her at once. Fleeing arrows and spears, he and his companions sailed away.

The voyage home was full of trials. Hercules rescued a princess from a sea monster at Troy, killed Poseidon's son Sarpedon, and invaded the island of Thasos. Finally he gave

Hippolyte's belt to the herald Copreus, who presented it to Eurystheus for his daughter.

Next, Hercules had to capture the cattle of the monster Geryon, a creature with three bodies joined at the waist. This beast lived on an island in the great Ocean. No one had ever traveled that far west from Greece before. Eurystheus hoped Hercules would either be killed by the monster or become lost and die in the land of the setting sun.

The hero journeyed alone across the Mediterranean to Africa, then west across the desert until he came to the land of the giant Antaeus. This enormous bully was the son of Poseidon and Earth, and it was his habit to challenge every stranger to a wrestling match. In spite of his size, Antaeus was often thrown to the ground. Each time he touched his mother, the Earth, his strength was renewed. He killed every challenger and used their skulls to decorate the temple of Poseidon.

Antaeus wanted to add Hercules's head to his collection and demanded a wrestling contest. Hercules threw the giant time and again. Each time Antaeus grew stronger while Hercules grew weaker. At last Hercules understood what was happening. He held Antaeus high above his head so that he could not touch the ground. The giant weakened and Hercules snapped him in half like a twig.

After many weeks of travel, Hercules saw the vast Atlantic. He was so impressed by the sight that he erected two pillars on opposite sides of the narrow passage to the Ocean, one in Europe and the other in Africa. These Pillars of Hercules marked the edges of the world.

As he worked, Hercules grew so hot that he shot an arrow

at Helios. The sun god laughed, but he admired the hero's nerve. He loaned Hercules his golden bowl. Helios used this vessel to journey from the sunset lands to his home in the east so that he could rise again the next day. Hercules climbed into the bowl and followed the Iberian coast north until he came to Geryon's island kingdom.

He crept up on the cattle grazing on a riverbank, but nothing escaped the notice of the guard dog, Orthus. The hound rushed at Hercules. The son of Zeus smashed the dog's skull with one blow of his club.

Hades also had a herd of cattle nearby. His servant warned Geryon that a thief was stealing his cattle. The three-bodied monster stormed into the meadow. Hercules struck him down with poison arrows and then herded the cattle into the golden bowl. Once he was safely across the sea to the mainland, he returned the vessel to the sun god. It was time to begin his long journey by land back to Greece.

Hercules led the cattle across the Iberian peninsula, then over the Pyrenees Mountains to the land of Liguria below the Alps. There he was attacked by two sons of Poseidon who tried to steal the cattle. Hercules pounded them and their followers with so many stones that they were all killed and the land was covered with rocks.

Hercules then turned south into Italy instead of taking the route beyond the Po River into Greece. He crossed the Alps and followed the shore of the Tyrrhenian Sea past the cities of the Etruscans until he came to a quiet valley beneath seven hills on the banks of the Tiber River.

In a cave there, under a rocky crag, lived the fire-breathing monster Cacus. The ground around his cave was covered with blood and gore. The valley below was deserted, and Hercules had no idea anything lived there. He placed the cattle in a pasture and retired for the night. While he slept, Cacus grabbed four bulls and four heifers and forced them to walk backward just as Hermes had done with the cattle of Apollo.

The next morning Hercules realized eight of his best animals were gone. He saw their tracks, but was puzzled since they didn't lead away from the herd. Then one of the cows in the dark cave let forth a mournful *mooooo*. Hercules ran toward the sound. Cacus piled giant boulders at the entrance to his cave, but Hercules changed the course of the Tiber River to reveal a back door.

Cacus belched black smoke to create a thick cloud to hide behind. Hercules strangled him until his eyes popped out. He

then led his missing cattle back to the herd and continued on his way.

Hercules wasn't very good at geography. He made his way south to the straits separating Italy from Sicily and realized he was lost. He finally made his way back up the Italian shore of the Adriatic Sea and returned to the northern borders of Greece. There Hera drove some of the cows mad with a gadfly. They escaped across Thrace and swam the Hellespont to Asia. Hercules took the remainder of the herd to Mycenae. After he gave the cattle to Eurystheus, the king insulted Hercules by sacrificing the entire herd to Hercules's enemy Hera.

Hercules had now worked for Eurystheus for over eight years, performing impossible deeds to cleanse himself of guilt for murdering his family. The king had almost given up trying to kill Hercules. The next labor he assigned to Hercules would keep him away in distant lands for as long as possible. Hercules had to fetch the golden apples of the nymphs known as the Hesperides.

Few knew where the Hesperides lived. For Hercules to seize the apples, he would first have to find them. The pure gold apples grew on a tree given by Mother Earth to Zeus and Hera as a wedding present. A hundred-headed serpent named Ladon guarded the tree.

He began by asking sister nymphs where the Hesperides lived. They sent him to the ancient sea god Nereus. Nereus, a shape-shifter, didn't want to be disturbed. He changed into many terrifying forms to frighten Hercules away, but the hero stayed until the god revealed the location of the golden apples.

Nereus either gave bad directions or Hercules got lost

again. His search took him over most of the known world and beyond. His first stop was Egypt, where he entered the kingdom of Busiris. Years before, when Egypt had suffered a famine, a soothsayer had told the king to restore the land by sacrificing a foreigner to Zeus. Busiris took the advice and killed the seer on his altar. Fertility returned to the land, so the king sacrificed every foreigner who came his way. Hercules was seized and led to Busiris. While the king prepared to kill the hero, Hercules broke through the ropes holding him and grabbed one of the king's priests by the ankles. He used him like a club to kill Busiris and his sons.

Hercules next sailed north to the Greek island of Lindos and wandered east to the Caucasus Mountains. He found Prometheus chained to a rock with the eagle of Zeus eating his liver. Just as Prometheus had foreseen long before, the son of Zeus killed the eagle and broke his chains. As thanks, Prometheus pointed out that Hesperides meant "nymphs of the West." He told Hercules that he should find a way to have mighty Atlas retrieve the apples for him.

After a march west across the northern coast of Africa, Hercules found Atlas holding up the sky. Atlas agreed to fetch the golden apples and handed the heavens to Hercules. It didn't take Atlas long to come back with the fruit, but he told Hercules that he wouldn't take the sky back. Hercules groaned and asked Atlas to hold the sky for a minute while he placed a pillow on his shoulders as padding. Atlas wasn't very smart. Once he held the sky again, Hercules thanked him and went on his way. Atlas was left to hold up the heavens for eternity.

After another long journey, Hercules presented the apples to

the king. Eurystheus was too frightened to keep them. Hercules gave them to Athena, who returned them to the Hesperides.

The final labor of Hercules was the most terrifying of all. Eurystheus ordered him to go to the underworld and bring back Cerberus, the three-headed guardian of Hades. If Hercules failed, he would be trapped forever among the dead.

Before he started down the path to Hades, Hercules went to the city of Eleusis to be taught the mysteries of Demeter. The goddess had shown her followers how their spirits might escape the eternal night of the underworld. Hercules wanted this knowledge in case things did not go well on his last labor.

Leaving Eleusis, Hercules went to the cave of Taenarum near Sparta and began his journey. He walked through darkness for days until he reached the kingdom of shades. He found Theseus and Peirithous sitting trapped on their chairs after trying to steal Persephone. They reached out to him, but Hercules could save only Theseus.

Finally Hercules asked Hades if he might take Cerberus to fulfill his duty. Hades agreed, as long as Hercules didn't use his weapons. Hercules wrestled with the beast while wearing his lion skin. The serpent fangs on the tail of Cerberus could not penetrate the lion skin. Hercules held Cerberus so tight that the three-headed beast gave up. Hercules then carried Cerberus all the way to Eurystheus. The frightened king, still hiding in his jar, said the labors were finally complete. He ordered Hercules to take Cerberus and leave. The hero, now cleansed of his guilt, bade his uncle a bitter farewell and returned the guardian of the underworld to his home.

Now that Hercules was finished with his labors, he decided it was time to get married again. His old archery teacher, King Eurytus of Oechalia, offered his daughter Iole to anyone who could best him and his sons in a contest. Hercules went to the kingdom and won, but Eurytus refused to give him his daughter. The king was afraid that the girl would end up dead like Megara and her sons. Iphitus, a son of Eurytus, stood up for Hercules. The king still refused. Hercules stormed away swearing vengeance. He settled in the town of Tiryns not far from Mycenae.

It was only a short time later that Eurytus noticed twelve prized horses were missing. Iphitus again defended Hercules. He journeyed to Tiryns to prove the hero's innocence. Hercules welcomed Iphitus and promised to prove he wasn't hiding horses. He then led Iphitus to the top of the high walls of Tiryns. While Iphitus was admiring the scenery, Hercules pushed him to his death. He then went to the pasture to admire his stolen horses.

Hercules believed he could get away with anything. He asked King Neleus in Pylos to cleanse him of the crime of killing Iphitus. The ruler refused. Hercules soon developed a horrible disease as a punishment. He made his way to Delphi to ask what he must do to wash away the guilt. The priestess of Apollo wanted nothing to do with him.

Hercules grew angry. He grabbed the sacred altar from the temple and ran down the road. He said that he would establish his own oracle if the god would not help him. Apollo flew down to Delphi, grabbed the altar, and fought with Hercules. Zeus sent a lightning bolt to break up the fight. Apollo unwillingly told Hercules he could be cured if he would serve as a slave for three years. Apollo led him to the nearest slave market where he was bought by Queen Omphale of Lydia.

During his three years as a slave, Hercules cleared the countryside of bandits and other evildoers. One such pair were the Cercopes, bandits who attacked travelers. One day they saw Hercules sleeping beside the road and decided to rob him. Before they knew what was happening, he had hung them upside down by their feet from a pole over his shoulders. As he carried them down the road, the two began to joke with each other. Hercules laughed so hard that he decided to let them go. Zeus later turned the pair into monkeys.

After he had served his three years as a slave, Hercules settled some old scores. The first was against King Laomedon of Troy, who had cheated him of his reward when he rescued the king's daughter Hesione from a sea monster. Hercules filled eighteen ships with soldiers to attack the city. He killed Laomedon and all the princes of Troy save one, a young boy named Podarces. When the princess Hesione was brought before Hercules, he offered to let her buy the freedom of one of the Trojan captives. Hesione chose her brother Podarces to preserve the royal line, giving Hercules her veil as his price. The lad was thereafter known as Priam, Greek for "ransomed one." He became king of Troy and ruled the city during the Trojan War.

After attacking other kings and princes who had offended him, Hercules collected a large army. He marched against Augeas who had refused to give him his reward when he had cleaned Augeas's filthy stables. He killed the king and his sons, then started a series of athletic contests in nearby Olympia to celebrate. These contests were repeated every four years and came to be known as the Olympic Games.

After so many adventures, Hercules still did not have a wife. He heard of a beautiful princess named Deianira in western Greece and decided to make her his. The maiden had another suitor, a river god named Achelous. Hercules fought him for the hand of Deianira. It was a difficult contest, as the river god had the body of a water serpent and a deadly horn on his forehead. The two fought until Hercules grabbed Achelous by his horn and ripped it from his head.

Hercules took his new bride and traveled east to settle in the city of Trachis. Along the way they came to the swift Evanus River where the centaur Nessus ferried passengers across the stream on his back. Nessus had served as a beast of burden for travelers since Hercules drove him out of Arcadia after the battle at the cave of Pholus. The last person he wanted to see was Hercules, but he had little choice but to ferry Deianira across the river.

Halfway across, Nessus tried to force himself on Deianira. In an instant Hercules shot him through with one of his poisoned arrows. As he lay dying, Nessus told Deianira to take some of his blood. "It is a powerful love potion in case you ever need it," he said.

After they reached Trachis, Hercules made a home for himself and Deianira. In time he decided on one last act of revenge. He was still angry at his old archery teacher, Eurytus, who had refused to give him his daughter Iole. Hercules raised an army and took the king's city, killing Eurytus and his surviving sons. He then took Iole home to Trachis as a slave.

Deianira knew it was time to use the blood of Nessus. She smeared it on a cloak and presented it to Hercules. Her husband draped it around his shoulders. The cloak burned his skin like a blazing fire. Hercules screamed in agony, but he could not remove the cloak. The poisonous blood ate his flesh until Hercules built a funeral pyre. He dragged himself to the top and asked a young man named Philoctetes to set it on fire. In an instant Hercules was consumed by the flames and his torture finally ended.

When his friends and family went to collect his bones and ashes after the fire had cooled, they could find nothing. Zeus had snatched his son and taken his soul to Mount Olympus, where he became an immortal god. He made peace with his stepmother, Hera, and married Hebe, the goddess of youth.

There in the heavens, Hercules at last found the eternal glory he had sought all his life.

Oedipus

Long before Hercules was born at Thebes, the city was founded because of a wandering cow and an angry dragon. After Europa was kidnapped by Zeus, her brother Cadmus searched everywhere for her. Finally, he went to the oracle at Delphi to ask Apollo where to find her. The oracle said to forget about Europa and instead seek out a cow. Cadmus had to follow the cow until it collapsed. Wherever that was, he had to establish a city.

This seemed very strange, but Cadmus couldn't ignore the orders of a god. He walked down the mountain road until he came upon a herd of cattle. One cow had a mark on its side like a full moon. This seemed like a sign, so he bought the beast and followed it as it wandered away. The cow made its way down the mountain, past lakes, over hills, and across plains. At last it lay down on a ridge above a broad plain north of Athens.

It was a good spot for a city, with a fortress for protection and fields all around. Cadmus built an altar and sent some of his companions to a spring to draw water. Suddenly he heard a scream. His friends lay dead at the feet of a mighty dragon.

Cadmus attacked this guardian of the spring. After a fierce battle, he slew the dragon.

Athena appeared and told him to knock out the dragon's teeth and sow them in a field like seeds. Cadmus was used to strange orders by now, so he planted the teeth.

He had no sooner sown the last tooth than the tips of hundreds of spears broke the ground. They were followed by helmets, then faces, chests, and legs. A whole army of warriors rose from the dragon's teeth. Cadmus grabbed his own sword to defend himself.

"Stay out of things that aren't your business," said the soldier closest to him.

The warriors started killing each other. At last only five fighters were left alive on the bloody field. At Athena's command, the survivors laid down their weapons. These five warriors became the founding fathers of Thebes, under the rule of Cadmus as king.

A city of men alone has no future. Women were found for the warriors along with a queen for Cadmus. Her name was Harmonia, the beautiful daughter of Ares and Aphrodite. The gods themselves presented gifts to the happy couple, including a necklace and robe for Harmonia. She and Cadmus lived a long and tragic life together. All four of their daughters—Autonoe, Ino, Semele, and Agave—led lives marked by violence, madness, or sadness. Only Polydorus, their son, passed his days in peace, fathering a son named Labdacus. Labdacus in turn fathered a future king of Thebes named Laius.

Cadmus and his wife Harmonia ended their days exiled to Illyria and were finally turned into snakes. But the family of Cadmus thrived until his descendant Menoeceus bore two children, Creon and his sister Jocasta. Jocasta married her distant cousin Laius.

After Laius became king of Thebes, the oracle at Delphi told him that he would die at the hands of his own son. When Jocasta gave birth to a boy, Laius ordered that the baby be left to die on the slopes of Mount Cithaeron. He fastened the baby's feet together with an iron pin and gave him to a shepherd to leave in the wilderness.

The kindly shepherd could not bear to leave the baby to die. He gave him to a friend from the city of Corinth. The friend in turn gave the boy to Polybus, the king of Corinth, and his wife Merope. They loved him as their own and gave him the name Oedipus ("swollen foot") because of the injury from his pierced ankles.

Oedipus grew up happily as a prince of Corinth, but one of his friends told him that he was not a true son of the king. Oedipus went to Polybus, but he wouldn't tell Oedipus anything. Eager to discover the truth, Oedipus journeyed to the oracle at Delphi to find out if he was adopted. The priestess did not answer his question. She gave him the terrible news that he was going to kill his father and marry his mother. Oedipus loved his parents, so he fled Delphi vowing that he would never return home and commit such terrible acts.

Oedipus made his way east feeling sad and hopeless. At a place where three roads met, he was forced into a ditch by a man in a chariot who hit him with a stick. Oedipus pulled the man from the chariot and killed him with his sword. Then he killed the rest of the party, except one who got away.

When Oedipus came to Thebes, he found the city in an

uproar. A terrible creature called the Sphinx had arrived. This beast—with the head of a woman, the body of a lion, and the wings of an eagle—was an offspring of the ancient monsters Typhon and Echidna. The Sphinx perched on a mountain outside the city and swooped in to catch her victims. The creature always asked the terrified citizen a riddle, promising she would let him go if he answered correctly. Of course, no one knew the answer and so all were eaten by the Sphinx.

King Laius had left town to ask the oracle at Delphi what the city could do to rid itself of this murderous beast. When he didn't return, the people believed he was dead. The acting king, Jocasta's brother, Creon, offered the kingdom and the hand of Queen Jocasta to anyone who could drive the Sphinx away.

When Oedipus arrived, the winged creature flew down to block his way. The Sphinx expected him to be terrified, but Oedipus calmly sat down on a stone and waited. The monster posed the riddle: "What walks on four legs in the morning, two legs at midday, and three in the evening?"

The Sphinx was ready for another tasty meal, but Oedipus said: "The answer is man. An infant crawls on all fours during the morning of its life, then walks on two legs as an adult, then finally uses the third leg of a cane in his twilight years."

The Sphinx was defeated. She threw herself off a cliff to her death, and Oedipus entered Thebes as a hero. He took the crown and married the still-young queen. In time the couple had four fine children, two boys and two girls. It seemed to Oedipus as if all of his troubles were over.

Thebes was a happy, wealthy city for many years. One day things began to go terribly wrong. The cattle stopped bearing young and so did the women. A plague settled on the city, killing young and old. Sacrifices to the gods changed nothing, and the local oracles had no answers. Finally the people asked Oedipus to do something. He had saved them from the Sphinx—could he not rescue them again? "Oedipus, protect us. Come, save our city! You have brought nothing but good fortune to us. If you can't help us, you will soon rule over a wilderness."

And Oedipus replied: "My friends, I know about the ills that plague this city, but no one is more sick than I. I have sent my brother-in-law, Creon, to the oracle of Apollo at Delphi to see if the god might reveal to us the cause of this evil."

Creon returned to Thebes with the oracle's advice. The oracle said the citizens were suffering because they allowed the murder of King Laius to go unpunished. Unless the city brought his murderer to justice, the curse would remain. Oedipus knew very little about the previous king. Creon explained that Laius had been killed by a band of robbers while he was on the way to Delphi. His whole party had been killed, save for one servant who ran away. The city, then suffering under the Sphinx, could not spare any men to chase the murderers. After the monster was gone and a new king was on the throne, it seemed best to forget the murder.

Oedipus scolded the people for failing to avenge their king. He vowed that he would find the murderer and cleanse the city. The first thing he did was call together the citizens. Whoever had information about the death of Laius was to come forward and tell everything he knew.

No one did. The people suggested the king seek the counsel of the prophet Tiresias. Oedipus had already sent for the seer and expected him at any moment. Tiresias arrived but was reluctant to speak.

"Tiresias, you must help me," Oedipus said. "Tell us who killed Laius."

"Let me go home, Oedipus. The words I have to say would not please you but only add to your sorrows," Tiresias said.

"My sorrows? How could you make matters worse when my city is suffering? Reveal what you know or face my anger," Oedipus commanded.

"All right, I'll speak. It's you, Oedipus. You're the murderer you seek!"

"That's impossible, you liar! Did Creon pay you to say this? Is this a plot to seize my throne?" Oedipus asked.

"Forget Creon," Tiresias answered. "I may be blind in my eyes, but you are blind in your ears and mind! Let me leave or I'll tell you even worse things."

Oedipus was outraged. "Get out of here!"

After Tiresias left, Oedipus accused Creon of trying to steal his throne. Creon said he was innocent, but Oedipus did not believe him. Jocasta scolded both men—her husband and her brother—for arguing in public. She assured Oedipus that his fears were foolish. She believed the prophet's words were worthless. She told Oedipus that Laius had been told that his own son would kill him, but that was impossible. His only son had died as a baby. Laius was murdered by bandits at a place where three roads met.

A chill went down the spine of Oedipus. He demanded details. Finally he asked if there were any witnesses still alive. Jocasta said there was a shepherd who had seen the murder. He had asked to be sent far into the fields when Oedipus became king.

Oedipus insisted that she send for the shepherd. He explained that he had once killed a man at a crossing place of three roads, but he had been alone. If the witness told him there was one man, and not a group of bandits, then Oedipus would be afraid he might have killed the king. But he knew the king could not have been his father.

Before the shepherd arrived, an elderly messenger from Corinth came to Thebes. He bore the sad news that King Polybus had died of old age. Oedipus wept to hear about the death, but he was happy that the prophecy of Delphi could not come true. He could not kill his father if the king were already dead. Jocasta told him she had been right all along and oracles were worthless. Oedipus confessed that he was afraid he might still marry his mother by some horrible twist of fate. Jocasta dismissed the idea: "Oedipus, seers have no knowledge of the future. It's best to enjoy one's life not worrying about the fears buried deep inside us."

The messenger from Corinth asked if there was anything he could do to ease the king's mind. Oedipus told the old man about the prophecies and how he fled Corinth to make sure they would not come true. The old man said he knew for certain that Polybus and Merope were not the true parents of Oedipus. He himself had given Oedipus to them as a baby. The messenger had received him from a shepherd who had rescued him from death in the wilderness. He could prove it, because Oedipus would still have a scar on his ankles.

Jocasta turned white as a ghost. She ran into the palace crying out that Oedipus should never learn who he really was. But Oedipus was determined to unravel the mystery.

The shepherd who had witnessed the murder of Laius at last arrived. Oedipus began to question him in the presence of the messenger from Corinth. The shepherd confessed that he had given the baby Oedipus to the Corinthian messenger. He had also seen Oedipus kill Laius.

Oedipus forced the old man to tell him who his real father was. The shepherd said it was King Laius himself.

Oedipus realized that he had fulfilled the prophecy. He had murdered his father and married his mother. "No! No! No! O radiant sun, may I look on you today for the last time. I am cursed in my birth, cursed in my marriage, cursed in my killing."

Jocasta was so upset to learn that she had married her own son that she hung herself. Oedipus found her dead and then gouged out his own eyes. He exiled himself from Thebes to roam the earth as a penniless beggar. His only companion was his daughter, Antigone. He left the kingdom and the care of his other children, Ismene, Eteocles, and Polynices, in the charge of Creon. Oedipus and Antigone wandered Greece for years, shunned by all.

The sons of Oedipus, Eteocles and Polynices, inherited the rule of the city from their uncle Creon when they came of age. The brothers agreed to share the throne, taking turns as king year by year. When the first year was over, Eteocles refused to step down and drove his brother from the city. Polynices fled to Argos, but not before he stole the necklace and robe the gods had given to his ancestor Harmonia.

In those days Adrastus ruled over Argos. He welcomed refugees from many Greek cities. Aside from Polynices, he also gave a home to Tydeus, a son of the late King Oeneus of Calydon. Tydeus had murdered a relative in anger and fled to Adrastus for protection. Neither Tydeus nor Polynices were happy living in exile. They often fought.

One day when they had set upon each other with swords drawn, Adrastus came either to stop the fight or to encourage them to kill each other. Suddenly he noticed that Polynices had a lion painted on his shield. The shield of Tydeus was decorated with a boar. The oracle at Delphi had once told him to "bind his daughters to a lion and boar," but he had not understood the message. He now married his two daughters to Polynices and Tydeus. Then he promised both men he would help them regain their kingdoms, starting with Thebes.

Adrastus recruited the finest warriors in Argos, including his brother-in-law Amphiaraus, a gifted seer. Amphiaraus could foresee the grim outcome of the war and refused to go. His wife Eriphyle had an eye for fine gifts. Polynices came to her secretly and offered her the necklace and robe of Harmonia if she would change her husband's mind. She took the bribe and talked her husband into joining Adrastus. Amphiaraus made his son vow to avenge what he knew would be his certain death before the walls of Thebes.

Seven warriors set out leading a vast army. They were King Adrastus, the seer Amphiaraus, Polynices, Tydeus, and three nobles named Capaneus, Parthenopaeus, and Hippomedon. Each warrior would lead an assault on one of the seven gates of Thebes.

With an army marching on Thebes, Apollo once again spoke through his oracle at Delphi. The priestess declared that whichever side possessed Oedipus—or at least his bones—would win the war. Oedipus had become a prize desired by both his sons.

Oedipus and Antigone had wandered to an outlying district of Athens called Colonus. Here the old blind man sat down on a rock in a sacred grove and declared to his daughter he would never leave. He had been told that one day he would die in a place sacred to the dark Furies. The local people were horrified when they discovered Oedipus lived among them. Theseus, the king of Athens, promised to protect Oedipus from harm.

Ismene, the other daughter of Oedipus, found her father

and told him of recent events in Thebes. Soon Creon arrived to urge Oedipus to think well of Thebes and Eteocles. Oedipus told Creon to leave him alone. Then Creon revealed that he was holding Antigone and Ismene hostage to make sure that Oedipus returned to Thebes. Fortunately, Theseus returned to rescue the women and drive Creon away.

It wasn't long before Polynices arrived and begged his father for help. He said he was the elder son, and Eteocles should give up the throne to him: "I know I have been a poor son, father, but that can change. We are both exiles, you and I, driven from our city unjustly. Please, come with me and we will win!"

Oedipus cursed his son, saying he and his brother were doomed to slay each other before the walls of Thebes. Polynices realized his fate was sealed. He left Colonus, making his sisters promise to give him a decent burial.

With only Theseus in attendance, Oedipus walked to a hidden part of the grove and prepared to die. He saluted the life-giving earth and the shining sky. Then suddenly, Oedipus was gone. How he died or where his body lay, none could say except Theseus, who was pledged to silence. When Oedipus died, so did all hope for his sons. For his daughters, it seemed that only suffering lay ahead.

When Polynices arrived at Thebes, the seven captains met before the city. They swore by Ares, Hera, and the god Panic that they would either reduce Thebes to rubble or die. Then they drew lots to see which gate each leader would attack. By chance or by the curse of Oedipus, Polynices was assigned the gate held by his brother Eteocles.

Tiresias informed the people of Thebes that the only way they could save their city was by human sacrifice. The victim must be a descendant of the warriors who grew from dragon's teeth. Menoeceus, a son of Creon, had a deep love for Thebes and killed himself outside the walls in view of the enemy.

The slaughter that followed was brutal. The Argive leader Capaneus scaled the walls of the town, shouting that not even Zeus could stop him from taking Thebes. In answer, a lightning bolt killed the boastful warrior. A huge boulder crushed the skull of another Argive captain, Parthenopaeus, while his fellow captain Hippomedon was also slain. A Theban warrior named Melanippus attacked Tydeus and mortally wounded him. As Tydeus lay dying, Athena asked Zeus to make the young man immortal. Zeus agreed, but the seer Amphiaraus knew Athena's plans. He hated Tydeus for dragging him into this war, so he cut off the head of Melanippus and brought it to Tydeus. Tydeus broke open the skull and ate his enemy's brains. Athena was so disgusted she smashed the vial containing the potion of immortality. Tydeus died in the dirt. Soon after, Amphiaraus avoided a spear in the back only to be swallowed by a great opening in the earth.

Of the seven who had marched against Thebes, only Adrastus and Polynices remained. The king of Argos fled the battlefield on the divine horse Arion, offspring of Demeter and Poseidon. But Polynices stood before the walls of the city and called forth Eteocles. In the no-man's-land between the two armies the brothers met.

Polynices and Eteocles ran at each other with spears ready. They threw and missed, then clashed like wild boars with swords drawn. Whenever one would strike, the other would meet the weapon with his shield. Then Eteocles slipped on a pebble and gave Polynices the chance to drive his spear through his brother's calf. Wounded, Eteocles hurled his own spear through the breast of his brother. Both wounded men stumbled across the dust in agony, then took up their swords to continue the fight. Eteocles stepped back with his left foot, then swung his sword and pierced his brother's side. The elder brother fell to the ground, seemingly dead. Just as Eteocles dropped his own weapon, Polynices rose with his last breath and plunged his sword into his brother. Side by side the two sons of Oedipus lay in death, ruling the bloody battlefield.

Creon once again assumed rule of Thebes and gathered the bodies of the fallen Theban warriors for burial. He ordered that the enemy—including his nephew Polynices—be left to rot on the battlefield. Anyone who buried them would be killed. Everyone was shocked. Without burial, the dead were doomed to wander the far banks of the River Styx for a hundred years in misery. No Greek would deny burial to even their worst enemy for fear of offending the gods.

Antigone and Ismene returned to Thebes, having nowhere else to go. Antigone was determined to give Polynices a decent burial. Even her engagement to Creon's son Haemon and the pleas of Ismene to reconsider would not change her mind. She sprinkled dust on the body of her brother.

Creon was shocked to discover his own niece had disobeyed him: "Antigone, do you admit that you did this shameful deed or do you deny it?"

"I admit it proudly," she answered. "Zeus and Justice demand a proper burial for the dead. You are a fool to think you can stand against the gods!"

"And you are a fool to think you can stand against me!" Creon said.

Antigone stood firm. "Go ahead and kill me! I would rather die honoring the gods than live under your wicked rules."

Creon ordered her to be sealed in a cave until she was dead. Haemon pleaded with his father to spare his bride, but his words couldn't bend Creon's will.

Tiresias appeared before the new king and told him he was offending the gods. "Change your mind," he warned, "or you will suffer more than you can imagine."

Creon hesitated, and by then it was too late. Antigone had hung herself in her cave. Haemon, seeing his love dead, struck out at his father with his sword and then plunged it into his own heart. When Creon's wife heard that their son was dead, she committed suicide. Like Oedipus before him, Creon at last realized that men were helpless before the will of the gods.

Jason and the Argonauts

Deucalion and Pyrrha, the couple that escaped the great flood sent by Zeus, had a great-grandson named Athamas. Athamas became king of Orchomenus, not far from Thebes. He married a woman named Nephele ("cloud") and together they had a son named Phrixus and a daughter named Helle. Later Athamas married Ino, daughter of King Cadmus of Thebes. She bore Athamas two sons and then began to plot the death of Phrixus to put her own boys on the throne.

Ino bribed the women who stored seed grain for the kingdom to dry the seeds. Naturally, the grain did not grow and Orchomenus faced starvation. Athamas sent heralds to Delphi to ask Apollo how to save his kingdom. Ino convinced the heralds to tell the king that the only way to save Orchomenus was to sacrifice Phrixus to Zeus.

The people of the land cried out that Phrixus must die so they could live. Athamas reluctantly led Phrixus to the altar with a sharpened knife. At that moment, a golden ram appeared. Phrixus and his sister, Helle, climbed on the ram's back and flew high into the sky.

While the brother and sister soared over the sea near Troy, Helle lost her grip and fell to her death in the straits between Europe and Asia. This passage was known ever after as the Hellespont. But Phrixus flew across the Black Sea until he came to the land of Colchis beneath the Caucasus Mountains. The ruler of this kingdom was Aeetes, a son of Helios. He happily received Phrixus and gave him one of his own daughters to be his wife. In gratitude, Phrixus sacrificed the golden ram to Zeus and gave its fleece to Aeetes. The king of Colchis hung the priceless gift on a tree in a grove sacred to Ares. There it was guarded by a fierce dragon.

Athamas had a beautiful niece named Tyro. This princess was married to Cretheus, but she was in love with a local river god named Enipeus. She would often sneak away to wander by her lover's river, waiting for him. Poseidon saw her there and disguised himself as Enipeus to make love to her. Afterward, Poseidon revealed his true identity and told Tyro she would have twin sons.

Tyro's sons Pelias and Neleus grew into strong men. Pelias

became king of Iolcus on the coast of Thessaly. Neleus founded a kingdom in sandy Pylos in the far southwest of Greece. Tyro also had two sons, Aeson and Pheres, by her mortal husband, Cretheus.

Pelias kept his half-brother Aeson under careful watch because many people thought he was the rightful heir to Iolcus. Aeson knew his life depended on keeping a low profile. When his wife bore him a son, the couple announced that the infant had died so that Pelias would fear no future threat to his throne. Aeson secretly took the baby to be raised by the wise centaur Chiron on the slopes of Mount Pelion. The boy, named Jason, was educated and grew into manhood.

Pelias was always on guard against threats to his power. He had learned from an oracle that if a man wearing only one sandal ever arrived in his kingdom, his rule was in danger.

When Jason grew up, he boldly decided to journey to Iolcus and claim the throne from his uncle. He came to a stream swollen with spring rains where he saw an old woman. She asked him to carry her across. She had asked many before him, but all had said no. Jason was in a hurry, but he carried the woman to the far shore. Along the way, he slipped and lost a sandal in the mud. The old woman thanked Jason, and he went on his way, not realizing that he had just helped Hera. The goddess was angry at King Pelias, so she tested Jason to see if he was worthy to replace his uncle. After Jason showed her kindness, Hera set a plan in motion to do away with Pelias.

Jason arrived in Iolcus just as the king was making a sacrifice to his father, Poseidon. Pelias noticed the young man in the crowd wearing only one sandal. After discovering who he was, he welcomed Jason. Pelias then asked his nephew what he would do, as king, if he knew someone was going to kill him.

Jason laughed and thought of a plan to get rid of such a man: "I would send him to capture the Golden Fleece."

"An excellent idea, " responded the king. He looked Jason in the eye and said, "Go fetch the Golden Fleece."

Jason accepted the challenge and began to prepare for the long, dangerous journey. He asked his cousin Argus to build a fifty-oared craft to sail to Colchis. The goddess Athena fitted a special prow made of oak onto the ship. The wood came from a sacred grove of Zeus and had the gift of speech. When the ship was complete, Jason christened it the *Argo* in honor of its builder.

There are many different stories about who joined Jason on the *Argo*. All agree that he invited the greatest warriors in Greece. First there was Hercules, who interrupted one of his labors to make the journey. Next were the great bard Orpheus and the two brothers of Helen, Castor and Pollux. Zetes and Calais also came, two winged sons of Boreas, god of the north wind. Peleus, the grandson of Zeus and father of Achilles was there, as was his brother Telamon, the sire of Ajax. Some say Theseus of Athens sailed with Jason, while others say the famous female warrior Atalanta accompanied the men. Everyone agrees that Meleager, brother of Hercules's wife Deianira, joined Jason. Idmon the seer was among the chosen, as was Tiphys, who served as helmsman. The band of sailors was known as the Argonauts.

The sailors elected Hercules as their leader, but he refused. He said he would only go on the quest if Jason was their captain. The young prince accepted and made a long speech. Soon even the ship was tired of listening to him and the oak prow shouted that they should begin. The men took their places on the rowing benches, and the *Argo* slipped away from the port of Iolcus and into the Aegean Sea. King Pelias watched from shore, certain he would never see Jason again.

After a few days, the Argonauts came to Lemnos in the northern Aegean. The people of the island panicked. The women on the island had killed their husbands, and ever since, Lemnos had been an island of women alone.

The men of the *Argo* knew none of this when they sailed into the harbor looking for fresh water. They sent their herald, Aethalides, a son of the god Hermes, to speak to the ruler. He was surprised to find himself speaking to the beautiful Hypsipyle instead of a man, but Aethalides explained that the Argonauts simply wanted to take on supplies. Hypsipyle was in favor of giving the sailors what they needed and sending them on their way, but a wise old woman suggested a different plan. She said they should think of the future. Did they want to grow old without children and grandchildren? The old woman said they should welcome the Argonauts into their homes so that the women could become pregnant. Only then would they send the men on their way.

So, the Lemnian women invited the Argonauts into their homes.

One night turned to a week and a week to a month, and the men were still there. Hercules finally brought them to their senses. He had stayed on the boat and cared nothing for the native women: "You fools! We are on this voyage to sail distant seas and accomplish deeds worthy of eternal glory. The Golden

Fleece lies there, beyond the far sunrise, not on this island. I'm sailing to Colchis!"

The Argonauts gathered their gear and said farewell. Most of the women were pregnant and ready to see the men go. They waved good-bye as the *Argo* sailed away.

The Argonauts sailed northeast across the Aegean to the Hellespont, the first of two narrow passages leading to the Black Sea. The winds were strong and the waves choppy as they fought their way past Abydos where Leander had swum to his secret love Hero. Once beyond the Hellespont, they entered the inland sea of the Propontis and sailed to a place called Bear Mountain. On this mountain lived creatures of great strength known as the Earthmen. Each had six powerful arms.

Instead of monsters, the Argonauts were met on the beach by a friendly folk called the Doliones. Their young king, Cyzicus, had been advised by an oracle that if foreign heroes ever landed on his shore, he should welcome them. Cyzicus did so and struck up a warm friendship with Jason, who was the same age as the king.

Jason and his men left Hercules to guard the ship in a sheltered cove and entered the town of the Doliones. The Earthmen, looking down from Bear Mountain, decided the ship was an easy target. The creatures did not bother the Doliones, but strangers were fair game. The Earthmen tossed huge boulders into the mouth of the cove to prevent the *Argo* from escaping. Hercules pulled out his bow and began to shoot every Earthman in sight. The Argonauts heard the uproar and rushed back to join the battle. Soon there was a pile of dead monsters on the beach.

The next morning the Argonauts cast off with thanks and

pledges of friendship to the Doliones. Cyzicus had described the kingdoms and lands that lay ahead as far as the entrance to the Black Sea. The Argonauts sailed around the great bulk of Bear Mountain all day until they passed the northern point of the peninsula and headed east. When evening came, a great storm blew them back to the west. The wind was strong and the rain heavy. They had no idea where they were, only that they had to find land. Finally they saw a harbor. The men of that unknown land saw the strangers make shore. Unwelcome guests from the east could only mean raiders, so they attacked. The Argonauts fought back but had no idea who they were killing.

When the sun rose, Jason and his men saw that they had been fighting the Doliones. Jason saw that his own spear had pierced the chest of Cyzicus. The Argonauts wept and cut their hair in mourning for the terrible mistake, then built funeral pyres for the Doliones with their own hands. They laid out a special tomb for Cyzicus and marched around it three times in their bronze armor to honor him. The Argonauts then sailed away, leaving the Doliones alone in their grief.

To help forget the disaster, the Argonauts competed to see who could row the longest and hardest. One by one the men dropped away, but Hercules kept rowing until he alone drove the ship over the calm sea. Just as they reached the land of Mysia, his oar snapped in two. The hero fell onto the deck while his friends laughed. The voyagers pulled to shore and were welcomed with a feast of roasted mutton and sweet wine. Hercules was in no mood to eat. He and his friend Hylas went into the woods to cut a new oar. Hercules found a towering pine tree that was just the right size. He grabbed the tree around its base and pulled it out of the ground with his bare hands. Taking it on his shoulder, he headed back to the ship to shape it into an oar.

Hylas had gotten bored and went in search of water. He found a beautiful spring to fill his bronze pitcher. A water nymph immediately fell in love with him. She leapt out of the spring to kiss him and pulled him into the water.

One of the Argonauts, Polyphemus, heard Hylas scream and rushed to the spring. All he could see were ripples on the surface. He ran to Hercules, who dropped his tree and searched for his friend all night.

When dawn broke, the Argonauts cast off with a fair wind behind them. It was several hours before they realized that three of their crewmen were missing. A fierce argument broke out about what they should do. Most wanted to turn the ship around. Calais and Zetes, sons of the North Wind, declared that such a fair breeze was a gift of the gods and should not be scorned. The men turned to Jason, but he was unable to make a decision.

Suddenly Glaucus rose out of the waves. The fisherman who had turned into a sea god after eating magical grass told them that everything had unfolded according to the will of Zeus. Polyphemus was to found a great city among the Mysians, while Hercules needed to get back to his labors. Hylas was now the husband of a water nymph and was lost to the world of men. Reluctantly, the Argonauts continued on their way without their companions.

For almost two days a west wind blew the *Argo* across the Propontis Sea until, at last, the sailors came to the land of the

Bebryces near the entrance to the Bosporus straits. A brutish king named Amycus ruled that land. He met the Argonauts at the shore and told them it was the law that strangers must box with him in a fight to the death.

Pollux, the twin of Castor, accepted the challenge. Amycus was the stronger of the two men, but Pollux was quick and smart. He dodged the king's blows and kept him off balance. Amycus raged and threatened. The king charged Pollux with all his might. Pollux stepped aside at the last second and struck Amycus on the back of the head, killing him in an instant.

The Bebrycian men rushed at the Argonauts with spears and swords. Jason and his comrades drove them back. Soon the Greeks had finished off the men of Amycus. They camped on the beach while Orpheus sang songs of victory. When morning came, they pushed off and sailed into the swirling Bosporus, the final obstacle before they entered the mysterious Black Sea.

On the west side of the Bosporus straits was the land of the Thynians, ruled over by old King Phineus. He was said to be brother to King Cadmus of Thebes. Like Cadmus, his was a life of great suffering. Apollo had given him the gift of prophecy, but Phineus revealed too much of the future. Zeus punished the king by blinding him and by sending Harpies to torment him. These hideous creatures had the heads of women and the bodies of large birds. Whenever food was set before Phineus, the Harpies swooped down and snatched it in their talons. They left only enough to keep Phineus alive and prolong his pain. He was little more than skin and bones. He trembled from weakness and old age and was covered in the Harpies' waste.

Phineus told the Argonauts that if they would drive the
Harpies away, he would tell them what lay ahead on their
journey. So, the Argonauts prepared a feast and waited for the
Harpies to appear. When they did, Zetes and Calais flew after
them with swords drawn and chased them out of sight. Some
say the sons of the North Wind slew the Harpies, but others
say they spared the monsters in exchange for a promise never
to trouble Phineus again.

In gratitude, the seer told the sailors how to overcome the
dreaded Clashing Rocks at the exit of the Bosporus. Then he
described the lands and peoples along the southern shore of
the Black Sea and the kingdom of Colchis where the Golden

Fleece lay. He warned that a great monster guarded the treasure, one that no man had ever escaped alive.

Jason asked if he should turn around and go home rather than face certain death. The king asked what sort of hero he was if he ran away from danger.

"Put your trust in the gods," Phineus said, "especially Aphrodite."

The Argonauts made their way up the Bosporus. A cold fog enveloped them, but soon they began to hear a strange sound. It was like the pounding of a giant drum. When they finally rowed around a bend in the straits, they saw the Clashing Rocks. These two enormous stone guards stood on opposite sides of the entrance to the Black Sea. They rushed across the waterway and crushed anything that came between them. Phineus had told them their only hope of sailing between the rocks was to first send forth a dove from their ship. If this bird could fly between the rocks and survive, there was a chance that the *Argo* might also make it through.

The sailors were terrified, but to give up would bring shame on them forever. They released the dove. At first it seemed as if the Clashing Rocks would not notice the small creature, but suddenly they began to rush together. There was a sound as if the earth itself had split apart, but the dove lost only the tip of its tail feathers.

The Argonauts cheered for the bird as the rocks moved back, but they knew their boat could not fly as swiftly as a dove. They took oars in hand and prepared to row. Not even if Hercules had been aboard would the *Argo* have cut through the waves so fast. The rocks were even faster. The Argonauts shouted to each other to press on even as the rocks were almost on top of them. At the last moment, just as their strength was almost gone, they shot into the Black Sea. The Clashing Rocks met with a thunderous crash, cutting off the banner that flew from the stern of the *Argo*.

The gods had declared that if a ship ever sailed between the rocks, the rocks would never move again. So they withdrew to opposite sides of the straits where they would remain forever. The Argonauts gazed at the sea stretching before them and wondered how they would escape the new dangers that lay ahead.

As soon as they had passed the Clashing Rocks, Jason fell into deep despair. He told the helmsman, Tiphys, that he didn't know how they were going to make it all the way to Colchis. Tiphys assured Jason that everything would turn out well in the end, especially with the help of the gods. At that moment they saw Apollo flying high in the sky. Everyone but Jason took this as a sign of divine favor.

Several days later they came to the land of the Mariandynians where King Lycus ruled. This country was known for a dark cave from which an ice-cold wind blew. It was an entrance to Hades, but the Argonauts went instead to the palace of Lycus. The king welcomed the weary travelers and feasted them in grand style. He was so impressed by Jason and his companions that he sent his own son to join them on their quest.

Great sadness befell the Argonauts in that land when their seer, Idmon, was wounded by a huge white-tusked boar as he hunted in the woods. His friends killed the beast, but not before it had killed the soothsayer. They had just said their final farewells to Idmon when Tiphys suddenly died of a fever. Jason lost all hope. He urged the Argonauts to turn back, but the sailors instead asked the experienced seaman Ancaeus to guide the *Argo*.

A few days later the crew passed the tomb of Sthenelus, who had died during Hercules's battle with the Amazons. The spirit of the dead warrior rose from his grave. The sailors were terrified by the ghost and offered sacrifices to him hoping he would let them pass in peace, and he did.

Many more miles down the coast they came to the Assyrian colony of Sinope and took on supplies. There they met three survivors from Hercules's war on the Amazons, who gladly accepted an offer to join the Argonauts and advised Jason to sail away from the Amazon kingdom. Luckily, Zeus sent a wind that bore them safely past the coast held by the women warriors.

The Argonauts sailed for weeks past many different lands and tribes. The blind seer Phineus had told them they would find an island sacred to Ares where they should stop to receive a great blessing. When the Argonauts attempted to land there, they were attacked by birds. One of them remembered that Hercules had told of similar birds. When they landed on the beach, the Argonauts beat their shields and shouted to scare the birds away just as Hercules had done.

Moving inland they saw four skinny men. They were the shipwrecked sons of Phrixus, the young man who had flown to the land of Colchis years earlier on the golden ram. Jason invited them to join his quest, but the brothers warned the Argonauts that Aeetes was a cruel and clever king who would never let them have the fleece. They urged Jason to sail back to Greece, but the Argonauts were determined to press on. The four brothers joined only to escape the island of birds.

Jason and his men sailed on until they saw the Caucasus Mountains in the distance. At last they pulled the *Argo* into the mouth of the Phasis River, a swift stream that flowed through the heart of Colchis and the kingdom of King Aeetes. The long journey was over, but even the bravest among them wondered if they would live to sail the *Argo* home.

The goddess Hera had been following Jason's journey. Both she and Athena wanted the Argonauts to succeed, but they let mortals make their own way through the difficulties of life. Still, the wife and daughter of Zeus met secretly to find a way to help Jason. They knew that it would take extraordinary measures to capture the Golden Fleece, so they chose the one thing that could melt the hearts of both men and gods—love.

They asked Aphrodite to send her son Cupid to Colchis. They wanted Medea, the daughter of King Aeetes, to fall hopelessly in love with Jason. Medea was a powerful young witch and could use her magic to help the Argonauts. Aphrodite offered her son a golden ball that threw a flaming trail through the air like a comet. Cupid accepted the bribe and flew to Colchis to find Medea.

Meanwhile, the Argonauts had left the *Argo* and were making their way to the palace of Aeetes. Hera helped the men by covering them in a mist so that they could approach the king's city unseen. When they arrived at the gates of the palace, Hera blew the mist away and revealed a marvelous city built by the god Hephaestus himself. Medea looked out her window and saw Jason. Cupid let his arrow fly and she fell in love instantly with the handsome visitor from Greece.

Aeetes laughed at Jason and the Argonauts when they said they meant him no harm and politely asked for the Golden Fleece. The king told Jason he could have it if he could pass a small test of bravery. Jason had to yoke a pair of fire-breathing oxen. Then he had to use them to plow a field and sow it with dragon's teeth left over from the beast Cadmus had killed at Thebes. Armed warriors would spring from these teeth. Jason would have to kill them or be slain himself. When he had accomplished all this, Jason could try to take the fleece from the dragon.

Jason sat in an empty corner of the palace weeping and cursing the day he had ever left his home on Mount Pelion. Medea found him and swore that she would help him. Jason was overcome with gratitude and promised to love the princess forever. Medea then gave him a magic ointment to protect him from the oxen's fiery breath.

The next day Jason and his men found the field where Aeetes had placed the bronze yoke—wood would burn away in an instant—and fixed his spear in the ground. He hung his helmet, full of dragon's teeth, from its point. Then, with only his shield, he came to the dark cave where the oxen lived. The oxen stormed out bellowing fire, but Jason trusted in Medea's ointment and was not harmed. He waited until the oxen stopped to take a breath, and then, quick as lightning, wrestled one ox to the ground. He kicked the other hard on its leg and brought it to its knees. With the help of Castor and Pollux, he lifted the heavy bronze yoke onto the necks of the oxen and led the animals to the field.

As the oxen broke the sod, Jason sowed the dragon's teeth. When he finished, he let the oxen go and put on his armor. Men were slowly rising from the earth. Medea had told Jason what to do next. He threw a large boulder into the middle of the field. The warriors turned toward the stone. Some began fighting with each other, but most were unable to move. Jason rushed into the field and began hacking at the warriors. Soon they were all dead, with only Jason left alive to glory in his victory.

Aeetes spent the whole night plotting the death of Jason and his men. He knew that Medea's magic was behind Jason's success. Medea snuck out of the palace dragging her little brother Apsyrtus behind her. The sleepy child trusted his sister completely.

Medea made her way barefoot through the empty streets until she was at the banks of the river. She climbed onto the *Argo* and fell to her knees, begging Jason to take her to Greece. She would help him get the Golden Fleece, but they had to act quickly. Jason gladly agreed. Medea put her brother to bed on board and led Jason to the sacred grove of Ares.

The Golden Fleece hung on a huge oak tree, but the largest snake anyone could imagine was curled up around it. The serpent's hiss sent shivers down Jason's spine. Medea ran to the giant snake, fixing it with her eyes. Medea knew she could not hold its attention for long. She dipped a juniper branch into a powerful potion and then sprinkled it on the serpent's head while she chanted spells. Even this magic had its limits, so she told Jason to hurry. He grabbed the fleece and backed away while Medea continued to work her magic on the snake. The beast slowly raised its head and bared its fangs, but the spell was too strong and it collapsed.

Jason and Medea ran like the wind. He cut the ship's ropes and ordered the crew to cast off. The Argonauts manned the oars and pulled with all their might down the Phasis into the sea. They knew that Aeetes would show no mercy to the foreigners who had stolen his most valued possession.

By dawn the Argonauts were well along the coast, but Aeetes had gathered his ships. The Colchians closed the gap between the ships and overtook the *Argo*. It was now that Medea brought her little brother onto the deck in view of their father. Aeetes may have been ready to kill his daughter, but he would never harm Apsyrtus. Medea plunged her dagger into her brother's heart while both the Argonauts and the king watched in horror. She then cut Apsyrtus into little pieces, casting one of his arms into the sea. Aeetes screamed in anguish and ordered his ship to slow so that he could pick up the limb floating on the waves. Medea repeated this until little chunks of Apsyrtus were all over the sea. Aeetes fell farther and farther behind as he collected the pieces. The Greek sailors were grateful to Medea for saving them, but wondered what sort of woman they had taken on board.

Jason knew that the Colchians would follow him to the Bosporus straits, so he made instead for the mouth of the Danube River on the western coast. The king suspected he might take this route, so he sent a warship to the Danube, commanded by one of his sons. After a long voyage across the sea, the Argonauts entered the mouth of the Danube only to find that the Colchians had arrived first. Medea told Jason she could get them through if he had the courage to act without mercy. At this point, Jason was more afraid of the young witch than he was of her father's men, so he agreed.

Medea sent a messenger to her older brother to come alone to an island to discuss terms for the return of the fleece. When the brother arrived, Jason cut him down with his sword. Medea told Jason to cut off her brother's fingers and toes and suck the blood from each three times, spitting it onto the ground. This magic would keep the ghost from pursuing them. With the bloody deed done, the pair returned to the *Argo* and Jason ordered his men to row up the Danube deep into the unknown wilderness.

Stories say the voyage took the Argonauts through the dark forests and snow-covered mountains of Europe, far up the Danube to the foot of the Alps and beyond. Some say they sailed as far as the land of the Celts and through Gaul until they came to the Mediterranean coast of Liguria. From there they held to the Italian shore past the land of the Etruscans and the future site of Rome. Then they arrived at the island of Aeaea, home of the dreaded witch Circe.

Circe was sitting on the beach washing her head with seawater. She had never had such horrible dreams as she had the night before. She came down to the shore that morning followed by the wild creatures she had created from the strangers who came to her island.

When she saw Jason and Medea approaching, she signaled them to follow her. They fell down before Circe with hands over their faces like those seeking to wash away the sin of murder. Out of respect for Zeus, Circe began to purify them. She bathed their hands in the blood of a suckling pig. Next she prayed to Zeus and then burned cakes to soothe the Furies who follow after those who kill their own relatives.

When Circe finished, she asked her guests to tell of their terrible crime. She was especially eager to learn who Medea was, for she saw in her the fire of someone descended from the sun god Helios, her own father. Medea told Circe that she was indeed the granddaughter of Helios and daughter of Aeetes, and therefore Circe's niece. She told of the voyage of the Argonauts from Greece in search of the Golden Fleece and how she had helped them. Medea did not mention the murders, but Circe could see into her heart: "You foolish girl, truly you have embarked on a voyage of shame. How could you slay your own brothers and expect to escape the wrath of your father? I have unknowingly purged you of this crime and cannot punish you, but your life will be full of misery. Get off my island and take this wretched fellow with you!"

Jason took Medea by the hand and led her back to the ship. Medea pulled her robe over her eyes and wept. She had murdered her own kin and lost her home and family forever, all for the love of a stranger.

Hera sent a fair wind, and the *Argo* sailed south along the Italian coast. The bard Orpheus sang loudly as they approached the island of the Sirens. He drowned out the sweet songs that lured men to their death. The ship then passed between the monster Scylla and the giant whirlpool, Charybdis, with the help of the goddess Thetis. They also avoided the Wandering Rocks that crushed vessels off Sicily.

Warships sent by King Aeetes caught up with the Argonauts after they entered the harbor of the kindly Phaeacians. The Phaeacian queen, Arete, was very proper. She promised her husband would not turn the Argonauts over to the Colchians if Jason and Medea married. That night the couple were wed, and the Phaeacian king, Alcinous, agreed to protect them. The Colchians didn't dare challenge such a powerful ruler, but they were afraid to return home empty-handed. Alcinous granted them land for a colony nearby so they would not have to face Aeetes. The Phaeacians then sent the *Argo* on its way with gifts and fresh provisions.

Jason and the Argonauts were almost home. As they rounded the tip of the Peloponnesus, a fierce storm blew them all the way across the Mediterranean to Africa. One enormous wave carried the ship many miles into the desert, leaving it far from the sea. The men were so depressed that they lay down in the sand to die.

Jason had gone away from the others to face his end alone when suddenly he thought he saw three beautiful nymphs. They smiled and said they were the divine guardians of that land. They advised him not to worry: "Get up and rouse your comrades, Jason! As soon as Amphitrite unyokes the horses of Poseidon, then you and your companions must pay back your mother who has carried you so long. You may yet return to Greece!"

Then they vanished. Jason thought he was losing his mind, but he told the Argonauts what the nymphs said. The men were doubtful until a magnificent horse ran toward them and galloped into the distance. Peleus said this was the horse of Poseidon, and that the mother the nymphs spoke of must be the *Argo*. They should put the ship on their shoulders and carry her until they came to water.

Anything seemed better than dying in the desert. The men picked up the ship and set out through the wilderness. After nine days they came to an oasis. It was the Garden of the Hesperides, the very place Hercules had visited to gather the famous golden apples. The nymphs of the garden told them they had just missed the hero.

The sailors picked up the ship again and carried it until they came to inland Lake Tritonis and paddled around for days. Eventually the god Triton, Poseidon's son, took pity on them and carried the ship to the Mediterranean where they set sail for Greece. Along the way, they tried to take on fresh water in Crete, but were attacked by the bronze giant Talus who threw boulders at anyone who came near. Zeus had given Talus to Europa as a gift to protect her. The girl was long dead, but the mechanical monster still took his job seriously. The Argonauts were desperately thirsty. Medea once again came to their rescue and cast a spell. Talus struck his heel on a rock and the magic fluid that gave him life drained from his body. The men pulled to shore and refilled their water jars for the end of the voyage. They sailed north through the Aegean for several days until they came at last to Thessaly and Jason's own city of Iolcus beneath Mount Pelion, where they had set out from so long ago.

There are many different stories about what happened next, but most say that Jason gave the Golden Fleece to his uncle Pelias to fulfill his vow. The Argonauts then delivered their faithful ship to Corinth and dedicated it to Poseidon before going their separate ways. Jason and Medea returned to Iolcus. Jason's father, Aeson, was still alive, and at Jason's request, Medea rejuvenated him with her magical powers. This so impressed the daughters of King Pelias that they asked her to restore the youth of their own aged father. Medea was glad to help.

She took an old ram and cut it into pieces, then threw the parts into a large pot full of magical herbs. Moments later the witch reached in and pulled out a spring lamb. The daughters were thrilled and agreed she should do the same to their father. They entered his bedroom with swords and gathered around him while he slept. Before he could wake, they cut him into little pieces, then hurried to Medea. She placed the pieces in the cauldron, sprinkled herbs, and chanted spells above the boiling brew. The daughters looked into the pot, but all they saw was a bubbling stew. Medea explained that sometimes the magic didn't work. She then ran back to Jason to tell him the throne was his.

The sons of Pelias had other ideas and chased Jason and Medea out of Iolcus. Jason had lost his home in Hera's elaborate plan to punish Pelias, but Medea urged him to seek out another city. Corinth seemed like a good choice, since the king of that town—named Creon like the king of Thebes—admired Jason. So the couple made their way south to the Peloponnesian peninsula with nothing but the clothes on their backs. Medea took comfort in the fact that Jason's love for her would never fail.

Jason and Medea lived together in Corinth for ten happy years. Their lives were humble, but they found joy in their two sons. On days when their work allowed, they would take the boys down to the shore to show them the *Argo* and tell them stories of their great adventure.

Jason longed for the life of royalty and missed the days when men looked up to him. In Corinth, the people laughed at him behind his back because he had taken a foreign witch for a wife. By Greek law his sons could not even be citizens. There had to be some way he could set things right.

One day Jason came home and announced to Medea that he was going to marry Glauce, the daughter of King Creon of Corinth. He said that their own marriage didn't count because she was a foreigner. The king and his daughter were eager to make a match with the hero who had brought back the Golden Fleece. His new bride understandably didn't want Medea and her children around the city, so she would have to leave Corinth.

Medea exploded in outrage. She was the one who had gotten the fleece and brought Jason safely back to Greece through many dangers. She had given up her life for him. How dare he think he was going to get away with this!

Jason claimed that she should be grateful. He had gotten her away from that backward kingdom of her father and brought her to the glorious land of Greece. He then ran back to the palace and hid.

Medea was furious. She was being cast aside after all she had done for Jason. She knew that both she and her boys would wander the roads of Greece, starving. There was only one way to have her revenge.

She sent a message to Jason saying she had spoken out of anger. She knew he had her best interests at heart, so she wanted to make things right. She even had a wedding gift for the bride, a robe of the finest cloth.

Jason was glad to see that Medea had come to her senses. He carried the gift to Glauce himself. When she put on the robe, she started foaming at the mouth. The cloth burned her skin and the girl screamed and screamed. The king tried to help, but his own flesh began to melt. Both father and daughter died while Jason and the rest of the family looked on in horror.

Jason rushed to the home he had shared with Medea. He found her with a bloody sword in her hand. He felt a chill run down his spine and asked where their sons were. Medea calmly told him that they were dead. It was the hardest thing she had ever done, she confessed, but she could not leave them to suffer without a proper father.

Jason fell to the floor and cried in anguish. He hardly noticed that Medea had disappeared—some say on a chariot drawn by dragons sent by the sun god. Now Jason had truly lost everything.

As the weeks and months passed, Jason was scorned by all as a man cursed by the gods. He took to sitting beneath the rotting remains of the *Argo* on the beach at Corinth. He tried to remember the old days full of adventure and romance. At last one day the heavy oak prow from the grove of Zeus, now long silent, fell to the ground and crushed him. Jason's life was over.

Troy

I t all began with an apple.
Zeus gave his mortal grand-
son Peleus, who had sailed on the
Argo, the hand of the sea goddess
Thetis in marriage. The only prob-
lem was that Zeus had failed to ask
Thetis.

To help Peleus win over his bride,
the gods told him of a secret place where she danced with
sea nymphs in the moonlight. Peleus hid himself among the
rocks. When Thetis and the nymphs lay down to sleep, Peleus
crept up on the goddess and claimed her as his wife. She used
her powers to change into terrifying shapes, but Peleus hung
on until the goddess agreed to marry him.

They had a splendid wedding on the slopes of Mount
Pelion. The fifty sisters of Thetis sang, the Muses danced,
and Ganymede, the cupbearer, poured wine for all into golden
goblets. Everyone was there—except for one goddess. Zeus
had kept Strife, born at the dawn of the world, off the guest

list. In revenge she snuck up to the wedding and rolled a golden apple across the floor. On it were written the words, "For the fairest."

Hera, Athena, and Aphrodite fought over the apple. Zeus stopped them with his voice of thunder and declared that the matter must be decided by someone who had an eye for beautiful women. As judge, he chose a young Trojan prince named Paris.

Troy had struggled for many years to rebuild after it was destroyed by Hercules. Priam, the one surviving member of the royal family, married many wives and rebuilt his city to its former glory on the shores of the Hellespont. One of his wives was Hecuba, who gave him a fine son named Hector. A soothsayer told her that her second son would cause the downfall of Troy. So Priam and Hecuba gave the newborn infant, named Paris, to a shepherd to abandon on Mount Ida above the city.

The shepherd could not bring himself to kill the innocent baby. He raised Paris as his own, teaching him to watch over flocks and drive off wild animals. Paris was a beautiful child and popular with the local girls. He was also skilled with animals. A pet bull he raised became known throughout the region.

One day men from the court of the Trojan king came to take the bull. Priam needed it as a prize for funeral games in honor of a long-dead son he had been forced to abandon.

Paris decided to compete in the games to win his bull back. He went down to Troy and won every contest of strength and skill. The many sons of Priam were furious. One, named Deiphobus, drew his sword to kill the peasant, and Paris jumped on an altar of Zeus for protection. At that moment Cassandra, the soothsaying daughter of Priam, declared that the young stranger was the long-lost son. Everyone was so glad to see Paris alive that they forgot about the prophecy and welcomed him into the palace.

As much as he enjoyed life in the Trojan court, Paris still enjoyed the countryside. One night while he was playing his flute for his sheep, Hermes appeared along with three of the most beautiful beings Paris had ever seen. Hermes explained that Zeus wanted Paris to decide which of the three goddesses was the most beautiful. Hera, Athena, and Aphrodite were all perfect, so he could not choose. The goddesses whispered in his ear.

"Choose me," said Hera, "and I will make you king of all the lands."

"Choose me," said Athena, "and I will make you the greatest warrior men have ever seen."

"Choose me," said Aphrodite, "and I will give you the most beautiful woman in the world."

Paris declared that Aphrodite was the fairest. Hera and Athena stormed off, swearing vengeance. Aphrodite told the young shepherd that his bride waited across the sea in Greece. She was Helen, the daughter of Leda and Zeus, sister of Castor and Pollux. She was his—except for the fact that she was already married to King Menelaus of Sparta. The goddess of love assured Paris that Helen's marriage wasn't a problem.

The prince raced back to Troy and told everyone he was sailing to Greece. He arrived at the palace of Menelaus, brother of the great king Agamemnon, and was welcomed as a royal guest. Menelaus trusted Paris. But when Menelaus sailed to Crete for a funeral, Paris told the beautiful Queen Helen that he wanted to make her the happiest woman in the world. That night, with her young daughter Hermione, she left Sparta and sailed for Troy with Paris.

A few years earlier, the greatest kings and warriors from all of Greece had sought to win Helen's hand with magnificent gifts. Her mortal father, Tyndareus, had a problem. Helen's powerful suitors would be angry if they were not chosen.

Odysseus, the king of the tiny island of Ithaca, had a solution. If Tyndareus would arrange for Odysseus to marry Tyndareus's niece Penelope, he would draw up an oath for Helen's suitors. They would swear to accept the choice of Tyndareus, and if any man ever took Helen by force, they would fight to regain her for her husband.

This seemed like the perfect solution to Tyndareus, so he arranged for his niece to marry Odysseus. Then he made every suitor take the oath. Menelaus, who had given Tyndareus the most valuable gifts, was chosen as Helen's husband. The rest of the suitors sailed home and married other women.

When these powerful men heard that Paris had taken Helen to Troy, they realized they had vowed to go to war to get her back. Some were angry, but others were pleased. They were warriors with a thirst for battle, and Troy was rich beyond anyone's dreams. Agamemnon, the greatest of the Greek kings, was especially thrilled. He had long dreamed of gathering an army to take Troy and its treasures.

Agamemnon sent word to all those who had taken the oath to gather their armies at the Greek port of Aulis on the coast of Boeotia. Most came gladly. Odysseus, who had settled into married life, enjoyed spending time with Penelope and his newborn son, Telemachus. The walls of Troy were strong and the men of the city were great fighters. The war would be long and difficult. Odysseus knew that many men would not return home, and he did not want to be one of them.

When Menelaus and his comrade Palamedes arrived at Ithaca to collect Odysseus, they found the young king sowing a field with salt. Penelope said her husband had gone mad, but Palamedes suspected a trick. He grabbed Telemachus from Penelope's arms and placed the infant in the path of Odysseus's plow. Odysseus headed straight for his son, but at the last moment he turned the plow aside and picked up his baby. Menelaus and Palamedes knew that Odysseus was sane and fit for duty.

Once he was discovered, Odysseus prepared for war. He gathered twelve shiploads of men and outfitted them for a long fight. He made Penelope promise that she would wed again if he did not return by the time Telemachus began to grow a beard. He then kissed his wife and son, took one last look at Ithaca, and sailed away. He knew in his heart it would be a long time before he gazed on its shores again, but he swore he would make it home.

The marriage of the sea goddess Thetis and her mortal husband Peleus had been a happy one until their son Achilles was born. Some say that Peleus discovered his wife was secretly dipping their son in ambrosia and roasting him in a fire to make him immortal. When Peleus saw them, he cried out in terror and grabbed the boy from the flames. Thetis was so angry that she left her husband and returned to the sea. Others say that the goddess tried to make her son immortal by dipping him into the river Styx, but she held Achilles by his heel so that this one part of his body did not get wet and could be hurt.

Peleus took his young son to Mount Pelion to be raised by the wise centaur Chiron, just as Jason had been. His half-human, half-horse teacher instructed Achilles in music and poetry, athletics and war. While he was still a youth, Achilles returned to his father and completed his education under an aged tutor named Phoenix. While there, he met a young man named Patroclus, who became his best friend.

When preparations for the Trojan War began, the Greek leaders received an oracle that they needed Achilles on their side to take Troy. Thetis knew that if her son sailed to Troy, he would die. The Fates had said that Achilles would either live a long, quiet life, or he would become the greatest hero of the age and be remembered forever, even though his life would be short. Thetis sent her son to the small island of Scyros and dressed him up like a girl to keep his identity a secret.

Odysseus received word that Achilles was hiding there and set out to find him. He came as a merchant to the palace and spread out his wares in the courtyard for the king's daughters to examine. Among the jewelry and per-fumes he placed a fine sword and spear. At a prearranged signal, his herald sounded a trumpet as if the palace were being attacked. The girls screamed and ran, but one tall young woman grabbed the weapons and ran to the walls to fight. Odysseus knew he had found Achilles. Achilles was relieved—he longed to prove himself in battle. Childhood was over and he was going to war.

The men who had sworn the oath to Tyndareus formed the heart of the Greek expedition, but many others flocked to Aulis. They all hoped for fortune and glory. Agamemnon brought a hundred ships full of men from Mycenae. His brother Menelaus came with sixty from Sparta. Young Achilles brought many brave warriors from the kingdom of his father Peleus, including his friend Patroclus. Ajax, the son of Telamon, was there along with the son of Oileus known as Little Ajax. Old King Nestor led ninety ships from Pylos, while the great warrior Diomedes of Argos came with thirty ships. Menestheus brought fifty long black ships from Athens. Agapenor led enough men to fill sixty ships from the mountains of Arcadia. Idomeneus, king of Crete, arrived with eighty ships. Philoctetes, who had once kindled the funeral pyre of Hercules, brought the weapons he had received as a gift from the great hero. Agamemnon also brought Calchas, the great prophet from Megara. Besides these, there were countless other kings, princes, and warriors gathered on the beach at Aulis to launch a thousand ships for the sake of a beautiful woman.

The vast armada set sail across the Aegean and in a few days arrived on the coast of Asia Minor near the Hellespont. They immediately began to lay waste to the countryside. But they were not at Troy at all. They were somewhere on the shore of Mysia to the south. By the time they started back to the ships, the king of Mysia, a son of Hercules named Telephus, launched an attack and killed many of the invaders.

Achilles did manage to wound Telephus with his spear when the king tripped on a vine, but it was not a good beginning for the Greeks.

The ships were tossed by storms on their retreat. At last they made their way back to Aulis where the men grumbled that this was no way to start a war. To make matters worse, the winds had begun to blow against them so that they could not set out to sea again.

One day they were surprised to see King Telephus arrive on the beach. He explained to Agamemnon that he was in terrible pain from the wound Achilles had given him. The oracle of Apollo had told him he could only be healed by that which had harmed him. Achilles said that he was no doctor, but Odysseus suggested they scrape the rust from Achilles' spear into the wound. Soon the pain stopped and the injury began to heal.

The Greeks had just received their own oracle saying that they could not win the war unless the Mysian king came with them. Telephus owed a debt to the Greeks for healing him, but also had family duties to the Trojans. He agreed to guide the armada to Troy, but not to fight on their side. So Telephus readied himself to lead the ships across the Aegean—if only the wind would stop blowing.

Weeks went by in the Greek camp. Food ran short, disease set in, and the soldiers grew restless. Agamemnon knew they would have to sail soon or the army would go home. He prayed and sacrificed to the gods, but the wind still blew.

At last Agamemnon sent for the seer Calchas. He said that Artemis was angry because Agamemnon had boasted that he could hurl a spear better than the goddess. Agamemnon demanded to know what he must do to make peace with Artemis. Calchas begged him to send the army home instead. The king threatened to strangle Calchas unless he spoke. The soothsayer finally declared that the only way to win the favor of Artemis was for Agamemnon to sacrifice his own daughter, the beautiful Iphigenia.

The other captains demanded Agamemnon sacrifice the girl. The king reluctantly agreed. He sent a message to his wife, Clytemnestra, that he had decided to marry Iphigenia to handsome Achilles. The queen brought their daughter to Aulis. When they arrived, Agamemnon bound Iphigenia for the altar. The priests placed a gag around her mouth so she could not curse them.

Agamemnon recited prayers to the goddess of the hunt. The priests lifted the maiden in her wedding dress, a bride of death, onto the altar. The girl pleaded with Agamemnon with her eyes. With tears rolling down his cheeks, Agamemnon raised the knife and slit his daughter's throat.

Some say that at the last moment Artemis rescued the girl. But most agree that the maiden met her end on a bloody altar at Aulis, a sacrifice to the ambition of men.

The wind died away, and the Greeks sailed once again to Troy. They stopped at the island of Lemnos to offer sacrifices to the gods. Philoctetes helped with the preparation of the sheep, goats, and oxen, but a snake bit him on the foot. It swelled to twice its normal size and began to ooze smelly pus. The men could not stand the stench and abandoned Philoctetes on the island.

The fleet made its way past the small island of Tenedos just off the Asian coast, then to the mouth of the Scamander River that flowed near Troy. The men could see the great city on its hilltop overlooking the plain above the sea. Few had ever gazed at walls so tall and strong, and none had ever seen an army like the one that had gathered to meet them. More than one brave man in the Greek army wondered why he had ever left home.

The Greeks had received an oracle that the first man to land on Trojan soil would die. Everyone hung back, afraid to be the first. At last Protesilaus, king of Phylace, jumped onto the beach. Hector met him with a spear through his heart, shedding the first blood of the war. Achilles was there in an instant to drive Hector away, then he attacked Cycnus, a ruler of a nearby town. Poseidon had made it impossible to harm Cycnus with weapons, so Achilles strangled him with his own helmet strap.

The rest of the Greeks soon reached the shore and began to drive the Trojans back. It was slow, bloody work. By nightfall the Trojans had withdrawn into their city. The Greeks made camp on the shore. Priam and his subjects knew the walls of Troy could not be breached by any man. It was going to be a long war.

The Greeks were unable to take the city, and the Trojans were unable to drive the Greeks from their shores. Battles were fought on the plain in front of the town, but neither side was winning. The Greeks began to attack the lands of the city's allies, hoping to keep Troy from getting supplies. The Greeks, led by Achilles, raided over twenty cities, killing their men, taking their treasure, and marching their women and children back to camp as slaves.

For nine years the war continued. The Trojans were able to bring food and luxuries into the city in spite of Greek efforts to stop them. Everyone grew weary.

One of Agamemnon's favorite slaves was the daughter of Chryses, a priest of Apollo. It was the custom of the time to ransom slaves for gold if there were any relatives alive to make a payment. Chryses made his way to the Greek camp bearing gifts and holding the sacred staff of Apollo. He asked Agamemnon to release his daughter, as it would be pleasing to the god. Agamemnon rose from his throne and knocked the ransom from the priest's hands: "Get out of my sight, old man, and never let me see you in this camp again! I will never give up the girl!"

Chryses prayed to the god: "Apollo, god of the silver bow, if ever I have offered pleasing sacrifices to you, hear my prayer! Strike down these Greeks who mock your priest. Rain your arrows down upon them!"

Apollo heard the prayer and flew down from Olympus. He knelt on a hill above the Greek camp and shot arrows of plague among the tents. The men began to fall, then die. Soon the funeral fires burned day and night.

At last Achilles called an assembly of the Greek leaders and said they should sail home unless they could find out why the gods were punishing them. The seer Calchas said he would reveal the truth, but first Achilles had to promise to protect him from the wrath of the one at fault. The young warrior agreed, then Calchas said that Agamemnon was to blame. If the king would return the daughter of Chryses, Apollo would stop the plague.

Agamemnon complained that it wasn't fair that he should have to give up his favorite slave: "I like this young woman even better than my own wife, Clytemnestra. But I'm a reasonable man. I'll give up the girl if I receive a slave of equal beauty and quality from one of you."

Achilles shot back: "And just who do you expect to give up his slave, you greedy pig? For once think of the troops more than yourself. Surrender the girl."

Agamemnon would not change his mind: "You're telling me how to lead an army? I was killing men on the battlefield while you were still wetting your pants. I'm going to take your slave, Achilles. Have the girl made ready and I'll send my men for her."

Achilles was about to kill Agamemnon when Athena appeared, visible only to him, and ordered him to stop. So Achilles obeyed Athena and sent his slave to Agamemnon. He said he was leaving the war along with all his men. The other leaders begged him to reconsider, but he would not. He urged his divine mother, Thetis, to ask Zeus to help the Trojans. He wanted to see thousands of Greeks lying dead on the plains of Troy so that Agamemnon would beg him to fight for them again. Thetis flew to Olympus and asked Zeus to help the Trojans. Zeus agreed, even though he knew it would get him into trouble with Hera, who supported the Greeks.

Zeus sent a misleading dream to Agamemnon telling him that if he attacked the Trojans at once, a great victory would be his. The Greek leader jumped from his bed and told the soldiers that they would crush the Trojans that very day. After years of waiting, the Greek warriors cheered and put on their armor. The great battle was upon them at last.

Hector was watching from the walls of Troy and saw the rush of activity in the Greek camp. He gathered the Trojan army to meet the enemy. Both sides faced each other across a narrow no-man's-land between the armies. Agamemnon stood in his chariot at the center of the Greek lines. His brother Menelaus was beside him. Ajax, Odysseus, Diomedes, and all the other Greek captains—except Achilles—waited at the front of their own troops. Hector and his brother Paris faced them with Trojan troops and allies gathered all around.

For nine years Menelaus had fought against the young Trojan who had charmed Helen away. The Spartan hated Paris. When he saw the prince standing opposite him, he jumped from his chariot. Paris ran behind Hector to hide from the Greek warrior, but Hector called him a coward and a fool. Paris answered: "Ah, Hector, you're right. I know this war is because of me, so I should end it. Send a herald to the Greeks telling Menelaus that I will fight him to the death in single combat. The winner takes Helen, and everyone can go home at last."

Both armies rejoiced at the idea of the war ending. Sacrifices were made and oaths taken that Greeks and Trojans alike would respect the outcome of the fight. Then the armies watched as the warrior of Sparta marched to face the young prince of Troy. Helen stood on the walls beside King Priam to see what her fate would be.

Menelaus hurled his oak spear straight at Paris. The shaft flew so fast it broke through the Trojan's shield and struck his breastplate, but Paris turned aside at the last moment and avoided the deadly point. Then Menelaus drew his silver-studded sword and ran at Paris, bringing the blade down on his helmet. The sword broke into pieces. Paris was stunned, and Menelaus was without a weapon. Then Menelaus rushed at Paris and grabbed his helmet strap. He began to drag Paris back to the Greek lines to kill him, but Aphrodite whisked Paris to safety.

Paris woke to find himself on his bed and knew the goddess had helped him. Menelaus meanwhile stalked up and down the lines looking for Paris. A Trojan archer named Pandarus saw his chance for glory and shot his deadly arrow at the Spartan king. It was only a glancing blow, but the Greeks shouted that the Trojans had broken the truce. All hope of a peaceful end to the war vanished as both armies rushed together like two giant waves crashing. Soon the field was littered with bodies.

Greek warrior Diomedes cut through the Trojan lines taking on man after man as the gods watched, invisible on the battlefield. He would have slain Aeneas, but his divine mother, Aphrodite, picked him up before Diomedes could drive home the fatal blow. Then Athena, who favored Diomedes, lifted the mist from his eyes so that he could see the gods on the plain. She whispered to him to stab Aphrodite.

Diomedes began to stalk Aphrodite through the killing fields. When he was close enough, he stabbed her through the wrist, forcing her to drop Aeneas. Gods cannot die, but they can be wounded. Aphrodite shrieked and fled from the battle. Diomedes mocked her: "What's the matter, goddess, giving up war so soon? Maybe you should stick to ruining people's lives with your petty schemes." Soon after, Diomedes rammed his spear into the gut of the war god Ares. Aphrodite and Ares flew to Olympus to complain to Zeus that Athena let a mortal man attack them. Athena joined them to defend herself, and Zeus sent them all away.

Back on the battlefield, Diomedes was about to kill Aeneas when he saw Apollo beside the Trojan warrior. Diomedes tried three times to drive Apollo away. On the fourth attempt, Apollo spoke: "Think, Diomedes. You are a man and I am a god. I don't want to destroy you, but I will. Stop before it's too late."

Diomedes came to his senses and turned his attention to mortal enemies.

The Trojan prince Hector saw his men falling all around him. When the Greeks were pressing close to the gates of the city, Hector told his captains to hold the line while he told the women to pray and sacrifice to the gods. He ran through the gates of Troy and up to the citadel. He saw his brother lounging on a couch: "Paris, what are you doing here while the enemy is at our very walls? Get up and join the battle, before the city is burned to ashes around you!"

He then ran to find his wife, Andromache, and tell her to organize the women to beseech the gods. He found her watching the battle, praying that her husband was still alive.

She held out their son, Astyanax, and begged her husband not to return to battle: "Dear Hector, think of your son and stay with us. I don't want to be a widow. You know what will happen if the Greeks kill you and take the city. Stay here, please, where it is safe."

Hector held her close and said: "My beloved, I must return to the battle. I would die in shame before my men if I stayed here safe while they fought. In my heart I know there will come a day when sacred Troy will fall. My blessed father, Priam, will perish along with my brothers, while my aged mother, Hecuba, will be taken to Greece to spin flax as a slave. None of that compares to the pain I feel when I think of some Greek tearing you away from your home to work his loom. Still, I cannot give up the fight. It may well be my fate to die here, but I will never be called a coward."

No sooner had Hector made his way back to the battle than Ajax, son of Telamon, challenged him to combat. The Trojan prince turned to the giant who towered over him. Hector threw his spear first and struck the shield of Ajax, but could not pierce it. The Greek then set his spear flying until it pierced Hector's shield. Hector turned away just as the mighty shaft cut through his armor. The two warriors then set on each other with swords and fought until night began to fall. Heralds from both sides called on the pair to stop because of darkness. Each hated to back down, but both withdrew to fight another day. After the Greeks dragged themselves back to their camp, they feasted and raised a toast to their many friends who had fallen that day. "Come sunrise," they boasted, "we will storm the walls and take the city of Troy."

It was now that Zeus remembered his promise to Thetis to make the Greeks beg Achilles for help. When Agamemnon and his men were ready to storm the city the next morning, Zeus sent down lightning bolts. The shafts of fire threw men and horses into a panic. No man can fight Zeus. The Greeks fell back while Hector and the Trojans chased them across the plain, killing countless warriors.

What seemed like certain victory for the Greeks had now turned to defeat. All hope seemed lost as they gazed out at hundreds of Trojan fires spread across the plain like stars in the sky. Hector and his men had not even returned to the city that night. They were ready to strike at dawn.

Many Greek captains wanted to sail away that very night, but Nestor urged them to beg Achilles to return to the fight. If only Agamemnon would set aside his pride, the Greeks might be able to drive the Trojans back. Agamemnon admitted he had been wrong. He would send heralds to Achilles to apologize and offer splendid gifts to win the young warrior over.

Odysseus and others found Achilles playing the lyre, singing songs of glorious heroes of old. He greeted them warmly and listened to their words carefully. Then he addressed Odysseus: "Son of Laertes, let me say this plainly and quickly. Will Agamemnon's generous offer win me over? Not for all the world. I have my honor. I'm going to sail away tomorrow at daybreak. All of you should as well, for the Trojans are going to crush you."

Aged Phoenix, who had once been the tutor of Achilles, told a story of another man who had been unforgiving. This was Meleager, king of Calydon, who had sailed with Jason on the *Argo*. When he returned from that voyage, he married a beautiful woman named Cleopatra. He ruled his land with wisdom, but one day he slew his uncle after the man tried to take the hide of the Calydonian boar from him. Meleager's own mother cursed him for killing her favorite brother.

Meleager was so angry at his mother that he refused to fight when his uncle's tribe attacked his city. His family and friends begged him, but he would not hear their words. When this uncle's tribe were about to take the palace, his wife, Cleopatra, urged him to rejoin the fight. She asked if he wanted to see her killed or taken into slavery. Meleager then led his warriors to victory, for he realized that anger and pride would cost him that which he held most dear.

Achilles listened to the story, but he did not understand the meaning. If the Greeks were going to face the Trojans, they would have to do it without him.

The Greek warriors hardly slept as fear walked among them that night. When dawn came, Zeus sent the goddess Strife down to the Greek camp to stir up their courage. Strife was delighted with how events had unfolded since she had rolled the apple into the wedding celebration of Peleus and Thetis. Now she stood on the hull of Odysseus's ship and let out a cry, great and terrible. It put the lust for battle into the hearts of the Greek invaders. Moments before, the fight had seemed hopeless Now they yearned to meet the Trojan force—just as Zeus had intended.

The Greek captains led their men against the army of Hector with promises of victory. But soon, even though the Trojans took their share of casualties, the best of the Greeks began to fall. A Trojan spearman slashed Agamemnon on the arm down to the bone, forcing him to withdraw from battle. Next, mighty Diomedes was struck in the foot with an arrow, making him retreat behind the lines. Odysseus was surrounded by Trojans eager to claim the glory of slaying the son of Laertes. He fought off many, but one cut through his armor. The king of Ithaca then also withdrew, leaving few Greek officers to encourage the men.

Achilles sent his dearest friend, Patroclus, to Nestor to ask the old man for news of the battle. Nestor told Patroclus that the Greeks were losing and could not keep the Trojans from the ships much longer. If they set the Greek ships ablaze, he warned, they were doomed. He begged Patroclus to join the fight. The sight of Achilles's friend might be enough to drive the Trojans back.

As Patroclus ran to Achilles to ask his friend if he might fight, Hector smashed through the rampart guarding the Greek ships. He ordered the Trojans to make for the ships, torches in hand. The Greeks fought to hold the enemy back, but yard by yard the Trojans came closer.

Nothing could keep the Trojans away as they broke over the walls of the Greek camp. Finally they reached the closest of the Greek ships and threw their torches inside the hull. The flames lit up the sky. The Greeks held the enemy back from the rest of the fleet, but they all knew they would not live to see another day.

Zeus had forbidden the other gods to get involved in the war. Those who favored Agamemnon's men, such as his wife Hera, could not stand to see their side losing so badly. Hera knew she could not challenge Zeus directly, so she tried a more subtle approach.

She went to her chamber and bathed in the most enticing perfumes known to the gods. She next applied a magical elixir she had gotten from Aphrodite. Then she went to the god Sleep, and promised him one of the beautiful Graces as his wife if he would put her husband to sleep at just the right moment. At last she strolled past the mountain meadow where Zeus was sitting.

Zeus saw her and decided the mortals could wait: "Hera, why hurry away? Never have I seen a goddess or mortal woman who has made my heart pound so. Europa, Semele, Leto—they were all nothing compared to you."

Crafty Hera had Zeus spread a thick mist around them,

to cover them from the sight of gods and men. Then Sleep poured his potion on Zeus so that he fell into a deep slumber.

Hera flew down the slopes of Olympus and stirred the Greeks to hold back the Trojans. Back and forth the tide of battle shifted as one moment the Greeks pushed the Trojans from the ships, then the next they were driven back to the sea.

Achilles had agreed to let Patroclus join the fight and even gave him his own armor to wear. He warned his dear friend only to drive the Trojans back from the ships, not to take the battle to the city. Patroclus put on the shining armor and led many hundreds of fresh troops into the fight.

The appearance of Patroclus and his men brought hope to the Greeks and terror to their enemies. The Trojans thought that Achilles was rejoining the fight. With a tremendous roar, the Greeks pushed the Trojans over the ramparts and back onto the plain. The men began to believe they might take Troy itself that day. Patroclus forgot the warning of Achilles and ordered the men to follow him to the walls of the city.

The Greeks would have taken Troy then if Zeus had not awoken and sent Apollo to stand before the ramparts of the city. The young god came up behind Patroclus and slammed him between the shoulders. A Trojan warrior then struck him with a spear but did not bring him down. Immediately Hector was there with his own bronze-tipped spear. Patroclus fell into the dust, his soul flying down to the house of Hades, leaving life behind.

Hector stripped the armor off the dead soldier and would have taken his corpse back to Troy, but Menelaus drove Hector away. He put the body into a chariot to return it to the

Greek camp for proper funeral rites. Hector gloried in the fact that he had killed Patroclus, one of the greatest of the Greek warriors and the friend of Achilles.

The wail that went up from the Greek lines told Achilles that his friend was dead. He sat in the dust tearing his hair. His cry was so loud that Thetis heard it in the depths of the sea and came to comfort her son. She told him that as horrible as things seemed, he had gotten what he wanted. Agamemnon had suffered and the Greeks realized they could not win the war without him.

That meant little to Achilles now. Phoenix had been right. His own pride had cost him that which he loved the most. At last he agreed to set aside his anger and rejoin the fight, with his sole purpose to destroy Hector. Nothing mattered now but revenge.

Thetis flew to the home of the divine smith Hephaestus to ask the god to make new armor for her son. Hephaestus created a set of armor like no man had ever seen. The enormous shield was embossed with figures telling stories of two noble cities, one at war, one at peace. All the world was there, encircled by the mighty river of Ocean. He also forged a breastplate, a sturdy helmet, and greaves to cover the warrior's legs. Thetis winged back to Troy to present the gifts to her son, who armed himself for battle.

Zeus knew his promise to Thetis had been kept. The Greeks honored Achilles as he marched onto the battlefield. The first enemy he met was Aeneas, son of the goddess Aphrodite. Achilles would have killed him, but the gods saved Aeneas. Achilles then slaughtered other Trojans like sheep.

The Scamander River became so clogged with his victims that the god of the river rose up and ordered Achilles to stop. When he refused, the river leaped out of its banks and pursued him across the plain like a tidal wave. Hephaestus used fire to force the river back.

At last Achilles reached the walls of Troy and called Hector forth. Hector donned his armor to face the greatest warrior of the age. The two fought like lions. Hector knew he could not match the rage of Achilles. He fled and ran three times around the walls of Troy while Achilles chased him. Then the goddess Athena appeared to Hector in the form of his brother Deiphobus and told him they would fight together. Hector turned to make his stand, but Deiphobus vanished. Hector was doomed. He fought bravely, but Achilles triumphed. As Hector breathed his last, Achilles promised the fallen soldier that the dogs and birds would soon feast on his corpse. When the soul of the Trojan had departed, Achilles dragged his body back to the Greek camp while Hector's family on the walls looked on in horror.

The funeral rites for Patroclus were splendid. All the while the corpse of Hector lay unburied. Zeus favored Achilles, but he could not allow him to dishonor the dead. He sent Thetis to demand he accept a ransom for the body of his enemy. Achilles agreed, but only if a Trojan warrior was brave enough to cross the lines and claim him.

Later that night, King Priam had a vision telling him to go to Achilles. Guided by Hermes, Priam drove a cart across the plain, alone in the darkness. He fell down on his knees before Achilles, kissed the very hands that had killed his son, and asked him for Hector's body.

Achilles thought of his own aged father, Peleus, across the sea. He thought of all the young men who had died on the battlefield in hope of eternal glory. And at last he thought of his friend Patroclus. Tears poured down the faces of both men as they realized the true cost of war.

Achilles carried the body of Hector to Priam's cart and laid him gently inside. He then sent Priam back to Troy, granting him ten days of peace to mourn and bury his son. The women of the city wailed songs of sorrow. Hector was the best among them, both as warrior and as a man. The Trojans built a great funeral pyre and burned his body. When the flames died away, they gathered his white bones, wrapped them in purple cloth, and laid them in a grave within a golden chest.

Hector was dead, but the walls of Troy still stood, and new allies arrived to join the army of King Priam. Penthesileia, ruler of the Amazons and a daughter of the war god Ares, rode onto the plain with her warrior women and killed many of the best Greek fighters. Achilles mortally wounded the queen and then fell in love with her as she lay dying. Achilles also slew Memnon, king of the Ethiopians, who had brought his army all the way from the headwaters of the Nile.

It seemed as if nothing could strike down Achilles. But Apollo knew where he was weak and guided an arrow of Paris to his heel. The greatest of the Greek warriors bled to death beneath the walls of Troy. The Trojans would have seized his divine armor, but Ajax and Odysseus drove them back and carried the corpse to their camp by the shore. All the Greeks mourned Achilles and burned his body on a funeral pyre, afterward mixing his ashes with those of his friend Patroclus.

The Greeks then held a contest to see who would receive Achilles's glorious armor. Ajax argued that he had killed more Trojans than anyone save Achilles and therefore deserved the prize. Odysseus won the armor with his smooth tongue, claiming that his brains had helped the Greeks more than anyone's brawn. Ajax became crazed with jealousy. That night he attacked his old friends, slaughtering Agamemnon, Menelaus, and Odysseus. When dawn came, he returned to his senses and discovered he had in fact killed only a herd of sheep. Ashamed, he went to a cave and killed himself with his own sword.

The Greeks were no closer to taking the city of Troy than they had been ten years earlier. They asked the seer Calchas what they must do to win the war. He said they needed the weapons Hercules had left with Philoctetes—the very man they had abandoned on the island of Lemnos. A group sailed to bring Philoctetes to the Greek camp in spite of his still-stinking wound. Once on the beach at Troy, the injured man was healed. He then used his weapons to kill Paris.

Two brothers of Paris, the seer, Helenus, and the warrior, Deiphobus, quarreled over who would be the third husband of the most beautiful woman in the world. Deiphobus won, and Helenus left the town in bitter disappointment to live alone on the slopes of Mount Ida. The Greeks knew Helenus was a powerful prophet, so they sent Odysseus to kidnap him and bring him to the Greek camp. He revealed that for the Greeks to take the city, they would first need to transport the bones of Agamemnon's grandfather, Pelops, to their camp from Greece. Second, they would need to bring Achilles's son Neoptolemus to join them. Finally they would need to steal the Palladium, the wooden statue of Athena, from her temple in the city. "These three things are necessary," said Helenus, "but they are not enough. You will still have to discover for yourselves what no man or god knows—how to breach the walls of Troy."

The Greeks collected the bones of Pelops and found young Neoptolemus eager to join them. Stealing Athena's statue from her temple in the center of Troy was a problem. Odysseus and Diomedes disguised themselves as beggars and snuck into the city. Some say that Helen recognized them and helped them, but others claim they stole the statue on their own. Now they had everything they needed to take the city of Troy—if only they could find a way to get their army through its walls.

How the idea of the wooden horse occurred to Odysseus no one ever knew. When the Greeks heard it, they knew it would work. It was daring and insane, but it was also simple and cunning. Odysseus instructed a craftsman named Epeius to build a wooden horse big enough to hold fifty men. It had to look solid from the outside but needed a secret door that could be opened by those hiding inside.

When the horse was complete, Odysseus, Menelaus, and four dozen other Greeks sealed themselves in the creature's belly. The rest of the Greeks burned their tents and sailed away to anchor on the far side of the island of Tenedos and await the signal.

When dawn rose the next morning, the Trojans could see the smoldering ruins of the Greek camp and a giant wooden horse in the distance. They rode out to the shore and wondered why their enemies should have built such a thing. Suddenly a man named Sinon came running to them from the bushes and threw himself at the feet of Priam. He said the wooden horse was left behind as a peace offering to Athena. The Greeks had realized that they could never take the city and only wanted to sail home in peace with the blessing of the goddess.

The prophetess Cassandra declared that Sinon was lying, but no one believed her. Laocoon, the Trojan priest of Poseidon, warned they should never trust Greeks, especially when they were bearing gifts. But Poseidon sent a sea serpent to devour Laocoon and his sons on the beach, a sign to all to reject his words. The Trojans then dragged the giant horse into the city.

At the victory feast that night there was music, dancing, and more wine than anyone had ever seen. Everyone sang and drank long into the night before stumbling back to their homes to sleep.

When the city was finally quiet, a door opened under the belly of the horse. Ropes were lowered and orders given to unbar the gates of the city. Sinon had already kindled a fire on the tomb of Achilles to signal the fleet. The Greek army had quickly sailed back and were waiting outside the walls.

The Greeks spread throughout the city to slaughter the Trojans and set fire to their homes. Aeneas, son of Aphrodite, gathered what men, women, and children he could and escaped. Most Trojans were not so lucky. King Priam was cut down at the altar of Zeus. Little Ajax found Cassandra in the temple of Athena and gave her to Agamemnon as a slave. Hector's mother, Hecuba, was led away in chains as was his wife, Andromache, but not before his young son, Astyanax, was thrown to his death. The Greeks took Priam's youngest daughter, Polyxena, and cut her throat over the tomb of Achilles, a sacrifice to the spirit of their friend. At last, when the city was a smoking ruin, Menelaus killed Helen's new husband, Deiphobus. He was ready to plunge his sword into his former wife, but Helen begged to be allowed to return to Sparta where she would make him a happy man. Menelaus hesitated, thinking of all the good men who had died for her sake. Then he took her by the hand and led her back to his ship.

The long war was finally over.

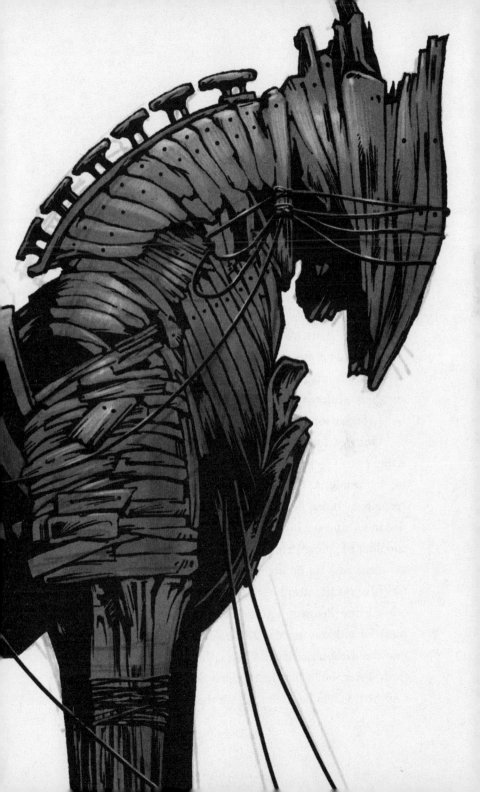

Mycenae

Many years before Agamemnon led the Greeks to Troy, his ancestor Tantalus ruled as king in Lydia. Tantalus was a mortal son of Zeus and one of his favorites. He took advantage of his father, stealing ambrosia and telling the gods' secrets to mortals. When Zeus overlooked this bad behavior, his son became more and more bold.

One day Tantalus invited the gods to dinner at his palace. Tantalus had slaughtered his own son Pelops and served him to his divine guests. The king was curious to see if the gods would recognize human flesh. Only Demeter was fooled because she was mourning the loss of her daughter, Persephone. She ate a shoulder of young Pelops before anyone could stop her.

Zeus rose up in anger and ordered Hermes to place the pieces of his grandson back into the stewpot. He then pulled out a living Pelops, minus a shoulder that Hephaestus later replaced with one made of ivory. Zeus then cast Tantalus down into the darkest corner of Hades. Tantalus stood in a pool of fresh water, but when he stooped down to drink, the water vanished. When he tried to grasp the fruits over his head, the wind blew them out of his reach. Thus for eternity Tantalus was tormented by food and drink he could not have.

Pelops was even more handsome after he was restored to life than he had been before. His good looks caught the eye of the god Poseidon, who took him to Mount Olympus to serve as his cupbearer. When he grew tired of the youth, Poseidon sent him away with a chariot so fast some said it could fly across the top of the sea.

Pelops used the chariot when he heard that King Oenomaus of Pisa was holding races to see who could win his daughter Hippodamia as a bride. The king had no desire to part with her, so he came up with an impossible contest to keep her unwed. Interested men had to race from Pisa to the Isthmus of Corinth before the king caught up with them. Oenomaus owned horses he received from the god Ares. When he caught up with the suitors—which he always did—he cut off their heads. Hippodamia was so beautiful that twelve warriors had already died trying to win her hand.

Pelops made his way across the Aegean Sea and knocked on the palace door. The heads of a dozen suitors hung from the palace walls. Hippodamia fell in love with Pelops. She asked her father's charioteer, named Myrtilus, to loosen the pins from the axel of her father's chariot. Myrtilus was desperately in love with the princess and did as she asked. Soon after the race began, the chariot collapsed. Oenomaus was thrown to the rocks beside the road and died.

Myrtilus went with the newly married couple as they made their way back to Lydia. At their first stop, he tried to force himself on Hippodamia while Pelops was fetching water. The prince caught him and tossed him off a cliff, but not before Myrtilus uttered the curse of a dying man upon Pelops and his descendants. Pelops later returned to Pisa with Hippodamia and took the crown. He was fond of his new land and named the entire peninsula for himself, calling it the *Peloponnesus* or "Pelops Island." He had many children with Hippodamia, including two sons, Atreus and Thyestes.

After the sons of Hercules killed Eurystheus, king of Mycenae, the people of the town received an oracle that they should choose one of the sons of Pelops as their new ruler. The Mycenaeans did not know which one to pick, so they sent for both. Atreus, as the eldest, said that he was the natural choice. Thyestes argued that whoever was able to present the citizens with the fleece of a golden lamb should be the new king.

Atreus thought this was a wonderful idea. Several years earlier he had made a vow to sacrifice the finest lamb born to his flock to Artemis. A ewe gave birth to a lamb with fleece of gold. Atreus knew he should offer the lamb to Artemis, but he couldn't bring himself to part with such a miraculous gift. He strangled the golden lamb and hid its fleece.

Unknown to Atreus, his wife, Aerope, was in love with Thyestes. Aerope had secretly given the golden fleece to her lover. When Atreus tried to prove to the Mycenaeans that he should be king, the fleece was gone. Thyestes then presented it to the city elders, who offered him the crown. Atreus was furious. So was his great-grandfather, Zeus.

Zeus sent Hermes to Mycenae. He told him to ask Thyestes if he would give up the throne if Atreus could make the sun move backward. Thyestes laughed at such a silly idea and agreed. The next day, after the sun traveled halfway across the sky, it began to move backward. The people of Mycenae wanted a king who could change the course of the heavens. Atreus became ruler and banished Thyestes from the land.

The new king could not forget his brother's dishonesty. He lured him and his family back to Mycenae with an offer to make peace. Atreus invited his brother to join him at the head of the table at a great banquet. Atreus had killed his brother's three young sons. He had cut off their heads and limbs and boiled the rest in a stewpot. After much wine, song, and tender meat, Atreus asked his brother how he liked his dinner. Thyestes replied it was the best he had ever eaten. Atreus clapped his hands and had a platter brought out with the heads and limbs of Thyestes's sons. He had just dined on their flesh. The younger brother cursed Atreus and his sons, and was cast out of the kingdom once again.

Alone and wretched, Thyestes traveled to Delphi to find out how he could have revenge. The oracle told him he had to father a child by his own daughter Pelopia, whom he had not seen in years. Thyestes dismissed the idea and traveled to the land of Sicyon in the northern Peloponnesus. As he passed by a forest he happened upon a group of young women celebrating the rites of Artemis. He hid behind a tree and watched. The leader of the dancers was a particularly pretty girl who slipped on sheep's blood and left the group to wash her robes in a nearby stream. Thyestes followed her and forced himself upon her. The girl could not fight back against such a powerful stranger. She stole his sword before he left and placed the weapon under the altar at the temple of Artemis.

Back in Mycenae, the crops were failing because of the

blood-guilt Atreus had brought on the land when he killed his nephews. Atreus traveled to an oracle near Sicyon to seek relief for his kingdom and was told that he must bring Thyestes back. The oracle did not say dead or alive, and Atreus did not ask. Before he left, he saw a beautiful young woman standing near a temple. He didn't realize that she was his niece, Pelopia, and that she was pregnant by her own father, Thyestes. He asked if she would become his wife. The woman agreed. A little less than nine months later, she bore a son named Aegisthus.

Years went by as Atreus searched for Thyestes. At last he sent his two sons, Agamemnon and Menelaus, to Delphi to ask the oracle where he could find his brother. Miraculously, Thyestes was also there and still seeking a way to have revenge. Agamemnon and Menelaus took their uncle back to Mycenae by force. Atreus threw his brother into prison. He then ordered his other son, Aegisthus, to take a sword and kill the man.

Aegisthus unwrapped the fine sword he had recently received from his mother. He went down to the palace dungeon and ordered the prisoner to kneel. Thyestes recognized the sword and asked where he gotten it. When Aegisthus told him, Thyestes revealed that Aegisthus was his son and that Pelopia was his own daughter. Aegisthus called his mother to the prison and she confirmed the story, then took the sword and plunged it into her heart. This was shocking to Aegisthus. He took the sword stained by his mother's blood and presented it to Atreus. The king believed that Thyestes at last was dead, but in his excitement did not notice Aegisthus come up from behind. Aegisthus stabbed him in the back.

Aegisthus then released Thyestes from prison and helped him seize the throne. Agamemnon and Menelaus took refuge with King Tyndareus in Sparta. In time they returned and drove their uncle Thyestes from Mycenae once again. Agamemnon became king and forgave his half-brother for murdering his father. Aegisthus seemed grateful and lived a quiet life serving Agamemnon loyally. His devotion was rewarded when Agamemnon sailed to Troy. The king left Aegisthus in charge of the kingdom until he returned. Aegisthus, whose anger at the family of Atreus boiled just below the surface, gladly agreed.

At Aulis, Agamemnon sacrificed Iphigenia, leaving only his daughter, Electra, and his son, Orestes, to comfort their mother. Anger grew inside Clytemnestra. Whatever love she had once had for Agamemnon died the day he killed their daughter. Now she turned to Aegisthus and found in him a willing partner in her revenge.

At last word reached Mycenae that Troy had fallen. Clytemnestra had long ago set up a series of signal fires to be lighted when Troy was taken so that she might know that Agamemnon was on his way back. Before the burning embers of Troy had died away, Clytemnestra prepared to welcome her husband home.

After a few weeks, Agamemnon landed at the port near Argos and made his way by chariot to his palace at Mycenae. Cheering crowds lined the way to admire the treasure he brought from Troy. Slave women marched behind to their grim, new life. But Cassandra, the daughter of King Priam, rode beside Agamemnon.

Clytemnestra welcomed Agamemnon home. She spread precious tapestries before him so that his feet would not have to touch the ground on the way to his throne room. Agamemnon objected that such honors were more fitting to a god, but his wife said that his victory at Troy had earned him this reward.

The royal party entered the palace except for Cassandra, who was left on the porch by the queen. Suddenly Cassandra cried that she saw blood everywhere. She saw babies butchered, murder and murder again, and even her own death. The people of the town assured her that the family of Atreus was now at peace. Cassandra heard none of these words but entered the chambers of the king to meet her fate.

Then, from inside the palace, there was a horrible cry. The citizens of the city gathered outside until Clytemnestra came out with a bloody sword: "The king is dead. Long have I waited for this day, ever since he killed my precious girl to fight his war. I struck him three times, a sacrifice to the restless spirit of my daughter. And I killed his little slave as well. Justice is done at last."

Aegisthus stood beside Clytemnestra with armed men and declared that they would rule together. The people could do nothing except bow to the new king and queen, but in their hearts they called on the gods for vengeance.

Before Clytemnestra murdered Agamemnon, she had sent her son, Orestes, to a kingdom near Delphi to remove any threat to her plans. Clytemnestra buried her husband near the palace, but first made sure his ghost was helpless to seek revenge. As the years passed no one dared to honor his grave except for Electra, who came in secret to pour wine for his troubled spirit.

One day two strangers appeared to lay a lock of hair on the grave. One was named Pylades, while the other was Orestes. While the two stood praying beside the mound,

Orestes saw Electra approach and hid himself behind a tree. She was startled to see footprints and an offering of hair on the grave. She knew her brother had returned.

Orestes asked for news of what had happened in the long years of his absence. Electra told him their mother had been troubled by dreams of late. In her dreams she gave birth to a snake that slashed her with its fangs. Orestes said that he was that snake, sent by Apollo. The prince had come to kill his wicked mother and the man who had stolen his father's throne. He told Electra to tell no one what she had seen. He would come to the palace in disguise to carry out his plan.

Soon Orestes and Pylades appeared before the gate disguised as travelers and speaking the language of Delphi. They asked to see the queen, for they had a sad message to give her. When they were led to the presence of Clytemnestra, they told her that Orestes was dead. Clytemnestra ran into the palace weeping, but beneath her tears she smiled. The one person who could avenge Agamemnon was now dead. She and Aegisthus could live out the rest of their days without worry.

But then Clytemnestra heard a cry from across the palace courtyard. She ran out to see the young stranger with a bloody sword. He revealed that he was Orestes and that he had just killed Aegisthus. Clytemnestra begged for her life: "I nursed you when you were a baby, cradled you in my arms. Yes, I killed your father, but only because he murdered your sister. I sought revenge for the blood of my own child!"

Orestes was torn. He had been ordered by the god Apollo to slay this woman, yet how could he kill his mother?

He raised his sword and brought it down on Clytemnestra, judging that the will of the god was greater than his own ties of blood. Yet as he stood over her body, he could not believe what he had done. Would this cycle of vengeance go on forever? His great-great-grandfather killed his own son and served him for dinner to the gods. Then Pelops had two sons who spent their lives plotting revenge on each other. His father killed his sister, and then his mother slayed his father. He had joined in by killing her. Who would now seek his life?

When the priestess of Apollo at Delphi arose that morning and purified herself, it seemed like it would be just another day at the temple. After praying to the earth mother, Gaia, to Themis, the guardian of justice, and to Apollo himself, she would sit on her stool above a fissure in the earth while she breathed in the sacred fumes that allowed her to commune with the god. There would be farmers asking whether or not to buy an olive grove, or fathers seeking advice on which suitor was the best choice for their daughters. The questions were always the same.

But when she entered the doors of the temple, she saw a man sleeping on the central stone, the very navel of the earth, with a bloody sword in one hand and an olive branch in the other. Around this altar were female creatures wrapped in black rags and a stench of death. They were the Furies, come to haunt Orestes for slaying his mother.

Apollo quietly entered and woke Orestes, telling him to make his way to Athens and the goddess Athena. When the young man had gone, the ghost of Clytemnestra woke the sleeping Furies. It was their sacred job to seek vengeance against those who had shed the blood of family. Apollo ordered them all out of his sanctuary. He told them to get to Athens where Athena would hear their case.

PHILIP FREEMAN

Athena called a trial on the hill of the Areopagus next to the Acropolis at Athens. Select men of Athens would be the jury, with Athena as judge. The Furies argued that without anger at the shedding of blood, there would be no reason for justice. What could be worse than a son killing his own mother? Allow him to go free, and the world would descend into chaos.

Apollo argued that Orestes had only sought revenge against the woman who had killed Agamemnon. Wasn't it justified to kill a woman who had murdered his father?

The Furies said that Clytemnestra's crime was wicked, but she did not kill someone related to her. Husbands and wives were joined by promises, not by blood. Orestes killed his mother and was therefore guilty of the greater crime.

Then Apollo made a shameless argument. He said that a child is not related to its mother. A woman carries her husband's baby until it is ready to be born. The baker makes bread, not the oven, he said. Likewise, a father is the true source of life, not the mother. He declared that his point could be proven by Athena, who was born from the forehead of her father, Zeus.

Athena considered the arguments. She judged that Apollo was right and that Orestes should be freed. She also said that there was a place for anger in a system of justice. She therefore invited the Furies to live in Athens, dwelling in honor under the Areopagus. They would be the basis of justice for her city.

Athena then declared that the long cycle of murder and revenge that had haunted the family of Tantalus for five generations had ended at last.

Odysseus

After ten long years of war at Troy, the Greek heroes sailed for home. Some returned to their families. Others met their deaths in the wine-dark sea.

Almost ten years had passed since the Greek ships sailed away from the ruins of Troy, but still Odysseus had not come home to his wife, Penelope, and his now-grown son, Telemachus. No one knew the fate of the king of Ithaca. Some said he had perished at sea, while others said he had founded a new kingdom in a distant land.

Most on Ithaca agreed that Odysseus must be dead and that Penelope should remarry. Many suitors came to woo the beautiful Penelope, but she and Telemachus still waited for the return of the king. The queen put off the suitors by saying she would make a choice once she had finished weaving a funeral cloak for Odysseus's father, Laertes. She worked her loom during the day. At night, she undid all she had woven. The suitors discovered her trick, but Penelope still managed to delay her decision. The ancient laws of hospitality insisted that all guests be welcomed and fed. The would-be husbands ate nearly everything she had.

The gods alone knew the fate of Odysseus. Athena, patron of war and trickery, cared most of all the Olympians for the clever king. Spying Telemachus sitting by himself while the greedy suitors feasted around him, she flew down from Olympus in the disguise of Mentes, lord of the sea going Taphians.

Telemachus saw the visitor and offered him an honored seat at the table. After Athena drank and feasted, Telemachus asked the visitor what brought him to Ithaca. The man said he was an old friend of Odysseus come to see if he had yet returned. When Telemachus shook his head sadly, the visitor urged him not to lose faith: "Odysseus is alive, my young friend! He may be long delayed, but he will come home. Sail to Pylos to ask Nestor if there has been word. Go to Sparta and find out if Menelaus has heard anything. Good news comes to those who seek it, not those who wait. Be a man, Telemachus, and find your father. When he does return, he will need a man at his side to drive away these suitors."

Telemachus was fired with courage. He asked the elders of Ithaca for a ship and sailors to make the journey. He declared it was time the islanders knew if their king was alive. If so, he would bring back news and maybe even his father. If not, he would marry Penelope to a new husband.

Penelope was proud of her son, though she feared losing him on the stormy seas. The suitors, led by Antinous, planned to kill Telemachus on his return. With him out of the way, Penelope would finally belong to one of them, along with the lands and crown of Odysseus.

Telemachus set sail for sandy Pylos. At last he saw the citadel of Nestor rising above the waves. The king was on the shore

offering nine black bulls to Poseidon. Athena had sailed with
young Telemachus, disguised as Mentor, a respected elder
and friend of Odysseus. The goddess urged him to approach
Nestor. Thus Telemachus landed and drew near to the gathering. He was welcomed by the king and by Prince Pisistratus.
The whole crew was made welcome with roasted strips of beef
and cups of wine.

When dinner was over, Nestor asked the strangers who
they were. Telemachus said he was in search of news about his
father Odysseus. Nestor was thrilled to have the son of his old
friend at his feast and told him stories of their times together
beneath the walls of Troy. But, alas, he could tell Telemachus
nothing of his father's fate. He urged the young man to travel
inland to the city of Sparta. There he would find King Menelaus and Queen Helen herself. Perhaps they could help him.

Telemachus accepted Nestor's son, Pisistratus, as guide.
They climbed into a chariot the next morning and set off
across the mountains. Telemachus had never seen such high
peaks as those that guarded the city of Meneleus, but at last
they made their way through the rugged passes until they
came to the valley of the Eurotas River and Sparta. The
splendid palace was easy to find, so the young men pulled up
before the gate and asked for the king.

Menelaus was easy to recognize with his head of bright
red hair. He welcomed his visitors and took them into his halls
to dine at his table. When supper was finished, he asked them
who they were. At that moment Helen entered the room and
declared Telemachus, who looked like his father, could be
none other than the son of Odysseus. Telemachus said that he
was indeed the child of that long-lost king and asked if they

might have any news. Like Nestor, Menelaus was overjoyed to meet the son of his dear friend and told him of all the two warriors had been through together at Troy. Tears ran down the cheeks of Telemachus as he heard stories of the father he could not remember.

Finally Menelaus told him that he had been delayed himself for several years for failing to honor the gods. The winds had blown him all the way to Egypt. He met a sea nymph on an island who told him where to find food and water for his starving crew. She also told him of her father, Proteus, who lived nearby, a god with knowledge of all things.

Menelaus snuck into the seaside cave of Proteus and hid among his pet seals. When the god entered and lay down to rest, Menelaus jumped on him and would not let go. The shape-shifting god became a serpent, a panther, a wild boar, a stream, and a tree soaring to the sky. At last he asked Menelaus what he wanted. The king declared that he was in search of news of Greece. Proteus told him that his own kingdom was safe, but that his brother Agamemnon had been murdered in Mycenae. Menelaus was sorry, but listened as the god told him of the fate of other great warriors, including Odysseus. Proteus had seen the king of Ithaca sitting on the shore of the island of the goddess Calypso, the hidden one, weeping for the home he could not reach.

"That is all that I know of Odysseus," Menelaus said. "Whether he is still on that island, has sailed away, or has gone down to the house of Hades, no man can say."

As dawn touched the top of Mount Olympus, Athena asked her father, Zeus, if it wasn't time to let Odysseus return to

Ithaca after almost twenty years away. Hadn't he suffered enough? Wasn't the anger of Poseidon satisfied? Zeus agreed and sent Hermes to the island of Calypso to tell her she must release Odysseus.

Hermes found the goddess braiding her hair, surrounded by nymphs. She didn't want to let Odysseus go, but she had no choice. She made her way to a beach where Odysseus sat on a rock, staring toward Ithaca far across the sea. He spent his days thinking of his wife and son, and of his aged father, Laertes.

Calypso told Odysseus that she would help him sail away, but she also tried to get him to stay—promising him immortality.

Odysseus answered: "Goddess, I long every day to see my Penelope again. What good is eternal life without the one you love? I would rather live a single lifetime with my Penelope than an eternity with anyone else."

He began to build a small boat. When it was ready, he stored one skin of wine and another of water aboard, along with a sack of food. Then he raised his single sail, and set off to the east toward Ithaca.

For eighteen days he sailed with a fair wind to his back. Just as his food and water were gone, he spotted an island. But at the same moment, the god Poseidon saw him on the waves and cursed his brother on Olympus: "So, Zeus, you decide to let Odysseus sail home? I may not be able to stop him, but I can still make his life miserable!"

Poseidon stirred up a storm that sent waves crashing over the little boat. The sail was torn away, then lightning split the mast in two. Odysseus was thrown into the sea and his clothes were torn from him in the waves. With the help of the sea goddess Ino, he reached the shores of the island. Naked, exhausted, and covered in seawater, he collapsed on the beach and fell into a deep sleep.

The princess Nausicaa was tired of life in the palace. She wanted a day at the beach. Her father, the great King Alcinous, wanted her to spend her time weaving and learning the things a young lady should know. She needed a good excuse, so she told her handmaids to go to her brothers' quarters and gather all the dirty laundry they could find. Then she went to her father and whispered in his ear: "Daddy dear, I'm worried about your sons. They are hopeless when it comes to their clothes, always leaving dirty things lying about and wearing whatever they can find. The girls will never give them a second glance. Let me take their laundry to the beach and give it a good cleaning. It may take all day, but I'm willing to do it to help my brothers."

Alcinous knew what his daughter was doing, but he loved her. He ordered the servants to take Nausicaa and her friends to the shore.

Once the princess and her companions reached the water, they rinsed the clothes quickly and threw them on the rocks to dry. Then they swam in the sea and spread a picnic on the beach. They traded gossip and teased one another about who their fathers would choose for them to marry. They gloried in the fact that they had a few hours to themselves.

Odysseus woke with a start when he heard young women laughing. He looked around and saw that he was lying in some bushes and that the sun was high. The raft he had made on Calypso's island had brought him to some new land. He decided it was best to approach the girls and ask if they could direct him to the king.

Nausicaa and her friends gasped when they saw the naked man. He looked terrible, but the princess noticed some noble bearing that stopped her from running away. Odysseus asked her for a few rags to cover himself and directions to the local palace. Nausicaa ordered her maids to give the man some of her brothers' old clothes and to show him a stream where he could wash.

When he was done, Nausicaa told Odysseus he was on the island of the Phaeacians, ruled by her father King Alcinous. It wouldn't look proper if she led a strange man to her home, but he could follow the road to find the palace.

The princess and her companions gathered their things and headed home while Odysseus considered what he should do. The girl seemed friendly, but he had been through much at the hands of those who had welcomed him. He decided not to reveal too much, and prayed to Athena that this would be his last stop before Ithaca. He asked the goddess to move the king to grant him a ship to sail home to his Penelope.

As Odysseus walked toward the splendid halls of Alcinous, a little girl offered to guide him. She warned him that the people of the island, descended from Poseidon, were suspicious of strangers. He should first go to Queen Arete, as she was more welcoming than her husband. As they entered the palace, the girl wished him well and disappeared. She was Athena in disguise.

Odysseus gathered his courage and walked into the throne room. Before anyone saw him, he fell down before the queen:

"Queen Arete, I come to you to beg for mercy. May the gods grant you prosperity and may your children be the pride of your life. I ask only for a ship to take me back to my native land. If you knew how far I've come and how much I've suffered, you would be kindly disposed to the man you see before you."

The queen and king were surprised, but they knew the laws of hospitality. They called for a chair and placed food and wine before him.

After he had eaten his fill, they asked the mysterious stranger who he was. Odysseus replied that he was a nobleman who had been held for seven years on the island of Calypso, daughter of the Titan Atlas. He had escaped and come to their shores, seeking a small ship to take him home to Ithaca. The king declared he would see that his visitor reached his home, but in the meantime told him to rest. The next day they would have a feast and send him on his way.

Odysseus thanked Alcinous and went to his chambers to sleep. Years of trouble seemed almost at an end. He knew that he would face trials in Ithaca, but at least he would be home.

The following evening the king held a banquet in honor of his guest with all the nobles of the land. After platters of food had been served and sweet wine poured, the king called his bard Demodocus to entertain them. The company rose to honor the blind singer who remembered the history and stories of their people. He knew songs of lands beyond, as well. Everyone cheered as he sang of how Hephaestus had once trapped his wife, Aphrodite, in a net with Ares on Mount Olympus. Then someone asked for a tale of Troy. Demodocus sang of the wooden horse built by the plan of the clever Odysseus. He told of how the Greeks had snuck from the belly of the beast and slaughtered the Trojans as the city went up in flames.

Odysseus listened to the words. In his mind he saw again the horror of that night—brave men dying all around him as they tried to defend their families—all for the glory of war. He began to weep. The Phaeacians watched him with sympathy and gave him time to collect himself. Then Alcinous asked him again who he was. "Great king, noble lady, kind people of Phaeacia. You ask who I am and what brought me to this land. It is a long tale full of pain, but if you want to hear it, I will tell you. I am Odysseus, son of Laertes, and I have suffered more than any man alive."

And with that, he began his story:

We set sail from Troy that day so long ago. The wind drove our ships west to the Thracian lands of the Cicones, allies of the Trojans. My warriors and I sacked one of their cities and killed the men, but kept the women and children as slaves. I shared everything with my comrades and urged them to sail before more Cicones came. Instead they drank wine until they fell asleep. The next morning the neighboring Cicones rode out of the mist and cut them down. We struggled to raise our weapons against the Cicones, but they forced us to flee. Many men who had fought at Troy for ten years died that day because of their foolishness.

Winds tossed our ships for two days and nights. We were exhausted when the sun finally showed us the Peloponnesus on our starboard side. The gale had carried us just where we wanted to go—almost home! I might have seen my family, but another storm hit us then, far worse than the first. It drove us for nine days. On the tenth morning we reached the land of the Lotus Eaters. I drew the ships onto the shore to collect fresh water and sent three scouts inland. When they didn't return, I set off myself with a group of armed men. The natives of that land offered us the honey-sweet fruit of the lotus. Some of my men tasted it, then lost their desire to journey home. All they wanted to do was stay and eat the lotus fruit forever. I forced them back to the ships. We cast off and rowed away.

The spirits of my men were low as we sailed to another strange shore. It was a lonely land with rough hills and wild goats. We anchored in a small harbor and caught goats for our supper. After a fine meal, we slept through the night. When dawn came, I left most of my soldiers on the beach and headed away with a few warriors to see what kind of men lived there. We hadn't gone far when we saw the entrance to a cave with a large stone rolled away from its mouth. There were sheep nearby, larger than any in Greece. I took a skin of wine and entered the cavern, hoping to trade for food. No one was home. My men discovered cheese drying on racks and spring lambs penned in the corner.

We built a fire to roast a sheep, then feasted on cheese and awaited the return of the shepherd. Late in the day, we heard something large approaching and quickly put out the fire. The creature that entered was taller than three men standing on top of each other and had a single, enormous eye in the center of his forehead. He entered the cave, then rolled the huge stone across the opening so that nothing could escape. My men and I hid in a corner while he milked his sheep. After he had lit his fire, the monster saw us huddled in the shadows.

"Who are you?" he demanded.

"We are Greek sailors," I answered, "making our way home from Troy. May it please Zeus, who watches over all guests, we would like to trade with you for food and be on our way."

"I am Polyphemus, a Cyclops, the son of Poseidon," the giant said. "I care nothing for Zeus." He grabbed two of my men and smashed their heads against a stone. He ate them raw, even the bones. We cried to Zeus for justice, but the Cyclops ignored us and fell asleep. I thought about killing him—but then who would move the stone away? We were trapped with a monster that was going to eat us all.

The Cyclops left the next morning, putting the stone carefully in place to seal us in. We tried everything to move that rock, but it was no use. While my men wept and prayed to the gods, I sat down to think. Just before sunset, I hit upon a plan and told my men to pour some wine into one of the Cyclops's bowls. When the giant entered and closed us in again, I spoke to him: "Mighty Polyphemus, son of the great god Poseidon, receive this gift from our hands."

The monster drained the bowl in a single gulp, then demanded more. After a second bowl, he asked my name.

"My name is Nobody," I said.

"A strange name," said the Cyclops. "I will eat you last!" Then he laughed as he ate two more of my men. With that he fell over in a drunken stupor and snored so loudly the cave shook.

"Courage," I whispered to my men. "Now we will have our revenge."

I ordered them to sharpen a wooden pole, then harden the point in the fire. When all was ready, I climbed on a rock above the sleeping Cyclops and plunged the stake into his single eye. The monster screamed in agony, then groped his way to the stone and rolled it away from the door just enough to shout to his neighbors.

"Help me!" he cried. "Nobody has attacked me! Nobody has blinded me!"

From the hills came cries in response: "Shut up you fool! If Nobody has hurt you, why are you bothering us?"

Polyphemus sank down on the cave floor and rolled the stone back in place. He tried to find us with his hands, but we moved too quickly. At last he settled into sleep in front of the door.

The next morning the sheep woke the Cyclops as they cried to be let out to pasture. I told my men to each grab the underside of one of the animals and hold on. Polyphemus rolled the stone away again and stood by the entrance. He carefully felt each sheep to make sure it was not a man, but he didn't search underneath. We all made it out of the cavern clinging to those wonderful sheep.

My men were overjoyed as we ran to our ships in the harbor. As we rowed away I could see Polyphemus stumbling down the path crying out that the man who had blinded him had escaped. My warriors urged me to keep quiet, but I couldn't help glorying over the stupid monster: "Polyphemus, you filthy cannibal, maybe now you'll learn to treat your guests with respect. My name isn't Nobody, it's Odysseus, raider of cities and hero of Troy."

The Cyclops threw giant stones at us, but they splashed off our stern. Then he fell to his knees and prayed to Poseidon: "Father, grant to me that Odysseus may never reach his home. If it is his fate to do so, at least make sure that day is far off and that he returns home alone, a broken man."

Poseidon heard his prayer. I foolishly gave Polyphemus my name to use in his curse and have suffered for it since.

From the land of the Cyclops we came to a beautiful island with cliffs reaching to the sky. This was the home of Aeolus, lord of the winds. He hosted us for a full month as I told him of the long war

at Troy and all that had happened since. As we left, he gave me a sack holding winds from all the corners of the earth, but the west wind he let loose to blow us home.

Nine days we sailed and on the tenth Ithaca was in sight! I had steered the ship the whole time and couldn't stay awake. I fell into a deep sleep. My men thought the gift Aeolus had given me was a bag of silver and gold. They opened it while I slept. The winds tossed the ships about in a hurricane that blew us far from home. Soon we found ourselves back on the island of Aeolus. I pleaded for another fair wind to send us to Ithaca, but the king sent us away empty-handed for seeking a gift twice.

Six days we rowed through calm seas and on the seventh came to the land of the Laestrygonians. Darkness never falls there. We sailed into a deep harbor and found the palace of King Antiphates. The people were giants, but they seemed friendly and welcomed us. Then the king entered, snatched one of my men, and tore him to pieces for dinner. The other Laestrygonians speared my men like fish. Some of us fought our way back to the harbor, but only my ship sailed away from that cursed land, one of the twelve ships that had left Ithaca many years before.

We were sick for our murdered comrades, but we journeyed on. Lost and alone, we spied another island and pulled up on the beach. The next morning I climbed the cliffs and saw smoke rising from the heart of the island. I sent my comrade Eurylochus and almost two dozen men to see what kind of people lived on these shores. A few hours later, he ran back alone and told us to launch our ship quickly. He said they had come across a palace in the woods with gleaming bronze doors. A beautiful woman surrounded by tame beasts opened those doors and invited them to enter. Only he stayed behind, sensing a trap. The others drank the wine she offered and turned into pigs.

I told my crew we were not leaving. We had lost too many men already and would make our stand here on this island. I forced Eurylochus to lead me back to the palace. The god Hermes, sent by Zeus, appeared and told me I was about to enter the halls of the great witch Circe. He gave me a magical herb to protect me from the witch's brew, then he vanished.

Circe welcomed me and gave me a goblet of her sweet wine. I drained the cup in one gulp, then threw it on the ground and raised my sword. She couldn't believe that I had not been turned into a pig, and swore she would change my men back and help me on my journey. I spared her life and watched as my men regained their human form. Circe then offered me the hospitality of her home

and called her nymphs to fetch the rest of the men from the ship. We welcomed the food and drink of Circe's house—a feast that flows on forever.

My men and I spent a year on Circe's island while we rested. I lost all track of time. But at last I told our hostess we must leave. Circe warned me of what lay ahead: "Odysseus, royal son of Laertes, to sail home to Ithaca you must first make another voyage, one no ship has made before. You must journey to the house of death, and there seek counsel from the ghost of wise Tiresias."

These words crushed my heart. I asked her how this was possible. She replied that an entrance to Hades's realm lay across the great river of Ocean far to the north. The spirit of Tiresias would tell me what I needed to know to make peace with Poseidon.

The men drank Circe's wine for the last time that night. One of the sailors, a foolish young man named Elpenor, fell from the palace roof and broke his neck in the early morning hours. There was no time to bury him. Once we set sail, I spoke to my crew: "Men, we are on our way to Ithaca, but there is one final journey we must first make. Circe has told me that we cannot find our way home until I have consulted the prophet Tiresias in the land of the dead."

The men thought I must be joking, then they saw that I was serious. How could anyone travel to the land of the dead and return, they asked? Hercules had journeyed there, as had Orpheus, but they were great heroes. We are just men, they cried. Even if we could sail this ship to Hades's realm, we would be trapped there forever.

Finally I convinced my crew we must travel to the dwelling place of ghosts or never see home again. With a last look at the world of the living, we turned our ship to the setting sun and sailed into darkness.

I don't know how long our voyage lasted, but at last we sailed to a land where the sun never shines. We beached our ship on a lonely shore. I found a sandy spot and dug a trench. I poured milk, honey, and wine into the hole for the dead, followed by water and barley. I took sheep and cut their throats over the trench so that the dark blood flowed in. Then I saw a sight to freeze your soul. Thousands of ghosts drifted toward me. I drew my sword and held them back from the blood they craved until I saw the ghost of young Elpenor who had fallen to his death on Circe's island. I let him sip the blood so that he could speak. He begged me to give him a proper burial if I made it back to the witch's home. I swore that I would do so.

The figure I saw next brought pity and fear to my heart. It was my mother, Anticlea, whom I had left alive when I sailed for Troy. She was only a ghost now. In spite of my desire to question her, I would not let her drink the blood until I had spoken to Tiresias.

The ghost of the prophet appeared and motioned me to lower my sword while he drank from the trench. At last he spoke: "Odysseus, son of Laertes, you have a difficult journey ahead of you. Many trials await you. You will come to an island where the cattle of Helios, god of the sun, graze. No matter how hungry you are, do not touch them. If you do come to rocky Ithaca, you will find things are not as you left them. If you become master of your house again, your journey will not be over. You must take an oar and carry it high into the mountains far from the sea. When someone at last asks you why you have a winnowing fan on your shoulder, plant the blade there and sacrifice to Poseidon. Then you will finally know peace."

The seer withdrew. Then I allowed my mother to drink the blood. When she had finished, I begged her to tell me of events in Ithaca and how she had come to the house of Hades. "My son, your home is overrun by wicked men who seek Penelope as their bride. She and Telemachus cannot hold them off forever. Your father, Laertes, has withdrawn in sorrow to a hut in the countryside. As for me, I could not wait for you any longer. My sweet Odysseus, I died of longing for you."

Tears rolled down my face as I tried three times to embrace her, but her ghost passed through my hands like smoke.

Others came to drink from the trench. Mothers of great heroes, such as Leda, who bore Castor and Pollux, and Jocasta, the mother of Oedipus. Then warriors marched forward, friends I had known at Troy. The spirit of Agamemnon told me of his murder at the hands of his wife. Then great-hearted Achilles drank the blood as I congratulated him on being the most famous of the ghosts in Hades. But he laughed at me: "Odysseus, you are a fool if you think there is any glory here. I would rather be a living slave to the poorest farmer in Greece than rule over the kingdom of the dead."

Mighty Ajax would not drink, still angry over the armor of Achilles I had won instead of him.

I saw countless others as they pressed forward to drink the blood. Terror gripped me and I called on my men to ready the ship before we were overwhelmed by all the ghosts of Hades.

We rowed for our lives as the spirits cried for blood. At last we left that dark land behind and began our long journey back to the world of light.

We returned to Circe's island and buried Elpenor, just as he had asked. The beautiful witch warned me of what lay ahead—temptations, monsters, and death for some, though I did not tell this to my men. The next morning we set out again for Ithaca.

A fair wind blew for many days, but suddenly it died in a strange sea. We took out our oars to row. Circe had told me what would happen next. I told my crew to fix beeswax tightly in their ears. I then ordered them to bind me to the mast with double ropes so that I alone could hear the song of the Sirens. These hideous creatures lured men to

their doom with words that no one could resist. The men rowed with powerful strokes away from the island of these creatures, but I heard them singing: "Welcome, Odysseus, come closer! We know what wonders you accomplished at Troy, and will sing to you of your glorious deeds. Come and lose yourself in the past."

I was driven mad by their voices and told my men to untie me so that I could go to them. My companions bound me all the tighter until we were far from their shore.

Scarcely were we safe from the Sirens than we came to a narrow strait. On one side lay the monster Scylla, a creature with six heads that ate men raw. On the other side lay the great whirlpool, Charybdis, that dragged ships to their doom. Our only hope was to row as swiftly as we could between them. Scylla took six of my brave men, all screaming my name with their last breath. She ate them

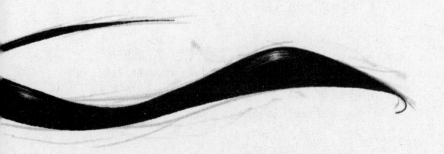

*alive. Of all the deaths I had seen, these were the
most horrible.*

*At last we found a green island and pulled on
shore. I had told my men we should row on, for
this was the island of Helios, lord of the sun. Circe
had warned me not to visit here, but my men
begged for rest and swore they would not touch the
cattle. At first they kept their word, but a fierce
south wind held us on the island for a month. The
food on our ship ran out and hunger racked our
bellies. At last while I slept, my men killed and
roasted one of the cattle. I awoke and told them
they were fools, but the deed was done.*

*The next day the wind finally died away and we
set out from the island. But Helios complained to
Zeus, and Zeus struck our ship with a lightning
bolt. My men were thrown from our craft and
cried as they sank down into the waves. I could
do nothing except cling to a few broken planks and
wait to die. But the gods had other plans. I washed
up on the shores of Calypso's island ten days later,
alone of all the men who had set out from Ithaca
so many years before.*

*That is my story, great King Alcinous and gracious
Queen Arete. You have heard the whole sad tale
and now I ask only that you grant me a small ship
so that I may find my way home.*

The king and his court sat spellbound as Odysseus finished his story. Alcinous told Odysseus he would have his sailors take him to Ithaca in his fastest ship. The king called on his nobles to give the penniless wanderer fine gifts of gold or silver so that he would not return to his home empty-handed. The lords of Phaeacia placed treasure on the ship. Then the king and queen led Odysseus to the docks and bid him a farewell.

The Phaeacian ship cut through the waters at great speed. The son of Laertes was so exhausted that he fell into a deep sleep. As the morning star rose in the east, the sailors spied the shores of Ithaca. They carried the sleeping Odysseus to the beach and laid him gently down. The treasure they stored in a nearby cave, then sailed away.

It was mid-morning before Odysseus awoke and found himself again in an unknown land. He thought the Phaeacian sailors had taken his treasure for themselves. He soon found the cave and counted his riches, but where was he?

A shepherd boy appeared. Odysseus asked him what country this was. The lad laughed and said he was on the island of Ithaca. Odysseus was overjoyed, but he did not show it. He would not reveal his identity until he knew who his friends were on the island: "Ithaca? Yes, I've heard of it. I'm from Crete. I killed a man there when he tried to steal the booty I won at Troy. I fled on a ship of Phaeacian traders who brought me here."

At that moment the shepherd boy laughed again and turned into the goddess Athena: "Odysseus, this is why I love you. Any other man would have rushed to his house after twenty years, but you are always thinking. You're right to be careful and trust no one—not even your wife, Penelope. Test them all before you reveal yourself. I will help you by transforming you into an old beggar. Then I'm off to Sparta to fetch Telemachus, who has been looking for you. Be careful. You have faced monsters and angry gods, but the dangers ahead are more treacherous."

The goddess touched Odysseus. His skin shriveled, his hair turned white, and his clothes turned into dirty rags. Athena gave him a staff and a beggar's sack. Then she disappeared.

Odysseus made his way to a nearby hut in the hills where his swineherd, Eumaeus, lived. The old servant welcomed the beggar—for Zeus watches over strangers—and gave him food. The king told the swineherd he was from Crete and had served beside Odysseus at Troy. He told Eumaeus he was blown off course to Egypt on the way home. He had lost everything—family, home, riches—before he washed up on these shores and only wanted directions to the palace so that he could beg for scraps.

Eumaeus warned him that Odysseus was long absent and that wicked suitors had taken over his home. They would not treat the beggar kindly. Odysseus thanked the shepherd, then asked instead if he might stay with him. Eumaeus made a bed for the stranger in a corner of his hut.

Athena meanwhile had flown to Sparta to send Telemachus home. The prince returned to his ship at Pylos and set sail for Ithaca. With the help of the goddess, he avoided the trap the suitors had laid for him and landed on the far side of the island. The young man wanted to question his old friend Eumaeus about what had happened at the palace during his absence.

The swineherd embraced the prince like a long-lost son and brought him into his simple hut for bread and wine. The old beggar rose to offer Telemachus his chair, but the prince told him to sit. The beggar watched the young man closely, noting his fine bearing and clear mind. When Eumaeus left to take care of the pigs, Athena removed the disguise so that Odysseus stood like Zeus himself before the startled prince.

"Friend," exclaimed Telemachus, "are you a god from Olympus? Be kind to us here on this humble island and we will offer you rich sacrifices."

The shining figure shook his head. "I am a man like yourself. You have borne a world of pain these last twenty years, but no longer. I am Odysseus, your father."

At first Telemachus did not believe these words, but Odysseus told of what he had been through and how Athena had transformed him. The prince saw that it was true and threw his arms around his father.

The two talked far into the night as Telemachus told him about each of the suitors who had tried to steal Penelope. Odysseus listened carefully and finally told his son what they would do. Telemachus had to return to his mother. The next day, when Athena had changed him back into a beggar, Odysseus would make his way to the palace. As soon as he had learned everything he needed to know, he would drive the suitors from his home. Telemachus was to say nothing about him to Penelope. Odysseus would reveal himself to her in his own time.

After Telemachus left, Eumaeus led his guest to the palace of Odysseus with a warning to be on his guard.

The wandering king at last entered the courtyard of his palace after twenty years away. He could hardly believe the tattered look of his beloved home or the crowd of suitors eating his food. It was then that an old dog in the corner pricked up his ears. He was Argos, trained as a puppy by Odysseus many years before. Now he lay blind and crippled on a pile of manure for warmth. Sometimes the servants threw him scraps of food. He heard the voice of his old master and used what little strength he had to raise his head. Odysseus dared not show any recognition. The faithful hound lowered his head and quietly died. His master wiped away a tear.

The suitors yelled at Eumaeus for bringing the old beggar into the palace. There was hardly enough food for them, let alone some castaway. Odysseus humbly reminded them that strangers were protected by Zeus. They hit him with a stool and laughed as he tumbled into the dust. They made him fight another beggar whom they used as a messenger. The messenger was a former boxer with a large chest and powerful arms. Odysseus circled him pretending to be afraid, then sent him crashing to the ground with one punch.

At that moment Penelope appeared on the balcony above, shining like a goddess. The suitors bowed to her, but she scolded them for their treatment of the beggar and went back to her quarters in disgust. Odysseus continued to gaze at the spot where she had stood. She was as beautiful as ever, with the same fire in her eyes. He did not dare to reveal himself to her yet. The suitors were well armed. It was better to wait and choose the right moment.

That night after the suitors had retired to their quarters, Odysseus sat alone. A maid told him the lady of the house would like to speak with him. He found himself alone with Penelope. She gave him a stool to sit on and apologized for the treatment he had received. She told him that when her husband was lord of the house, he knew how to welcome guests. He was gone now these twenty years and most said he was dead.

Odysseus thanked Penelope and suggested it was time she looked for a new husband. Penelope smiled and said she still longed for Odysseus. She had tried to put off the suitors, but she had run out of time. If she waited any longer, they would kill her son, Telemachus. The beggar told her of how he had met her husband long ago in Crete where he stopped on the way to Troy. Penelope listened to his story with tears running down her cheeks. Odysseus longed to tell her everything, but he sat silent until she withdrew to her room to find comfort in sweet sleep.

The old maid Euryclea then came to him at the bidding of Penelope and began to wash away the dirt from his feet. She had nursed Odysseus as a child. As she bent over to place his feet in the bath, she saw a childhood scar on his leg and knew in an instant that he was Odysseus. She started to shout for Penelope, but the clever warrior said he would strangle her if she said a word. She swore she would keep his secret and help him however she could. Odysseus told the old maid to stand ready, for the day of his revenge was about to dawn.

The next morning Penelope once again stood on the balcony to speak to the suitors. She declared that the long wait was over. Odysseus must be dead and she must remarry. But first her new husband would have to prove himself. She ordered her servants to take twelve long axes and stand them up in the courtyard in a straight line with their handles facing upwards. Whoever would marry her would have to string the bow of Odysseus, then shoot an arrow through the metal loops at the end of each axe all in a row. The suitors declared it was impossible. Penelope said that Odysseus had done it. Then she retired to her quarters.

Odysseus whispered to Telemachus that he should lock all the weapons away and order the gates to the courtyard barred to keep anyone from leaving. Then he sat in the corner while the suitors tried to string his bow. One after another they tried and failed. Then Odysseus spoke: "Gentlemen, would you mind if I tried? I'd like to see if there is any strength left in these old bones of mine."

The men did not object as he took the mighty bow in hand. The old beggar stroked the wood and in one swift movement strung the bow. He plucked the string, then took an arrow, notched it, and pulled back. It sailed clean through all twelve handles and lodged in the far wall.

Before the suitors could react, he took another arrow and shot their leader through the neck. The suitors moved in to kill him, but Odysseus leveled his gaze at them: "You fools! You bled my household dry and courted my wife while I was still alive, never fearing the gods above. You're all about to die!"

Odysseus was transformed back to his true self and began to cut the shocked suitors down. One after another they fell while Telemachus joined in the slaughter with his sword. The last to die pleaded with the king to let them pay for what they had done, but Odysseus would not listen. Bodies sprawled about the courtyard as on a battlefield. Odysseus told Telemachus to have the maids clean up the mess, then send his mother down.

When the courtyard had been scrubbed clean, fair Penelope took a seat facing Odysseus. She waited with folded hands. Telemachus asked his mother how she could be so cold, but

Odysseus said that if Penelope wanted to test him, then let her.

Penelope looked at Odysseus carefully. He did seem like the man who had left her twenty years ago. Still, she couldn't be sure. She said it would be best if her maids moved their bed into the courtyard for him since she wasn't going to share it with a stranger.

Odysseus was angry. Move his bed? He had built that bed himself from the living branches of an olive tree still in the ground. He built his bedroom around it, and around that he built his home. The bed could not be moved. No one ever entered their bedroom but themselves, so no one knew the secret. Had the bed been cut away?

That was the test. Penelope ran to embrace her husband. They held each other as if they would never let go and cried for joy. Odysseus was home at last.

Aeneas

Like the Greeks, the Romans had a story of a warrior who escaped after the Trojan War. He was Aeneas, son of Anchises and the goddess Aphrodite. He sailed from the ruins of Troy to found a new city in Italy. The gods said that this second Troy would give birth to a people who would rule the world.

These people were the Romans and they gave their own names to the gods. Zeus became Jupiter. Hera was known as Juno. Aphrodite became Venus, and Poseidon lorded over the seas as Neptune. By whatever name, the gods ruled the universe and played games with the lives of mortals.

Juno never forgave the Trojan prince Paris for giving the golden apple to Venus instead of to her. She became the enemy of Troy and wasn't even satisfied when the city was in ashes. It was predicted that Aeneas would found a new and glorious city, but Juno was determined to make his life difficult.

When she saw the Trojan fleet sailing toward the setting sun, Juno flew to the island of Aeolus, king of the winds: "Aeolus, the remaining Trojans are crossing the sea on their way to Italy. Blow them far off course, and I'll give you a gorgeous nymph to be your wife."

Aeolus stirred up a storm. The Trojan ships were tossed and scattered as the sky grew black. The winds drove them away from Italian shores toward Africa.

Aeneas stood on the bow of the lead ship and shouted to the heavens: "Oh my comrades who died at Troy, I call you blessed to have perished beneath our native walls rather than in unknown seas. I wish I had died there too, for I can't take any more of this!"

After a long struggle, a few of the Trojan ships were cast on an unknown desert coast. The rest of the fleet was lost. Aeneas feared these men and their families were dead.

Aeneas took his comrade Achates and headed inland. Soon they met a young girl hunting in the brush. They told her they were castaways. Could she tell them what king ruled this land, and where they might find him?

The girl laughed and said there was no king in this realm but a queen—Dido, ruler of Carthage. She had lately come from Phoenicia to found a new country. Her brother had murdered her husband and driven her from the city of Sidon with her followers. When she reached this land, the native chiefs offered to sell her only as much land as she could cover with the hide of a bull. Dido cleverly cut the hide into strips thin enough to circle a new city. The chiefs were furious at being outsmarted by a woman, but they could not go back on their word. The girl advised Aeneas to seek out this noble queen, then she threw off her mortal disguise and flew away as Venus. Aeneas cried after her: "Mother, why does it always have to be this way? Can't we ever embrace and speak together without disguise and trickery?"

Then he followed his mother's advice and made his way toward Carthage covered in a mist she provided.

The Trojan prince was impressed. Everywhere citizens worked like bees in a hive. Some raised the citadel, others laid out building sites and dug wells. Older men met in their senate to draft laws and elect judges. Aeneas wished his own city could be underway, but it seemed now as if the dreams of the Trojans had been lost. They could never establish a new home with only the men who had survived the storm.

As Aeneas entered the palace he was surprised to see pictures of the Trojan War carved on the temple of Juno. Here was the combat of Achilles and Hector, the cursed wooden horse, and weeping women driven away in chains. Suddenly Queen Dido appeared looking like a goddess. Aeneas was even more amazed when he saw the captains of his missing Trojan ships next to her. They were asking Dido for help in finding their leader, the great Trojan warrior Aeneas, whom they feared was lost forever. The queen pledged to help the men in their search.

Suddenly Venus swept away the mist and Aeneas himself stood before the queen and his men. He thanked Dido and praised the fine city she was building. The queen stood in awe of the Trojan hero. She invited him to send for the rest of his shipmates and join her for a feast in the royal halls. They were welcome to stay in her city as long as they wished—even settle there. Aeneas sent a messenger to tell his men to come to the city. He was especially eager for his young son Ascanius, called Iulus, to see the splendid town of Carthage.

Venus watched with worry in her heart. Juno would surely

find a way to turn the people of Carthage against her son and his men. She knew it was not the fate of Aeneas to live in Carthage, but to found his own kingdom in Italy. She needed a way to keep Dido friendly until her son was ready to sail. This was clearly a job for her other son, Cupid. She snatched Iulus and put him into a deep sleep in her own palace. Cupid took the form of the child and worked his magic on Dido. She was enchanted with the boy and fell in love with him and his father. By the time dinner was served, she was determined to make Aeneas her husband and have the Trojans and Carthaginians build the new city together.

While she held Iulus in her lap, Dido asked Aeneas to tell her of his adventures, leaving out no detail. Aeneas began his story.

It would take a man with the silver tongue of Ulysses—or Odysseus as the Greeks called him—to do justice to my tale. You know what the Greeks did to my city, since it is carved on the walls of your temple. Let me share with you the fall of Troy from the other side, along with all the pain and grief we have suffered.

You know well the story of the horse built by iron-hearted Ulysses. You know how no one listened to the warnings of Cassandra or the priest Laocoon to destroy the gift of the enemy. I will not retell the story of how we brought the horse inside our walls and feasted while Ulysses and his band waited for us to fall asleep.

But that night I lay beside my wife, Creusa, under the moon's quiet light when suddenly Hector appeared to me in a dream: "Aeneas, get out of Troy now! The Greeks are already in the city. Our home has fallen and you cannot save it. Take the images of the holy gods of our fathers with you along with all the Trojans you can gather and flee. You must survive to found a new city so that Troy may live again."

I awoke and ran to the window. I could see Greeks everywhere setting the homes ablaze and slaying everyone they could find. The fire roared and flames licked the sky. I grabbed my armor and weapons and prepared to fight. I found a few other Trojan warriors ready to make a final stand. We ran through the lanes fighting like madmen, then made our way to the palace of Priam. It was too late to save the king. The cursed Greeks murdered him, then killed all the men and marched the women back to their ships as slaves.

When I saw the body of Priam, I came to my senses and thought of my own father, Anchises, who was unprotected. On my way to our quarters, I saw Helen standing alone. I took my sword in hand determined that the cause of all this bloodshed would not live. But suddenly my mother appeared before me: "Sheath your blade, my son, and flee this city. Helen is not to blame, nor is Paris. The gods themselves are behind it all. Look, I will show you the truth."

She opened my eyes so that I saw Neptune prying loose the walls of Troy with his trident, shaking the city to its foundations. There was Juno leading troops through the gates. On the citadel stood Minerva, the goddess the Greeks call Athena, her savage shield freezing the hearts of the Trojans. Even Jupiter was stirring the Greeks to conquer and burn. What my mother said was true. All that was left was to rescue my family and escape from Troy.

I found my rooms at the palace still untouched among the burning halls and told my loved ones we must leave. My father said he had already lived too long if he was forced to see his city destroyed. I begged him to change his mind, but he would not budge. Then a tongue of fire flared up on the head of Iulus and danced about, though harming him not at all. My father thanked Jupiter for the holy sign and agreed to escape with me. I placed him on my back and carried him from the palace, with little Iulus holding my hand and my wife a few steps behind. We took the sacred hearth gods from the temple and gathered all the survivors we could find as we made our way through the streets.

We were almost to the walls when I saw that my wife, Creusa, was no longer with us. I searched for *her, but she was not to be found. There were Greek soldiers everywhere and the city burned. I told the rest to go on, then rushed back along the streets calling her name. I ran all the way to the palace as the flames swept over the city. Suddenly the ghost of my own wife appeared before me: "Aeneas, there is nothing more you can do for me. I'm so sorry I fell behind, but fate did not intend for me to make the journey with you. Go now, before it's too late! Look after our son. Farewell, my love, farewell."*

She slipped through my fingers as I tried to hold her one last time, then disappeared forever. I ran back to the rest of my family now outside the walls. The people gathered there—men, women, children—gazed back at the smoking ruins of our city. I told them our future lay ahead of us, not behind, and ordered them to follow me. I again took my father on my back and my son by the hand, then headed toward the mountains.

At a hidden spot on the coast beneath Mount Ida we built a fleet. I knew I was to found a new city, but I did not know yet where it should be. Trusting the gods, we set off into the unknown. Thrace seemed like a good choice since it was only a few days away and had been friendly to Troy in the past. We landed there and began to build. As I was sacrificing to my divine mother, something frightful happened. I

saw a grove of dogwood trees and was trying to tear off some green shoots to cover the altar. Dark blood began to ooze from the ground. A plea rose from the branches begging me to stop. It was a human voice saying he was Polydorus, a friend from Troy. He had been sent to the Thracian king with gold to secure him as an ally. When the ruler heard that Troy had fallen, he slew Polydorus and threw his body in a hole here. Polydorus urged me to flee this cursed land. After giving my friend a proper burial, we set out again across the Aegean.

We came to the island of Delos where there is an oracle of holy Apollo. The god's voice shook the trees. He told us to seek our ancient mother, for there I would build a city that would someday rule the world. My father said that our ancestor Teucer had sailed from Crete to Troy. Crete therefore must be our maternal land. We sailed there and began to build again. Then a plague struck and raged among us for a whole year. Why had the god sent us to this island to die?

That night I had a dream that the sacred images of our household gods rose up and spoke: "Aeneas, son of Anchises, Apollo never meant for you to settle in Crete. There is a land far to the west, fruitful in its soil and mighty in war. The native people call it Italy. It was the birthplace of Dardanus, your grandfather, six generations past. There lies your true home."

I told the dream to my father. He said he had made a terrible mistake sending us to Crete. Many times at Troy the prophetess Cassandra had proclaimed that our future lay on the Italian shores. At last we knew our true destination. We boarded the ships again and set off on Neptune's sea.

A storm blew us away from Crete along the southern coast of the Peloponnesus. The thunderclouds were so dark that even my faithful helmsman Palinurus couldn't tell day from night. Finally, on the fourth day, the winds ceased and we came to the Strophades islands off the coast of sandy Pylos. The Harpies had settled on these deserted shores after the Argonauts had driven them away from Phineus. We were so desperate for solid ground that we beached our ships and kissed the sweet earth. A fine herd of cattle grazed there, and we killed several for a sacrifice to Jupiter and as a feast for ourselves. When the table was ready, the Harpies swooped down and ruined the meal. We killed more cattle and drew our swords to guard our dinner, but it was no use. The creatures grabbed the food in their talons and left behind a trail of filth. Their leader, Celaeno, perched on a nearby tree and spoke to me: "My dear Aeneas, you would take up arms to drive us away from our rightful kingdom? This is our home, and those cattle belonged to us. Hear me well and remember what I say—as punishment, you will not find your new home until hunger drives you to eat your own plates." With that she shrieked and flew away, leaving me to puzzle at her words.

We sailed north past the coast of Ithaca, rocky island of cold-hearted Ulysses, and cursed the man who destroyed our home. Up the western shores of Greece we journeyed until we saw a small harbor. We anchored there and could not believe our eyes, for beside the banks of a stream was Andromache, widow of Hector, the best of Trojan warriors. "Aeneas, goddess-born, is it really you? Are you a man still alive or a spirit risen from Hades? If you come from the underworld, please tell me of my Hector. Is he well? Is our son Astyanax with him?"

I assured her I was alive, and we embraced as long-lost friends. She said Achilles's son had taken her as a slave. Then he married her to a fellow Trojan, Helenus, the noted prophet and son of Priam. They had settled here with a few others from Troy.

Helenus showed us all they had built. As I walked through their town, I marveled at the work—and yet I pitied them. It was a small Troy built of wood instead of stone. The walls were scarcely higher than a man. They called a dried-up creek after the great river Xanthus and honored an empty mound as the tomb of Hector. Still, even this shadow of Troy was a glorious sight. We feasted on their simple fare

*and shared stories of all that had happened to us
since the real Troy fell.*

*Helenus told us by his prophetic gift what lay ahead.
We had a long voyage yet before we could establish
our city. When we saw a sow the color of snow nursing thirty piglets beneath an oak on a riverbank,
our journey would be at an end. We must not sail
the shortest route to the western shores of Italy, for
that would take us through the straits between the
monster Scylla and the dreaded whirlpool Charybdis. Instead we were to voyage all the way around
Sicily and approach the blessed land from the west.
We must seek the river Tiber, but first we should go
to the prophetic Sibyl at Cumae. She would show us
the glorious future of the kingdom.*

*The Trojans from our ships and those from the
town exchanged gifts and wished each other well.
Andromache was the last to say farewell. She presented a fine robe to my son Iulus and choked back
sobs as she said how much he reminded her of her
own little boy, thrown to his death from the walls of
Troy. With great sadness we left our friends and
let the wind carry us toward our new home.*

*We sailed swiftly across the Adriatic Sea and
rejoiced to at last to see the shores of Italy. Our
course took us south along the heel of that great
peninsula and across its southern coast until we*

came to the island of Sicily. Before us loomed the fiery Mount Etna, said by some to hold the monster Typhon in its depths and by others to be the forge of the god Vulcan. We pulled through the pounding waves and came at night to a small harbor to refill our jars with fresh water. We were anxious to leave that desolate place, so as dawn arose I gave the order to push off. Just then, a man came running toward us from the inland hills. He was a wretched figure. He stopped when he saw I was a Trojan. I could see him think about running away. Finally he came forward and threw himself at my feet. "O Trojan warrior, strike me down with your sword if you wish. I am a poor Greek from Ithaca who fought against you at Troy, abandoned here by my captain Ulysses. Do what you will with me, but cut your lines and sail away now, before Polyphemus returns!" I was going to ask him who Polyphemus was when we saw a great Cyclops with his single eye gone. He had heard us and was making his way to the ships with surprising speed. I ordered my men to cast off and row for their lives. I took the man with me—I could not leave even an enemy to such a fate—and we pulled away while the Cyclops threw stones at us.

We sailed along the coast of Sicily until we came to a port on the westernmost part of the island. There the heart of Anchises at last gave out. Tears rolled down my cheeks as we sailed away from his tomb.

*I would never see him again unless it was in the
land of the dead.*

*Gracious Queen Dido, you know what happened
after that. A storm blew us to your friendly shores.
I have lost so much–city, wife, friends, and father–I
can only pray to the gods that better days lie before us.*

It was late and the stars shone brightly above Dido's palace. She handed young Iulus, fast asleep, to his father and ordered her servants to show the Trojan leader to the guest quarters. In the days that followed, Dido thought more and more of her love for Aeneas. Cupid had planted love in her heart, and she wanted to marry Aeneas. Her sister, Anna, pointed out that with the help of the Trojans Carthage could become the greatest city in the world.

Aeneas, also enchanted, found himself thinking less and less of sailing for Italy. His ships began to rot in the harbor as he supervised construction projects in Dido's city. There was little doubt that the two were in love. One evening when Aeneas and the queen were out hunting in the woods, they became separated from their followers in a fierce thunderstorm sent by Juno. Aeneas lit a fire in a cozy cave and they spent the night there. After they returned to the palace, Dido no longer hid her feelings for the Trojan hero.

None of this escaped Jupiter. He sent Mercury—Hermes to the Greeks—to Carthage to tell Aeneas it was time to set sail for Italy. The messenger god appeared suddenly: "Aeneas, I come from the throne of Jupiter to tell you that no woman is more important than your duty. Get your ship ready to sail to Italy. Your fate lies across the sea on the banks of the Tiber. Go now!"

Aeneas ordered his most trusted lieutenants to prepare the ships—though quietly so that Dido would not know he was leaving. As swift as the flight of a bird, word reached the palace that the Trojans were preparing to leave. Dido called Aeneas to her throne room: "Did you really think you could slip away unnoticed? I shared everything in my kingdom with you, and now you're going to sneak away in the night?"

Aeneas tried to explain: "Dido, it is the will of the gods that I establish a new home for my people in Italy. I'd love to stay, but I can't. I thought it would be easier if I just slipped away quietly."

Dido threw Aeneas out of the palace. After he had gone, she cried for hours. Her sister tried to comfort her, but Dido would have none of it. She prayed to the gods that they curse Aeneas and his city. Let there be everlasting hatred between the two cities, until one destroyed the other.

Dido ordered the servants to gather a great pile of wood and place it on the highest citadel of the city where the departing Trojans and their noble prince could see it like a beacon. She then took all the gifts that Aeneas had given her and carried them to the citadel herself. Finally she ordered her men to light the fire while she knelt on the top and stabbed herself. The flames swept over the queen, betrayed by love. Aeneas saw the great fire and knew in his heart that Dido was gone.

The Trojans sailed north and landed once again at the western tip of Sicily where Aeneas had buried his father, Anchises. Aeneas wanted to hold funeral games at the tomb. The ships pulled ashore, and the men honored the spirit of their late patriarch with sacrifices and athletic contests according to ancient tradition. From Sicily they struck a course for Italy, finding favorable winds and calm seas all the way. But Neptune insists on a price for safe travel. The helmsman, Palinurus, fell into the sea and was lost off the cape that later bore his name.

After losing their comrade, the Trojans saw Mount Vesuvius in the distance and soon arrived at Cumae, home of the Sibyl. Aeneas knew he must consult this oracle, but he was fearful. It was foretold to him that to learn the future, he must journey down to the land of the dead. Still, the captain of men entered the temple of Apollo and greeted the Sibyl, who told him that he would face a bloody war on the banks of the Tiber before he could establish his city. All the tribes of Latium, as the land was known, would be rallied against him by a new Achilles. But help would come to him from where he least expected it.

That was the immediate future, but if he wanted to learn the destiny of his kingdom, he must come with her to the underworld. First he had to visit her sacred grove and seek a tree like no other. "On this tree grows a branch of gold," said the Sibyl. "Fate has decreed this golden bough can be torn from the tree only by the one chosen by destiny."

Aeneas did as the Sibyl asked, and the bough slipped easily into his hand. Then he followed the prophetess to a nearby cave where they sacrificed to Hecate, goddess of darkness, along with the other powers there.

The cavern was as black as a moonless night. The ancient gods born at the dawn of the world dwelled there—Death, Strife, Disease, Hunger, War, and Fear. Aeneas heard blood-curdling shrieks and saw shadows of hideous monsters on the walls as they journeyed deep into the earth.

At last they found the boatman Charon at the River Styx. The old man told them to go away, but the Sibyl told Aeneas to show him the golden bough. The surly ferryman motioned them aboard, though the boat rode low in the water with the weight of their living bodies. Once on the far shore, Aeneas heard the cries of infants and the moans of those unjustly con-demned to die. Nearby were the fields for those who perished because of love. Aeneas wept when he saw the soul of Dido there and tried to speak to her, but she turned her back on him and faded into the darkness.

Among the countless souls Aeneas saw as he went deeper into the land of the dead were the ghosts of men he had fought with and against at Troy. The Sibyl led him on to a place where the path divided in two. She told him the road to the right led to the fields of Elysium, their destination. The trail to the left wound its way down to Tartarus, where the souls of the wicked were punished forever.

Aeneas was pleased to see the souls gathered at the pleas-ant fields of Elysium. But then the Sibyl pointed out to him one particular soul. He saw it was Anchises, his own father, looking splendid in shining robes. Aeneas tried to embrace him, but the old man laughed and explained that he no longer had a body. Anchises led his son to the crest of a hill and revealed to him all the souls that were waiting to be born, souls that would spring from the kingdom he would establish in Italy.

He showed him Silvius, a boy Aeneas would father in his old age by his beautiful Italian wife, Lavinia. Romulus and Remus, who would someday build the city of Rome, were there. There was also Brutus, who would overthrow a hated foreign king and establish the city as a republic. The great hero Camillus marched by, savior of the city from the dreaded Gauls. The spirit of Fabius Maximus appeared next; he would wear down Hannibal and the mighty elephants he would drive over the Alps. There was Julius Caesar, greatest of Roman generals, who would cross the Rubicon to crush his enemies. Last of all Anchises showed him Augustus, who would return mankind to the age of gold lost so long ago.

The shining spirit looked at his son and said: "Others in this wide world will forge bronze more skillfully and shape marble into human form. Others will speak with more elegant tongues and chart the course of the stars across the skies. But Romans will rule the people of the earth with power and justice. The gift of our people will be to establish peace, to spare the defeated, and to crush all who resist us."

Anchises then left his son to journey back to the land of the living. Aeneas swiftly climbed, eager to establish such a glorious future.

The Trojan fleet sailed north along the green coast of Italy until it came to the mouth of a river with broad trees along its banks and birds singing overhead. The captain ordered his ships to turn into this river and draw the ships to land. The place was so beautiful that Aeneas, his son Iulus, and all his people took food on shore and ate their meal beneath the boughs of shady trees. The women baked wheat cakes on the banks and heaped them with fruit they had gathered nearby. The men ate not only the fruit but even the cakes on which it was served. Little Iulus laughed and said, "Look, Father, we're so hungry we're eating our plates." It was then that Aeneas remembered the words of Celaeno the Harpy that they would know they had reached their final destination when they ate their plates. He was even more delighted when he saw a white sow nursing thirty piglets by the river, just as Helenus had foretold.

"Make camp," he shouted. "This is the Tiber River! This is where we are to build our new city. We are home!"

The people rejoiced to hear the long journey was at an end. While he supervised the building of a fortified camp, Aeneas sent his most trusted companions to find out what king ruled this land and how they might all live in friendship. The messengers soon found the town of King Latinus, a descendant of Saturn, called Cronus by the Greeks. He was a man of peace who had ruled many years, but had only one child, a daughter named Lavinia. His wife was determined to wed her child to Turnus, a powerful local ruler. But Queen Amata could not convince her husband. The king had once received an oracle that he should marry his daughter to a stranger who would come from afar.

The envoys of Aeneas presented Latinus with fine gifts. They said they were Trojans who had sailed west to seek out a new home. They sought a safe haven in which to build their city. If welcomed, they would be staunch friends of the king and allies against his enemies. Latinus agreed to all they asked. Moreover, he requested Aeneas come to him personally as he suspected the man was the one foretold to marry his daughter. The Trojans went back to report the good news to Aeneas.

Amata turned on her husband: "You old fool! You're going to give your daughter to some wanderer who washes up on our shore? You think these Trojans will help us defeat our enemies? By the gods, they're the ones who lost the Trojan War!"

Amata's anger suited Juno. The wife of Jupiter had not been able to prevent the Trojans from reaching Italy, but she might be able to kill them all yet. She went deep into the earth and found Alecto, most horrible of the Furies, and asked her to stir up trouble among the Latin tribes. Alecto told Turnus that Aeneas would steal his bride-to-be. She flew throughout the land raising the cry against the Trojans. Many tribes came together under Turnus to rise up against Aeneas. King Latinus was too old and weak to stand against them.

Aeneas reluctantly made preparations for war. He knew he could not stand against the tribes of Italy without allies of his own—but where to find them? That night, as he slept beside the river, the spirit of the Tiber spoke to him in a dream: "Fear not, Aeneas, for help is at hand. On my banks lies a city called Pallanteum ruled over by a king named Evander, who will help you. Do not be afraid to seek him out, even though he is a Greek."

Aeneas could hardly believe what the river god was telling him. Seek help from a Greek, the enemies of the Trojans?

But divine commands are not to be ignored. Aeneas fitted his best ship with troops and began to row up the river. By midday they had come to the city of King Evander beneath seven hills on the banks of the Tiber. The king and his son, Pallas, were making a sacrifice to Hercules when they saw the strangers pull up on the banks of the river. Pallas grabbed a spear and demanded to know whether they were friend or foe. Aeneas assured the brave lad they came in peace. Evander then welcomed them to his town and assured them he had no hatred for the Trojans. Dardanus himself sailed from this land long ago to found the line that gave birth to King Priam and to Aeneas himself. He was most welcome here.

Evander showed Aeneas his city and explained how he had struggled to build a home in a hostile land. He welcomed the Trojans as allies against their neighbors, especially the Etruscan tribe ruled by cruel Mezentius. Evander would stand beside Aeneas against such enemies. He even asked the Trojan leader if, along with troops from his city, he would take Pallas with him so that the boy could learn to fight from the best. Aeneas agreed and sealed a bond of friendship with Evander.

While Aeneas was away, things were not going well at the Trojan camp. The Trojan warriors had built a stockade around their ships on the banks of the Tiber. It was a strong position, but they could not hold out forever against an attack. Turnus taunted the Trojans: "Afraid to face us on the field of battle? Only cowards stay in camp! These are the brave warriors who fought against the Greeks at Troy? Scared to fight without Aeneas by your side?"

The Trojans were under orders from Aeneas not to fight the enemy until he returned. Two young Trojan warriors named Nisus and Euryalus snuck out one night. They killed a number of the enemy but were captured and killed before dawn. Turnus put their heads on poles in front of the Trojan camp. The men still did not leave their ships.

Turnus then launched an attack on the ships. He fought bravely but was forced to jump into the Tiber to escape death.

Soon Aeneas returned to camp with, Evander's son, Pallas, and the soldiers from Evander's city. It was then that the great battle began. Trojans and Italians met on the plain to fight and die in such numbers as Italy had never seen. Each side was full of courageous men. Pallas was at the front of his troops cutting down the enemy. Turnus came against him like a raging bull, ramming his oak spear clean through his chest. Turnus then hung the boy's sword-belt from his shoulder as a trophy.

Aeneas faced cruel Mezentius and his son in combat. He slew them both and turned to other foes. The battle continued for days. Among the bravest of the Italians was Camilla, a warrior-woman. She had grown up a child of the hunt devoted to Diana, whom the Greeks called Artemis. Camilla cut through the Trojan lines dealing death at every turn. At last an ally of Aeneas named Arruns sent a spear ripping through her, but he was soon cut down himself.

The battle raged on. Soon even the gods had enough. Jupiter called Juno before him and told her the killing must end. She agreed, but only if the hated name of Troy was left behind forever and the new city was Italian in title, language, and ways. The ruler of the gods nodded and Juno withdrew her support of Turnus and his men.

The mortals could sense that something had changed. Turnus realized he now stood without the favor of any god, but his pride would not allow him to surrender. He asked that Aeneas face him in single combat to end the war. Thus both men met on the bloody field between the lines. They fought with great courage, though neither could gain the upper hand. Finally Turnus picked up a rock that twelve men could barely lift, but he buckled under the weight. This gave Aeneas his chance. The Trojan captain sent his spear flying like a whirlwind through the breastplate of the great Italian warrior. Turnus lay in the mud looking up at Aeneas and spoke: "Strike the final blow, for you have conquered me. I do not plead for mercy. And yet, I would be grateful if you would send me back to die in my home with my own father by my side, a man much like your own great sire, Anchises. You have won, Aeneas. Lavinia is your bride. You don't need to kill me here."

Aeneas was moved by the courage of his fallen enemy. He started to sheath his sword when suddenly he saw the sword belt of Pallas across the shoulder of Turnus: "You ask a favor, Turnus, but did you give any to Pallas? Did you send him back to his father Evander? You dare to ask for kindness when you wear the sword belt of that dear boy as a trophy?"

Aeneas took his sword and planted it in the heart of Turnus so that it went down deep into the Italian soil beneath him, a foundation for his new kingdom and a message to all that Rome would never yield.

Rome

ROMULUS
AND REMUS

Aeneas married Lavinia and built a town named Lavinium in her honor. The Trojans and the Italians became one people, and Lavinium became a large and prosperous city. When Aeneas died, not long after founding the town, leadership passed to his son Iulus. In time, Iulus left to establish his own settlement called Alba Longa in the hills south of the Tiber. The descendants of Iulus ruled at Alba Longa for many generations until the time of Proca. Proca had two sons, Numitor and Amulius. He left the kingdom to Numitor, the eldest, when he died.

Amulius took the kingship from his brother, but kept Numitor alive. Numitor's sons were killed, but his daughter, Rhea Silvia, was spared on the condition she become a Vestal Virgin. These priestesses of Vesta, goddess of the hearth, kept the holy flame of the city burning and were not allowed to marry. Amulius wanted to be sure that Rhea Silvia would not have children to threaten his throne.

One day word came to the king that his niece had given birth to twins. Amulius demanded to know who the father was. Rhea Silvia claimed he was the god Mars. Her uncle laughed at her story and threw her into prison. He had his men take her twin sons to the banks of the Tiber to be drowned. By chance the river was flooding, and the servants could not approach the moving stream. They abandoned the boys on a mud flat beneath seven hills where the city of King Evander once stood. A female wolf heard the cries of the babies and came to investigate. She found the pair and nursed them until they fell asleep. Soon after, a shepherd found them with the she-wolf gently licking their faces. He brought them to his hut and gave them to his wife Larentia to raise.

The twins were named Romulus and Remus. They grew into great hunters and warriors. They were fearless and attacked local robbers, dividing their spoils among the poor shepherds of the region. The brothers gathered a merry band of youths to join in their adventures and

became famous for their courage. One group of robbers laid a trap for them during a festival. Romulus drove his attackers away, but Remus was captured and taken to King Amulius. The robbers claimed Remus had stolen goods from Numitor that they themselves had taken. Remus was given to his own grandfather for punishment.

Numitor liked the boy immediately. When he heard Remus's story, he realized that Remus and Romulus were the sons of Rhea Silvia. Remus sent for Romulus. Together with their followers they slew their great-uncle Amulius and restored their grandfather to the throne. The young men were happy for Numitor, but they wanted to found their own city at the place they had been raised.

The brothers could not agree which of them should be king of the new city. They decided to wait for a sign and so went to two separate hills, the Palatine and the Aventine, to watch for signs from the gods. Remus saw six vultures in the sky, an impressive sign. Then Romulus saw twelve. They argued about who had received the favor of the gods. The quarrel grew into a fight, and Romulus killed his brother. He named the new city Rome, after himself.

King Romulus welcomed bandits, fugitives, and runaway slaves to his new settlement. The town was full of wild young men who fortified their city with walls and built homes for themselves along with temples to the gods. Romulus appointed one hundred of the best men to be senators to help him govern the town, and these with their descendants were known ever after as patricians. But the king had little luck recruiting wives for his new subjects. So Romulus invited several villages of Sabines to a grand festival. The neighboring men came and brought their families. After the food and wine began to flow, the Roman men grabbed all the maidens. Then they drove the rest of the visitors outside the walls.

The Sabine fathers were furious. But the Roman men confessed their love to the Sabine maidens. They promised the women that together they would build a fine city and future for their children. Slowly the hearts of the women warmed to their new husbands.

The fathers were not so forgiving. They attacked the city to recover their daughters. One young woman named Tarpeia agreed to sneak the Sabine advance guard into the citadel on the Capitoline Hill if they would give her what they wore on their left arms, meaning their gold bracelets. Once they safely held the fortress, the Sabines piled their heavy shields—which they also wore on their left arms—on top of Tarpeia and crushed the life from her. The cliff where Tarpeia was killed became known as the Tarpeian Rock and was a place of execution ever after for those who betrayed their country.

The army of Romulus invited the Sabines to battle to settle the affair. Just as the fight was about to begin, the Sabine wives ran between the lines holding their babies in their arms. They cried that they would not be the cause of bloodshed between their fathers and husbands. Brought to their senses by the women, both sides joined together as one people.

The years passed and Romulus brought prosperity to his new city along with peace. The Romans also became known throughout the land as the fiercest of warriors.

One day when Romulus was holding an assembly on the Field of Mars, a great storm arose and turned the sky black. When the sun shone again, Romulus had disappeared. Some say he had been taken up into the heavens to live with the gods. Others claim that jealous senators had murdered him in the darkness, then cut up his body and smuggled the pieces away under their togas. In either case, Romulus was honored afterward as a god and worshipped among the Romans as the founder of their city.

THE HORATII BROTHERS

When Romulus died, Numa Pompilius became the leader of Rome. He was said to have given Rome many of its ancient religious traditions. After Numa, a great warrior king named Tullus Hostilius reigned. His goal was to include Alba Longa in Rome's growing state. The Albans, however, had no desire to join with their cousins. Both sides knew that a war would leave their towns weak and ripe for conquest by the hostile Etruscans to the north. So it was decided that each city would choose three men to fight to the death. Whichever town had the last man standing would surrender to the other. Both sides swore solemn oaths to the gods that they would honor the outcome of the contest.

Both Rome and Alba Longa had triplet brothers who were practiced warriors. The Horatii brothers of Rome agreed to stand against the Curiatii triplets of Alba Longa. The citizens gathered around the field of combat to see which city would rule. At the signal, shields clashed and swords flew. Two of the Romans soon fell dead. The remaining Horatii was surrounded by the Curiatii brothers, but the Roman warrior began to run. The Curiatii chased him around the field until they became separated from each other. This was just what the Roman soldier wanted. He struck down the first Alban to reach him, then the second, and finally the third, taking them on one at a time.

A tremendous cheer went up from the Roman side. The Albans were disappointed, but they agreed to stand by the outcome of the contest. The only one weeping was a sister of the surviving Horatii brother. She had been engaged to one of the Curiatii triplets. When her brother found out why she was crying, he plunged his sword into her heart. He said that should be the fate of any Roman woman who weeps for the enemy. The young man was put on trial for murder. His father said that his daughter's killing was just. But since the young man acted without the permission of Rome, the judges declared that he should be forced to march underneath a yoke as a sign of shame.

ONE-EYED HORATIUS

The next king of Rome was Ancus Marcius, who established a port on the sea at Ostia and built many aqueducts, along with a bridge across the Tiber. After his rule, an Etruscan king named Tarquin the Elder seized the throne, and a foreign dynasty ruled the city for the next three generations. The Romans didn't like being ruled by an Etruscan, but the city prospered and was united against other hostile Etruscan powers across the Tiber.

The most dangerous king in the region was Lars Porsenna, an Etruscan ruler just to the north. He was determined to conquer Rome and so marched his army to the single wooden bridge spanning the Tiber. The Romans could not hold the bridge against so many soldiers, so they began to tear it down from the Roman side as the Etruscans neared. A guard named Horatius Cocles ("one-eyed") volunteered to hold off the invaders to give his comrades precious minutes to complete the destruction.

Alone, Horatius fought the Etruscan warriors until the bridge fell apart. Then he dove into the river in full armor and swam to the Roman side. Afterward he was honored as a great hero who had risked everything for the good of Rome.

SCAEVOLA

Lars Porsenna was a very persistent king. When the bridge across the Tiber fell, he began a siege of Rome to starve the city into submission. As the weeks passed, the people of Rome grew hungry and desperate. It was then that a young man named Gaius Mucius came to the Senate with a plan. He would disguise himself as an Etruscan and sneak into the tent of Lars Porsenna. When he was close enough, he would kill the king and end the war. It was a suicide mission, but it was worth it if he could free Rome.

The elders agreed. That night the Roman slipped across the river and into the Etruscan camp. He came unnoticed into the tent, but he could not recognize the king. All the Etruscan nobility were dressed in such finery that everyone looked like royalty. He plunged his sword into a man sitting on a regal chair. Unfortunately, this turned out to be the secretary of the king. Mucius was seized and held before the true king, who demanded to know the details of any plot against him. If the Roman didn't speak, he would be burned alive. Mucius laughed and thrust his right hand into the fire. Mucius did not utter a sound or flinch as the fire burned his flesh.

The Etruscan king was so impressed that he decided to set Mucius free. Afterward he was known as Scaevola, or "lefty." The young man warned Lars Porsenna that there were three hundred other Romans who had pledged to assassinate the king if he failed. This so troubled Lars Porsenna that he immediately made a truce with the Romans and ended the siege.

CLOELIA

Part of the peace treaty with Lars Porsenna required the Romans to send hostages to live among the Etruscans to guarantee the good will of Rome in the future. If the city did not behave itself, the hostages would die. Among the nobility sent to Lars Porsenna was a maiden named Cloelia. She knew that she and the other girls would be abused by the Etruscan soldiers, so she organized an escape attempt and broke out of the Etruscan camp. After a chase, they made it to the Tiber and swam safely across to Rome. The Etruscan king was impressed by Cloelia, but demanded she be returned immediately or he would consider the treaty broken. As a gesture of kindness, he assured the Senate that he would send her back to Rome unharmed if they recognized his authority in this matter. He simply wanted to be sure that Rome would honor the peace treaty.

The Romans agreed and Cloelia returned to the camp, where she was treated well by the king. He honored Cloelia and said that he would allow her to take half the remaining hostages back to Rome with her. The girl considered which to choose, then decided on the youngest boys among the group. This was because it seemed more proper for a maiden to select boys than men. She led the hostages back to Rome, where a statue was raised as a tribute to her courage.

LUCRETIA

The third Etruscan king of Rome was Tarquin the Proud, who started a war against the nearby town of Ardea. The king's son Sextus Tarquinius fought in the conflict, as did his Roman friend Collatinus. One quiet night Sextus and Collatinus began to argue about which of their wives was the most virtuous. They decided to ride back to Rome and catch the women by surprise to see what they were doing.

They found the wife of Sextus at a grand party drinking wine and celebrating with her friends. The wife of Collatinus, a woman named Lucretia, was busy working wool in her modest home. After they returned to the camp, Sextus was ashamed of his own wife, but fascinated by Lucretia. He decided he must have such a woman.

A few days later Sextus returned to Rome alone. Lucretia welcomed the friend of her husband and had her servants show him to a guest room after dinner. When the house was quiet, Sextus crept into the bedroom of Lucretia and ordered her to be quiet or die. He claimed he was in love with her. Unless she allowed him to share her bed, he would kill not only her but one of her male servants and put his body in her bed. Then he would tell Collatinus that he had caught the pair together and slain them both out of outrage.

Lucretia knew she was trapped. She did as Sextus asked, then cried bitter tears. The next day she sent a message to her father and her husband asking that they come to her home immediately. Both arrived along with her husband's Roman friend Lucius Junius Brutus. She told them what had happened the previous night and said she was sick in her heart with guilt for bringing shame on her family. All the men told her that she was not to blame, but she would hear none of it. From beneath her robes she drew a sword and plunged it into her breast, falling dead to the floor.

As her husband and father held her body in their arms, Brutus picked up the bloody sword and swore an oath by it that the Tarquin family would be swept away. Soon Brutus led a rebellion against the Tarquins and drove them from the city. Rome put aside rule by kings and became a republic governed by the people.

The long age of monarchy stretching back to Aeneas and the Trojan War, to the Greek tradition and the earliest tales, had come to an end. The classical world now entered the age of history. But the ancient myths that shaped their lives—and still shape ours—were never forgotten.

Greek and Roman Gods

GREEK NAME	ROMAN NAME
Zeus*	Jupiter, Jove
Hera*	Juno
Demeter*	Ceres
Poseidon*	Neptune
Hestia*	Vesta
Artemis*	Diana
Aphrodite*	Venus
Ares*	Mars
Hermes*	Mercury
Hephaestus*	Vulcan
Apollo*	Apollo
Athena*	Minerva
Hades	Pluto, Dis
Dionysus	Liber
Eros	Cupid
Pan	Faunus
Heracles	Hercules

* Denotes the twelve
  Olympian gods

Directory of Gods, Goddesses, Monsters, and Mortals

Achilles (a-KIL-eez): Son of Peleus and the goddess Thetis, the greatest Greek warrior at Troy.

Acrisius (a-KRIS-i-us): Father of Danae, grandfather of Perseus, accidentally killed by a discus thrown by Perseus.

Acropolis (a-KROP-o-lis): The highest part of any city, but most commonly referring to the famous Acropolis of Athens, home to the sacred Parthenon temple of Athena.

Adonis (a-DON-is): Son of a union between Myrrha and her father, Cinyras. He was an extraordinarily handsome lad, beloved by both Aphrodite and Persephone. He was killed by a wild boar and the anemone flower sprang from his blood.

Adrastus (a-DRAS-tus): King of Argos and leader of the seven generals who fought against Thebes on the side of Polynices, son of Oedipus.

Aeacus (EE-a-kus): Son of Zeus and Aegina, he ruled over the island of Aegina. Zeus transformed ants into humans to be his subjects.

Aeetes (ee-EE-teez): Son of the god Helios, king of Colchis, and father of Medea. He had the Golden Fleece prior to Jason.

Aegeus (EE-je-us): King of Athens and father of Theseus, he aided Medea after she murdered her children and fled Corinth.

Aegina (EE-ji-na): Mother of Aeacus by Zeus and namesake of a small island near Athens.

Aegisthus (ee-JIS-thus): Son of Thyestes and his daughter Pelopia, he served as regent of Mycenae while Agamemnon fought at Troy. He helped Clytemnestra murder Agamemnon when he returned and was slain by Agamemnon's son Orestes.

Aeneas (ee-NEE-us): Son of Anchises and the goddess Aphrodite/Venus, he led the surviving Trojans to found a kingdom in Italy that would give birth to the Romans.

PHILIP FREEMAN

Aeolus (ee-O-lus): King of Thessaly who is sometimes identified with the ruler of the winds who tried to help Odysseus return home.

Aethra (EE-thra): Mother of Theseus, she became a slave to Helen.

Agamemnon (a-ga-MEM-non): Son of Atreus and brother to Menelaus, he was king of Mycenae and led the Greek expedition to Troy. He was murdered by his wife Clytemnestra on his return home.

Agave (a-GA-ve): Daughter of Cadmus, king of Thebes, and Harmonia, she was punished with madness by Dionysus and murdered her own son Pentheus.

Ajax (A-jaks): (1) Son of Telemon, a Greek warrior of immense strength in the Trojan War, he killed himself after losing the armor of Achilles to Odysseus; (2) Son of Oileus, also a gifted soldier at Troy, known as Little Ajax.

Alcinous (al-SIN-o-us): Phaeacean king, husband of Arete, and father of Nausicaa, he welcomed both Jason and Odysseus to his idyllic island kingdom on their travels.

Alcmene (alk-MEN-e): Mother of Hercules.

Alcyone (al-SEE-o-ne): (1) Daughter of Aeolus, she married Ceyx and was transformed into a kingfisher (halcyon) after he drowned.

Alecto (a-LEK-to): A divine Fury. By the will of Juno, she stirred up the native Italians against Aeneas and his Trojans.

Alpheus (al-FEE-us): Son of Ocean and Tethys, a river and a god of the Peloponnesus, who pursued the nymph Arethusa to Sicily.

Amazons (A-ma-zons): Women warriors who lived on the eastern edge of the Greek world.

Amphion (am-FI-on): Son of Zeus and Antiope, he and his brother Zethus avenged their mother's ill treatment at the hands of Lycus and Dirce to become corulers of Thebes.

Amphitrite (am-FI-tre-te): Sea goddess pursued by Poseidon, she bore him three sons.

Amphitryon (am-FI-tree-on): Grandson of Perseus and father to Hercules's half brother, Iphicles.

Amulius (a-MU-li-us): Great-uncle of Romulus and Remus, he drove his brother Numitor from the throne of Alba Longa and abandoned the twins on the banks of the Tiber River.

Anchises (an-KI-seez): Father of Aeneas.

Andromache (an-DRO-ma-kee): Wife of the Trojan hero Hector.

Andromeda (an-DRO-me-da): Daughter of Cepheus and Cassiopeia, she was rescued from a sea monster by Perseus.

Antaeus (an-TEE-us): Son of Earth and Poseidon, he was an African giant who was defeated by Hercules.

310

Antigone (an-TI-go-ne): Daughter of Oedipus who cared for her father in exile, then defied her uncle, King Creon of Thebes, by giving her brother Polynices a proper burial.

Antiope (an-TI-o-pe): Mother by Zeus to twin sons Amphion and Zethus.

Aphrodite (af-ro-DI-te) (Roman *Venus*): Goddess of love and the daughter of Sky.

Apollo (a-POL-lo): Son of Zeus and Leto, brother of Artemis, he was god of music, medicine, archery, and prophecy.

Arachne (a-RAK-ne): Young woman of Lydia who challenged Athena to a weaving contest and was turned into a spider.

Ares (AR-eez) (Roman *Mars*): Son of Zeus and Hera, the god of war.

Arete (a-RE-te): Phaeacian queen and wife of Alcinous, she kindly received both Jason and Odysseus on their travels.

Arethusa (a-re-THU-sa): Nymph who was chased across the sea by the river god Alpheus.

Argonauts (AR-go-nots): Sailors who joined Jason on the *Argo* to search for the Golden Fleece.

Argos (AR-gos): Aged and faithful dog of Odysseus that died when he heard his master's voice on his return.

Argus (AR-gus): Guardian of Io with a hundred eyes, he was killed by Hermes.

Ariadne (ar-i-AD-ne): Daughter of King Minos, she helped Theseus defeat her father and escape the maze of the Minotaur.

Arion (a-RI-on): Divine horse, born from Demeter and fathered by Poseidon.

Artemis (ART-e-mis) (Roman *Diana*): Daughter of Zeus and Leto, sister of Apollo, virgin goddess of the hunt.

Ascanius (as-KAN-i-us) (see **Iulus** [U-lus])

Asclepius (as-KLEP-i-us): Son of Apollo, god of healing, he was killed by Zeus when he dared to raise mortals from the dead.

Asopus (a-SO-pus): River god and father of the nymph Aegina.

Atalanta (a-ta-LAN-ta): Virgin hunter who raced hopeful suitors in a contest for her hand, then killed them if she defeated them.

Athena (a-THEE-na) (Roman *Minerva*): Daughter of Metis who was swallowed by Zeus. Athena sprung from the forehead of her father. She was the virgin goddess of war and crafts, as well as patron of the city of Athens.

Atlas (AT-las): Titan who held the heavens on his shoulders until, in some stories, he was turned to stony Mount Atlas by Perseus, who held Medusa's severed head before him.

Atreus (A-tre-us): Son of Pelops and Hippodamia, brother of Thyestes, and father of Agamemnon and Menelaus, he served the sons of Thyestes to their father at a banquet and took over the rule of Mycenae.

Atropos (A-tro-pos): One of the three Fates, she cut the thread of life.

Augeas (AW-je-as): King and owner of Aegean stables cleaned by Hercules.

Bacchus (BAK-kus) (see **Dionysus** [di-o-NI-sus])

Baucis (BAW-kis): Wife of Philemon. An elderly peasant woman who welcomed the disguised Zeus and Hermes to her home and was rewarded along with her husband.

Bellerophon (bel-LER-o-fon): Son of the king of Corinth who accidentally killed his brother. He was sent to Lydia to be killed but instead impressed the king with his heroic achievements, aided by the flying horse Pegasus.

Briareus (bri-A-re-us): One of the hundred-handed monsters who helped Zeus defeat the Titans.

Brutus (BRU-tus): Roman who expelled Tarquin the Proud, the last king of Rome, after the suicide of Lucretia.

Cacus (KA-kus): Monster who inhabited the future site of Rome and was killed by Hercules.

Cadmus (KAD-mus): Son of the Phoenician king, Agenor, he left his home to search for his missing sister, Europa, and founded the Greek city of Thebes.

Calais (KA-la-is): Brother of Zetes and a son of the North Wind who sailed with the Argonauts.

Calchas (KAL-kas): A gifted seer who accompanied the Greeks to Troy.

Calliope (kal-LI-o-pe): Muse of epic poetry and mother of Orpheus.

Callisto (kal-LIS-to): Follower of Artemis and unwilling lover of Zeus, she was turned into a bear by Hera.

Calydonian (ka-li-DO-ni-an) **boar**: Ferocious boar sent by Artemis to punish the people of Calydon for neglecting her worship. The greatest heroes of the age gathered to successfully hunt down the beast.

Calypso (ka-LIP-so): Divine daughter of Atlas who held Odysseus captive on the island of Ogygia.

Cassandra (kas-SAN-dra): Daughter of Trojan king, Priam, she was punished by Apollo for rejecting him. He granted her the gift of prophecy but made sure that no one would ever believe her. She was taken as a war prize by Agamemnon and murdered at Mycenae.

Cassiopeia (kas-i-o-PEE-a): Wife of Cepheus and mother of Andromeda.

Castor (KAS-tor): Brother of Pollux as well as Helen and Clytemnestra, he sailed with Jason and the Argonauts.

Cecrops (SE-krops): First king of Athens, born with a man's body and the tail of a snake.

Centaurs (SEN-tawrs): Creatures with the head and chest of a man, but the body of a horse, they were often described as uncivilized in Greek myths, but wise centaurs such as Chiron became the tutors of heroes.

Cephalus (SE-fa-lus): Husband of Procris who tested his wife's faithfulness, he failed a similar trial when his wife came to him in disguise.

Cepheus (SE-fe-us): King of Ethiopia, husband of Cassiopeia, and father of Andromeda.

Cerberus (SER-ber-us): The three-headed watchdog of Hades and the offspring of the monstrous Typhon and Echidna.

Ceyx (SEE-iks): King of Trachis and husband of Alcyone, he drowned but was revived and turned into a kingfisher along with his wife.

Chaos (KA-os): The ancient chasm from which sprang the first divine beings.

Charon (KA-ron): The ferryman of Hades who transported souls across the river Styx.

Charybdis (ka-RIB-dis): Deadly whirlpool opposite the monster Scylla in the narrow straits between Sicily and Italy.

Chimaera (ki-MEE-ra): A Lycian monster with the front of a lion, the middle of a goat, and the tail of a serpent, which was killed by Bellerophon.

Chione (ki-O-ne): A beautiful maiden who gave birth to sons by both Hermes and Apollo. She was later killed by Artemis for bragging.

Chiron (KI-ron): Wise centaur who tutored Jason and Achilles.

Circe (SIR-se): Daughter of Helios and a powerful witch who changed Scylla into a monster. She purified Jason and Medea, then entertained Odysseus after changing his men into pigs.

Clio (KLI-o): Muse of history.

Cloelia (KLOY-li-a): Roman maiden who was given as a hostage to the Etruscan Lars Porsenna, but escaped back across the Tiber River.

Clotho (KLO-tho): One of the three Fates, she spun the thread of destiny for each person.

Clytemnestra (KLI-tem-nes-tra): Wife of Agamemnon and mother of Orestes who joined with Aegisthus to murder her husband, she was later killed by her son.

Coeus (SEE-us): Son of Earth and Sky and father of Leto and Asteria.

Cottus (KOT-tus): One of the hundred-handed monsters who helped Zeus overthrow the Titans.

Creon (KREE-on): Brother-in-law of Oedipus and king of Thebes, he condemned Antigone to death.

Creusa (kre-U-sa): (1) Mother of Ion with Apollo; (2) First wife of Aeneas and mother of Iulus, she perished at the fall of Troy.

Cronus (KRO-nus) (Roman *Saturn*): Son of Earth and Sky who defeated his own father and then took his place as ruler of the universe. He was later tricked and overthrown by his own son, Zeus.

Cupid (KU-pid) (Greek *Eros*): Son of Aphrodite, he prompted irresistible desire in others with his arrows, but fell in love himself with the maiden Psyche.

Cybele (SI-be-le): Phrygian mother-goddess adapted into Greek mythology, sometimes identified with Rhea.

Cyclopes (si-KLOP-es) (singular **Cyclops** [SI-klops]): Sons of Poseidon who lived as brutes in the distant west. One of their number, named Polyphemus, killed some of Odysseus's men but was tricked and blinded by the hero when Odysseus escaped from the cave.

Cyparissus (si-pa-RIS-sus): Handsome boy who loved a pet deer, which he accidentally killed. Apollo turned him into a cypress tree to mourn the animal forever.

Daedalus (DEE-da-lus): Master craftsman and father of Icarus, he built the Labyrinth for King Minos in Crete. He later escaped prison on homemade wings with his son, but the boy plunged to his death when he flew too near the sun.

Danae (DA-na-e): Daughter of Acrisius, king of Argos, and the mother of Perseus.

Daphne (DAF-ne): Nymph beloved by Apollo, transformed into a laurel tree by Earth to save her from the god's advances.

Dardanus (DAR-dan-us): Italian-born ancestor of the Romans who migrated to Asia and became king of Troy. The Greeks claimed he was born on Crete or Samothrace.

Deianira (de-ya-NI-ra): Wife of Hercules who unknowingly gave him a poisoned cloak that caused his death.

Demeter (de-ME-ter) (Roman *Ceres*): Daughter of Cronus and Rhea, goddess of the bountiful earth and mother of Persephone.

Deucalion (du-KA-li-on): Son of Prometheus, husband of Pyrrha, and the lone male survivor of the great flood sent by Zeus to destroy humanity.

Diana (dee-AN-a) (see **Artemis** [ART-e-mis])

Dido (DI-do): Phoenician founder and queen of Carthage, she was loved and abandoned by Aeneas.

Diomedes (di-o-MEE-deez): (1) Greek king of Argos who fought at Troy; (2) Thracian king who was fed to his own flesh-eating mares by Hercules.

Dionysus (di-o-NI-sus) (Roman *Liber*): Son of Zeus and Semele, god of wine and a balanced life. Also known as Bacchus.

Earth (Greek *Gaia* or *Ge*): Sprung from Chaos, she bore Sky and then mated with him to produce many children, including Cronus, father of Zeus.

Echidna (e-KID-na): Monster born of Earth and Tartarus who produced many terrible children of her own, including Typhon, the Chimaera, and Cerberus.

Echo (E-ko): Nymph who loved and was rejected by Narcissus. She faded away into a voice that could only repeat the last words spoken by another.

Eileithyia (ee-li-THI-a): Daughter of Zeus and Hera, the goddess of childbirth.

Electra (e-LEK-tra): (1) Daughter of Agamemnon and Clytemnestra who helped her brother Orestes gain revenge on their mother; (2) Daughter of Atlas who bore two sons by Zeus, Dardanus and Iasion.

Endymion (en-DI-mi-on): Lover of Selene who, given whatever he wished by Zeus, chose to sleep forever, never growing old.

Eos (E-os) (Roman *Aurora*): Goddess of the dawn, most famous for transforming her lover Tithonus into a cicada.

Epimetheus (ep-i-ME-the-us): Brother of Prometheus, he accepted Zeus's gift of troublesome Pandora.

Erato (ER-a-to): Muse of lyric poetry.

Erebus (ER-e-bus): The dark underworld, he was born of Chaos.

Eris (ER-is) (see **Strife**)

Eros (ER-os) (Roman *Cupid*): The ancient spirit of rebirth, born of Chaos. Later authors depict him as a son of Aphrodite.

Eteocles (e-TEE-o-kleez): Younger son of Oedipus, killed by his brother Polynices at Thebes.

Eumaeus (u-ME-us): Faithful swineherd of Odysseus.

Europa (u-RO-pa): Daughter of Agenor, she was kidnapped by Zeus in the form of a bull and taken to Crete, where the god abandoned her.

Eurydice (u-RID-i-se): Wife of Orpheus, rescued from Hades then lost by her husband when he turned to look at her before they left the underworld.

Eurynome (u-RI-no-me): Mother of the Graces by Zeus.

Eurystheus (u-RIS-the-us): Cowardly cousin of Hercules and king of Argos. Hercules was forced to complete twelve labors in his service.

Euterpe (u-TER-pe): Muse of flute playing.

Evander (e-VAN-der): Greek king, ally of Aeneas, and father of Pallas, he ruled at the future site of Rome before the city was founded by Romulus and Remus.

Fates: The divine rulers of human destiny, they are usually described as three in number (Clotho, Lachesis, and Atropos), though there are conflicting stories.

Furies (Greek *Erinyes*): Avenging spirits of murder, especially among blood relatives. There are multiple stories of their creation.

Gaia (GE-a) or **Ge** (GE) (see **Earth**)

Ganymede (GAN-i-med): Handsome young man of Trojan royal blood, he was kidnapped by Zeus to be his cupbearer.

Geryon (JER-i-on): Monstrous creature who lived in the far west. Hercules robbed him of his cattle and then slew him.

Glaucus (GLAW-kus): Originally a mortal fisherman, he ate a magical herb and became a sea god who fell in love with the beautiful maiden Scylla.

Golden Bough: The magical branch used by Aeneas to gain entrance to the underworld.

Golden Fleece: The priceless fleece guarded by a dragon in distant Colchis. Stolen by Jason with the help of Medea.

Gorgons (GOR-gonz): Three ferocious, snake-haired creatures (Stheno, Euryale, and Medusa), the first two of which were immortal.

Graces (Greek *Charites*): Usually three in number, they were kindly divinities of various origins.

Graeae (GREE-ee): Ancient gray-haired hags who shared a single eye among them, which was stolen by Perseus.

Hades (HA-deez) (Roman *Pluto* or *Dis*): The name for both Zeus's brother, who served as god of the underworld, and the land of the dead itself.

Harmonia (har-MON-i-a): Daughter of Ares and Aphrodite, and the wife of Cadmus the founder of Thebes.

Harpies (HARP-eez): Foul female monsters with the bodies of birds, best known for ruining the food of Phineus, king of Thrace, and Aeneas on his voyage to Italy.

Hebe (HE-be): Daughter of Zeus and Hera who married Hercules.

Hecate (HEK-a-te): Goddess of the underworld and the dark forces of the universe.

Hector (HEK-tor): Son of Priam and the greatest hero of the Trojans.

Helen (HEL-en): Queen of Sparta who left Menelaus for Paris, causing the Trojan War.

Helenus (HEL-e-nus): Son of Priam and a Trojan seer.

Helios (HEE-li-os) (Latin *Sol*): Son of the Titan Hyperion, he was god of the sun and father of Phaethon.

Hephaestus (he-FE-stus) (Roman *Vulcan*): Crippled god of the forge, usually described as a son of Hera.

Hera (HE-ra) (Roman *Juno*): Daughter of Cronus and Rhea, goddess of marriage and women. She joined with her brother Zeus in an often quarrelsome marriage.

Heracles (HE-ra-kles) (see **Hercules** [HER-ku-leez])

Hercules (HER-ku-leez): Known in Greek as *Herakles* or *Heracles*, the greatest hero of ancient Greece.

Hermes (HER-meez) (Roman *Mercury*): Son of Zeus and Maia, messenger of the gods, and guide for the dead to the underworld.

Hero (HE-ro): Priestess of Aphrodite and secret bride of Leander, she killed herself rather than live without him.

Hesperides (hes-PER-i-deez): The nymphs who guarded the tree that grew gold apples, fetched by Hercules as one of his labors.

Hestia (HE-sti-a) (Roman *Vesta*): Daughter of Cronus and Rhea, she was the goddess of the hearth.

Hippolyte (hip-POL-i-te): Amazon queen who was killed by Hercules for her belt as part of his ninth labor.

Hippolytus (hip-POL-i-tus): Son of Theseus and the Amazon queen, Antiope. He died after refusing the advances of his father's wife, Phaedra.

Horatii (ho-RA-ti-i): Triplet brothers who fought as champions for Rome against three brothers from the town of Alba Longa. The last surviving Horatii brother killed the three enemy champions.

Horatius (ho-RA-ti-us): Called *Cocles* or "one-eyed," he held back the entire invading army of the Etruscan king, Lars Porsenna, on a bridge across the Tiber to protect Rome.

Hyacinth (HI-a-sinth): A prince of Sparta who was killed accidentally by Apollo, who then transformed him into a flower.

Hylas (HI-las): Friend of Hercules who accompanied the hero on the voyage of the Argonauts until he was lured into a spring by a nymph.

Hyperion (hi-PER-i-on): Son of Earth and Sky, he was the father of Eos, Helios, and Selene.

Hypermnestra (hi-perm-NES-tra): Daughter of Danaus who refused her father's orders to kill her new husband Lynceus.

Icarus (I-ka-rus): Son of Daedalus who died when he flew too close to the sun.

Inachus (IN-a-kus): River god in Argos, father of Io.

Ino (I-no): Daughter of Cadmus, sister of Semele. She became a minor sea goddess.

Io (I-o): Unfortunate lover of Zeus who was turned into a cow by the god. Long tormented by Hera.

Ion (I-on): Son of Creusa and Apollo. He became a priest at Delphi.

Iphicles (IF-i-kleez): Mortal brother of Hercules.

Iphigenia (if-i-je-NI-a): Daughter of Agamemnon and Clytemnestra, she was sacrificed at Aulis to gain a favorable wind for the Greek fleet sailing to Troy.

Iris (I-ris): Goddess of the rainbow and divine messenger.

Ismene (is-ME-ne): Daughter of Oedipus and sister of Antigone.

Iulus (U-lus): Also known as Ascanius, he was the son of Aeneas and his first wife, Creusa.

Ixion (iks-I-on): King of Thessaly who angered Zeus and was then chained to a fiery wheel that revolves in the sky.

Jason (JA-son): Leader of the Argonauts who retrieved the Golden Fleece with the help of Medea.

Jocasta (jo-KAS-ta): Mother and wife of Oedipus.

Juno (JU-no) (see **Hera** [HE-ra])

Jupiter (JU-pi-ter) (see **Zeus** [ZUS])

Lachesis (LA-ke-sis): One of the three Fates, she measured out the thread of life.

Laius (LI-us): Father of Oedipus who was murdered by his son.

Laocoon (la-OK-o-on): Trojan priest of Apollo who told his countrymen to beware of Greeks bearing gifts. He was killed by a sea monster sent by Poseidon.

Laomedon (la-O-me-don): King of Troy who cheated Apollo and Poseidon after they labored for him for a year.

Lapiths (LA-piths): A tribe in northern Thessaly who battled the centaurs at the wedding of their king, Peirithous.

Lars Porsenna (LARZ por-SEN-na): Etruscan king and enemy of Rome.

Latinus (LA-tin-us): Elderly Italian king who at first welcomed Aeneas to his shores, then withdrew his support when war began.

Lavinia (la-VIN-i-a): Daughter of Latinus and second wife of Aeneas.

Leander (le-AN-der): Secret husband of Hero who swam the straits of the Hellespont each night to be with her.

Leda (LE-da): Mother of Helen, Clytemnestra, Castor, and Pollox.

Leto (LE-to): Daughter of the Titans Coeus and Phoebe, and the mother of Apollo and Artemis.

Lucretia (lu-KRE-shi-a): Roman wife who killed herself after her husband's best friend forced himself on her.

Maia (MI-a): Daughter of Atlas and mother of Hermes by Zeus.

Mars (MARZ) (see **Ares** [AR-eez])

Marsyas (MAR-si-as): Foolish satyr who challenged Apollo to a flute contest and was killed by the god when he lost.

Medea (me-DEE-a): Daughter of Aeetes of Colchis, she sacrificed everything to help Jason retrieve the Golden Fleece and later murdered her children when Jason abandoned her.

Medusa (me-DU-sa): Once a beautiful maiden, she became a hideous Gorgon and was killed by Perseus. He used her head to turn his enemies to stone.

Megara (ME-ga-ra): First wife of Hercules, murdered by the hero in a fit of madness.

Melampus (me-LAM-pus): Greek seer who could understand the language of animals.

Meleager (me-le-A-jer): Greek hero who sailed with the Argonauts. The Fates told his mother he would live only as long as a certain log was not burned, but in anger she threw it on the fire.

Melpomene (mel-PO-me-ne): Muse of tragedy.

Menelaus (me-ne-LA-us): Son of Atreus, brother of Agamemnon, and husband of Helen before Paris took her to Troy.

Metis (ME-tis): Daughter of Ocean and Tethys, she helped Zeus overthrow Cronus. Zeus then married her, but swallowed her whole when she became pregnant. Their daughter Athena later burst from his forehead.

Mezentius (me-ZEN-ti-us): Cruel Etruscan king who fought against Aeneas.

Midas (MI-das): King in Phrygia who was granted the power to turn anything he touched into gold. In a separate event, Apollo gave him the ears of an ass.

Minerva (mi-NER-va) (see **Athena** [a-THEE-na])

Minos (MI-nos): Son of Europa and king of Crete, he ordered Daedalus to build the Labyrinth to house the Minotaur.

Minotaur (MI-no-tawr): Deadly half-human, half-bull offspring of Pasiphae and a bull.

Mnemosyne (mne-MO-si-ne): Wife of Zeus and mother of the Muses.

Muses (MUZ-ez): Goddesses who inspired poets, artists, and scholars. Includes Calliope, Clio, Erato, Euterpe, Melpomene, Polyhymnia, Terpsichore, Thalia, and Urania.

Narcissus (nar-SIS-us): Beautiful son of a nymph and river god. He fell in love with his own reflection in a pool and starved to death.

Nausicaa (naw-SIK-a-a): Daughter of King Alcinous and Queen Arete of Phaeacia, she helped Odysseus when he washed ashore on their island.

Nemesis (NE-me-sis): Goddess of revenge.

Neptune (NEP-tun) (see **Poseidon** [po-SI-don])

Nereus (NE-re-us): Sea god and father of fifty nymph daughters, the Nereids. He revealed the location of the golden apples to Hercules.

Nessus (NES-sus): Centaur driven from Arcadia by Hercules. He tricked Hercules's wife, Deianara, into giving her husband a cloak soaked in his poisonous blood.

Nestor (NES-tor): Aged king of Pylos who advised Agamemnon during the Trojan War.

Night (Greek *Nyx*): Born from primordial Chaos, she was the symbol of darkness and the mother of many children.

Niobe (NI-o-be): Proud and foolish mother of many sons and daughters. All were slain by Apollo and Artemis when she insulted their mother, Leto.

Numitor (NU-mi-tor): Grandfather of Romulus and Remus.

Nymphs (NIMFS): Minor female divinities of various origins and types, such as Dryads (tree nymphs) and Oceanids (daughters of Ocean)

Ocean: Son of Earth and Sky, he was the great river of boundless water that encircled the world.

Odysseus (o-DIS-se-us) (Roman *Ulysses*): Clever Greek warrior from Ithaca, husband to Penelope, and father of Telemachus. He spent ten years fighting at Troy and an equal time trying to make his way home.

Oedipus (ED-i-pus): Son of King Laius of Thebes and Jocasta. He unknowingly killed his father and married his own mother before discovering the truth and blinding himself.

Olympia (o-LIM-pi-a): Town in western Peloponnesus where the Olympic games were founded by Hercules.

Olympus (o-LIM-pus), **Mount**: Home of the gods, this series of peaks between Thessaly and Macedonia reaches almost ten thousand feet in height.

Orestes (or-ES-teez): Son of Agamemnon and Clytemnestra, he avenged his father's death by killing his mother.

Orion (o-RI-on): A giant hunter. Artemis killed Orion with a scorpion sting, then placed him in the heavens as a constellation.

Orpheus (OR-fe-us): Son of the Muse Calliope, he was the greatest bard in ancient Greece.

Orthus (OR-thus): Ferocious hound born from Typhon and Echidna.

Pallas (PAL-las): (1) Brother of Aegeus and the father of fifty sons; (2) Son of King Evander who was killed by Turnus and avenged by Aeneas.

Pan (PAN) (Roman *Faunus*): Shepherd god fathered by Hermes.

Pandora (pan-DOR-a): The first mortal woman, created as a beautiful punishment for men by Zeus.

Paris (PA-ris): Son of King Priam of Troy, he took Helen from her husband Menelaus and caused the Trojan War.

Pasiphae (pa-SI-fa-e): Wife of Minos who mated with a bull to produce the Minotaur.

Patroclus (pa-TRO-klus): Best friend of Achilles, he was killed by Hector at Troy.

Pegasus (PE-ga-sus): Winged horse sprung from the body of Medusa.

Peirithous (pe-RI-tho-us): King of the Lapiths, he was trapped in Hades forever when he attempted to take Penelope from the underworld.

Peleus (PE-le-us): Father of Achilles by the goddess Thetis, he accompanied Jason on the *Argo*.

Pelias (PE-li-as): Uncle of Jason who sent him on the search for the Golden Fleece.

Pelops (PE-lops): Son of Tantalus and father of Atreus, he was restored to life after he was cut up by his father and served to the gods.

Penelope (pe-NE-lo-pe): Wife of Odysseus and mother of Telemachus, she endured twenty years without her husband in Ithaca.

Pentheus (PEN-the-us): Grandson of Cadmus and son of Agave, he was lured to his death by Dionysus when he refused to worship the new god.

Persephone (per-SE-fo-ne): Daughter of Zeus and Demeter, she was kidnapped and taken to the underworld by Hades, but later released for part of each year

Perseus (PER-se-us): Son of Zeus and Danae, he beheaded Medusa, turned Atlas into a mountain, and rescued Andromeda from a sea monster.

Phaethon (FA-e-thon): Child of Helios and Clymene, he drove his father's chariot recklessly through the heavens and was destroyed by Zeus.

Philemon (fi-LE-mon): Elderly husband of Baucis who entertained Zeus and Hermes and was rewarded for his kindness.

Philoctetes (fi-lok-TE-teez): Set fire to the pyre of Hercules at his request and was rewarded with the hero's bow and arrows. He later joined the Greek expedition to Troy but was abandoned on the island of Lemnos because of his horrid stench.

Philomela (fil-o-ME-la): Sister of Procne who had her tongue cut out by her brother-in-law, Tereus.

Phineus (FIN-e-us): Thracian seer who was besieged by Harpies until rescued by the Argonauts.

Phoebe (FE-be): Daughter of Earth and Sky, she became the mother of Leto and Asteria by her brother Coeus.

Phoenix (FE-niks): Tutor of Achilles.

Pleiades (PLI-a-deez): Seven daughters of Atlas and Pleione.

Pluto (PLU-to) (see **Hades** [HA-deez])

Pollux (POL-uks) or **Polydeuces** (pol-i-DU-seez): Brother of Castor and Helen, he sailed with Jason on the *Argo*.

Polydectes (pol-i-DEK-teez): King of the island of Seriphus who sent Perseus to fetch Medusa's head.

Polyhymnia (pol-i-HIM-ni-a): Muse of hymns and pantomime.

Polynices (pol-i-NI-seez): Son of Oedipus, he was killed by his brother, Eteocles, when he attacked Thebes.

Polyphemus (pol-i-FE-mus): Cyclops blinded by Odysseus.

Pomona (po-MO-na): Roman goddess of fruit and orchards, she resisted the love of Vertumnus.

Poseidon (po-SI-don) (Roman *Neptune*): God of the seas, son of Cronus and Rhea, brother of Zeus and Hades.

Priam (PRI-am): Father of Paris and Hector, aged king of Troy during the war against the Greeks.

Priapus (pri-A-pus): Son of Aphrodite, a god of fertility.

Procne (PROK-ne): Sister of Philomela and wife of Tereus, she killed her son and served him to her husband when she discovered his treatment of her sister.

Procris (PROK-ris): Wife of Cephalus who tricked her husband in a test of marital faithfulness, just as he had tricked her.

Prometheus (pro-ME-the-us): Creator and patron of men, he stole fire from heaven for men, was chained to a distant mountain by Zeus as punishment, and had his liver eaten daily by an eagle.

Proteus (PRO-te-us): Shape-changing god of the sea.

Psyche (SI-ke): Bride of Cupid who could not resist the urge to see who her husband really was.

Pygmalion (pig-MA-li-on): King of Cyprus who carved a perfect woman out of ivory. She was brought to life by Aphrodite.

Pyramus (PI-ra-mus): Young man who loved the maiden Thisbe and killed himself when he believed her dead in a lion attack.

Pyrrha (PIR-ra): Wife of Deucalion and only female survivor of the great flood sent by Zeus.

Pythia (PI-thi-a): Name given to the priestess of Apollo at Delphi.

Python (PI-thon): Enormous guardian serpent at Delphi killed by Apollo.

Remus (RE-mus): Brother of Romulus and cofounder of Rome.

Rhea (RE-a): Daughter of Earth and Sky, mother and wife of Cronus, mother of Zeus and other gods.

Rhea Silvia (RE-a SIL-vi-a): Daughter of Numitor and a Vestal Virgin, she became pregnant by Mars and gave birth to the twins Romulus and Remus.

Romulus (ROM-u-lus): Cofounder of Rome with his brother Remus.

Sabine (SA-bin) **women**: Daughters of nearby Sabine villages kidnapped to be husbands for the single men of Rome.

Salmoneus (sal-MON-e-us): Arrogant king who pretended he was Zeus and was destroyed by the god.

Sarpedon (sar-PE-don): Poseidon's son, killed by Hercules.

Saturn (SA-turn) (see **Cronus** [KRO-nus])

Satyr (SA-tir): A half-man, half-goat creature.

Scaevola (SI-vo-la): Gaius Mucius Scaevola, a Roman warrior who proved his bravery to the Etruscan king, Lars Porsenna, by thrusting his hand into a fire.

Scylla (SI-la): Once a beautiful maiden. Circe turned her into a six-headed monster opposite the great whirlpool Charybdis.

Sea (Greek *Tethys*): Child of Earth and Sky who married her brother Ocean.

Selene (se-LE-ne) (Roman *Luna*): The moon. Daughter of Hyperion and sister to Helios and Eos.

Semele (SEM-e-le): Daughter of Cadmus who asked to see Zeus in all his glory. She died, but Zeus rescued their son, Dionysus, from her womb.

Sibyl (SI-bil): Beloved by Apollo, she tricked the god into giving her long life but forgot to ask for eternal youth. She was the oracle who led Aeneas to the underworld at Cumae in Italy.

Sinon (SI-non): Greek left behind on the Trojan beach to tell the Trojans the lie of the Trojan Horse.

Sirens (SI-renz): Women with wings of birds who lured sailors to their death with their beautiful singing.

Sisyphus (SI-si-fus): King of Corinth who was punished in Hades by forever rolling a boulder up a hill, only to have it roll back down once he reached the top.

Sky (Greek *Ouranos*, Latin *Uranus*): Child and husband of Earth, father of many children, including Cronus.

Solymi (SO-li-mi): A fierce people who were always at war with the Lycians on their borders.

Sphinx (SFINKS): Daughter of Echidna, a monster with a human head, lion's body, and eagle's wings, she killed herself after Oedipus solved her riddle at Thebes.

Sthenelus (STHEN-e-lus): Son of Perseus and father to Eurystheus, he took the throne of Argos when Amphitryon murdered Electryon.

Strife (Greek *Eris*): Goddess of discord, a child of Night, created at the beginning of the world.

Styx (STIKS): Chief river of Hades on which the gods swore unbreakable oaths.

Syrinx (SI-rinks): A nymph transformed into a flower to avoid the amorous advances of Pan.

Talus (TA-lus): Bronze giant who guarded Crete until disabled by Medea.

Tantalus (TAN-ta-lus): Lydian king and father of Pelops who served his son as a dish in a banquet for the gods.

Tarpeia (tar-PE-a): Vestal Virgin who betrayed Rome and was crushed to death by Sabine shields.

Tartarus (TAR-tar-us): God and the dark region sprung from Chaos, located far beneath Hades. It was the prison of the defeated Titans.

Telemachus (te-LE-ma-kus): Son of Odysseus and Penelope.

Tereus (TER-e-us): Evil Thracian king who married Procne, then cut the tongue from her sister, Philomela.

Terpsichore (terp-SIK-o-re): Muse of lyric poetry and dancing.

Tethys (TE-this) (see **Sea**)

Thalia (THA-li-a): Muse of Comedy.

Theia (THE-a): Daughter of Earth and Sky, mother of Eos, Helios, and Selene.

Themis (THE-mis): Daughter of Earth and Sky, onetime goddess at Delphi, she was associated with order and justice.

Theophrane (the-o-FRA-ne): Maiden turned into a ewe by Poseidon, she gave birth to the ram with the Golden Fleece.

Theseus (THE-se-us): Son of Aegeus, king of Athens, and the maiden Aethra of Troezen, he had many adventures and defeated the Minotaur in Crete.

Thetis (THE-tis): Sea goddess who gave birth to Achilles by her mortal husband, Peleus.

Thisbe (THIZ-be): Beloved by Pyramus, she killed herself after finding him dead.

Thyestes (thi-ES-teez): Son of Pelops and brother of Atreus.

Tiber (TI-ber): God and river that flows through Rome.

Tiresias (ti-RE-si-as): A great seer of Thebes, sought out by Oedipus and Creon in life, then by Odysseus in the underworld.

Titans (TI-tanz): Name given to the first generation of gods defeated by Zeus and his allies.

Tithonus (ti-THO-nus): Handsome prince taken by Eos to her palace as a lover until she turned him into a cicada.

Tityus (TI-ti-us): Giant who attempted to force himself on Leto. He was punished in Hades by being staked to the ground and having his liver eternally eaten by vultures.

Triton (TRI-ton): Sea god and namesake of Lake Triton in north Africa.

Turnus (TUR-nus): Italian foe of Aeneas and rival for the hand of Lavinia.

Tyndareus (tin-DAR-e-us): King of Sparta and husband of Leda.

Typhon (TI-fon): Powerful monster sprung from Earth and Tartarus, he challenged Zeus and was beaten after the war with the Titans.

Ulysses (u-LIS-seez) (see **Odysseus** [o-DIS-se-us])

Urania (u-RA-ni-a): Muse of astronomy.

Venus (VE-nus) (see **Aphrodite** [af-ro-DI-te])

Vertumnus (ver-TUM-nus): Roman fertility god who wooed and won the goddess Pomona.

Vesta (VES-ta) (see **Hestia** [HE-sti-a])

Vestal (VES-tal) **Virgins**: Roman maidens sworn to virginity who served the hearth goddess Vesta.

Vulcan (VUL-kan) (see **Hephaestus** [he-FE-stus])

Zephyrus (ZE-fir-us) or **Zephyr** (ZE-fir): God of the west wind, said to have caused the death of Hyacinth.

Zetes (ZE-teez): Argonaut and winged son of the north wind.

Zeus (ZUS) (Latin *Jupiter* or *Jove*): Son of Cronus and Rhea, brother of Poseidon and Hades, and husband of Hera. He was the most powerful of the gods.

Glossary

ambrosia: The food of the gods.

ancestor: A forefather. A person from whom a person is descended.

aqueduct: A structure for carrying water.

armada: A fleet of ships.

bard: A poet and singer of ancient tales.

citadel: A fort on high ground, often overlooking a city.

comrade: Friend, ally.

constellation: A group of stars.

cult: Religious worship of one particular god or goddess. Each had his or her own cult.

cupbearer: A person who serves wine to the gods.

democratic: A government ruled by the people instead of a king or another ruler.

descendant: A person who is the offspring of a certain ancestor.

destiny: The unchanging events that will happen to a person in the future. Fate.

divine: Sacred. Of or from the gods.

eternity: Forever, to the end of days.

fate: Destiny.

forge: To make or shape a metal object by heating it in an oven.

fortress: A heavily protected building or town. A fort.

funeral pyre: A wooden tower used to burn dead bodies.

heir: A person legally entitled to the property or rank of another person upon his or her death.

herald: A messenger.

hospitality: Friendly and generous entertaining of guests.

immortal: Living forever, never dying.

mortal: A human being, capable of death.

nectar: The drink of the gods.

oracle: A priest or priestess who gave advice from the gods. The place where such advice was given. Or a piece of advice from an oracle.

Palladium: A small, sacred wooden statue of Athena.

patron, patroness: A person, or god, who provides support.

prophecy: A prediction about the future from a prophet or prophetess.

prophet, prophetess: A person who was able to share the words of the gods.

purify: To cleanse someone, especially after they committed a crime.

rite: A religious act. Different gods and goddesses received different rites.

sacrifice: An offering to the gods. These included food, animals, and sometimes humans.

seer: A person who can see the future.

shade: A ghost or spirit.

sire: To father someone.

soothsayer: A person who can see the future.

suitor: A man who wants to marry a particular woman.

trident: A three-pronged spear.

typhoon: An ocean storm.

virgin: A person who has never been with a member of the opposite sex.

Genealogies

THE FIRST GENERATIONS OF GODS

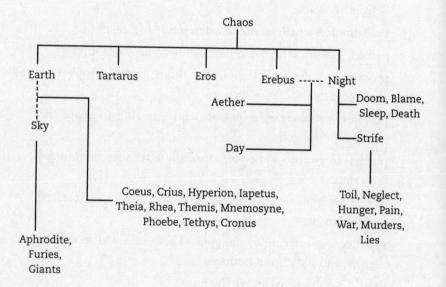

THE CHILDREN OF CRONUS AND RHEA

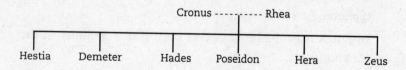

THE DESCENDANTS OF IO

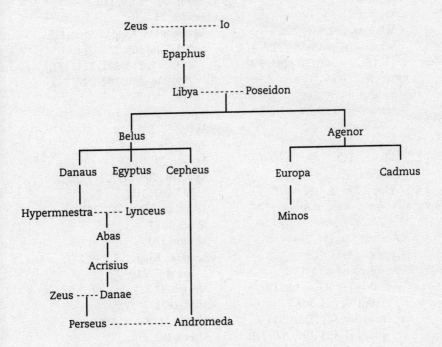

Index

Abdera, town of, 152
Abderus, 152
Abydos, 183
Achates, 275
Achelous, 162
Achilles, 107, 119, 181, 207–215, 218–227, 263, 276, 283, 309
Acoetes, 55–56
Acrisius, 84, 90, 309
Acropolis, 30, 47, 78, 97, 100, 242, 309
Actaeon, 71–72
Admete, 152
Admetus, King, 149–150
Adonis, 75–76, 309
Adrastus, King of Argos, 172–173, 175, 309
Adriatic Sea, 156, 284
Aeacus, 24–25, 309
Aeaea, island of, 195
Aeetes, King of Colchis, 179, 190–197, 201, 309
Aegean Sea, 51, 55, 102, 134, 152, 182, 183, 199, 209, 210, 233, 281
Aegeus, King of Athens, 90–91, 93–94, 96, 97, 309
Aegina, 24–25, 309
Aegisthus, 236–240, 309
Aeneas, 74, 216–217, 223, 229, 274–296, 305, 309
Aeolus, 121, 256, 257, 274–275, 310
Aerope, 234

Aeson, 180, 199
Aethalides, 182
Aethra, 91, 98, 99, 310
Aetolia, 26
Agamemnon, King of Mycenae, 205, 206, 209, 210–211, 213–215, 218–221, 223, 227, 229, 236–239, 242, 246, 263, 310
Agapenor, 209
Agave, 58, 165, 310
Agdistis, 82
Agenor, 20
Ajax, 181, 209, 215, 218, 226, 227, 263, 310
Alba Longa, 296, 300–301
Alcaeus, 137
Alcestis, 150
Alcinous, King, 197, 248–251, 266–267, 310
Alcippe, 47
Alcmene, 137–139, 310
Alcyone, 119–121, 310
Alecto, 292, 310
Alpheus, 130–132, 310
Alpheus River, 147–148, 310
Alps, 154, 195, 290
Althaea, 82
Amata, Queen, 291–292
Amazons, 97–98, 104, 152, 190, 226, 310
Amphiaraus, 173
Amphion, 23–24, 310
Amphion of Thebes, 37

Amphitrite, 30, 197, 310
Amphitryon, 137–140, 310
Amulius, 296–298, 310
Amycus, King, 184
Anaxarete, 133–134
Ancaeus, 190
Anchises, 73–74, 274, 278–282, 285–286, 288–290, 295, 310
Ancus Marcius, 301
Andromache, 217, 229, 283, 284, 310
Andromeda, 88–90, 137, 310
Anna, 286, 287
Antaeus, 153, 310
Anticlea, 262
Antigone, 172–174, 176–177, 311
Antinous, 244
Antiope, 22–24, 98, 311
Antiphates, King, 257
Aphrodite (Venus), 5, 10, 46, 47, 51, 58–60, 62–64, 73–76, 96, 108, 124, 165, 188, 191, 204, 205, 216, 221, 250, 274–279, 311
Apollo, 8, 15, 31, 32, 35–45, 48, 49, 71, 77, 91, 119, 135, 150, 155, 160–161, 173, 186, 189, 213, 217, 222, 226, 239, 240, 242, 281, 311
Apsyrtus, 193, 194
Arachne, 78–79, 311
Arcadia, 20, 39, 40, 47, 48, 50, 72, 108, 109, 146, 148, 162, 209
Arcas, 21, 22
Ardea, town of, 304
Areopagus "Hill of Ares," 47, 242
Ares, 8, 31, 46–47, 51, 109, 165, 174, 179, 190, 193, 216, 226, 233, 250, 297, 311
Arete, Queen, 197, 249–250,

(continued) 266–267, 311
Arethusa, 130–132, 311
Argive plain, 90
Argo (ship), 27, 181–185, 188–191, 193–195, 197–201, 203, 219
Argonauts, 31, 47, 107, 135, 182–192, 194–199, 282, 311
Argos, 29, 84, 90, 102, 107, 137, 138, 143, 152, 172, 173, 209, 237
Argos (dog), 270, 311
Argus, 17, 181, 311
Ariadne, 96, 97, 99, 311
Arion, 30, 175, 311
Arruns, 294
Artemis, 8, 20, 21, 26, 36, 37, 44–45, 71–72, 80, 107, 130, 131, 145–146, 210–211, 234, 235, 294, 311
Ascanius (see Iulus)
Asclepius, 15, 311
Asia Minor, 209
Asopus, 24, 311
Assyria, 75, 190
Asteria, 76
Asterion, 29
Astyanax, 217, 229, 283, 284
Atalanta, 82, 107–109, 181, 311
Athamas, King of Orchomenus, 178, 179
Athena, 8, 10, 25, 29–30, 32, 38, 47, 77–78, 85, 86, 90, 103, 127, 139, 142, 159, 165, 175, 181, 191, 204, 205, 214, 216, 225, 228, 229, 240, 242, 244–246, 249, 267–269, 279, 311
Athens, 29–30, 44, 47, 69, 78, 90–94, 96–100, 102, 109, 164, 173, 209, 240, 242

Atlantic Ocean, 153

Atlas, 7, 25, 26, 30, 47, 86, 88, 157, 250, 311

Atreus, 234–236, 312

Atropos, 81, 312

Attica, 97, 99

Attis, 83

Augeas, 147, 148, 161, 312

Augustus, 290

Aulis, 206, 209–211, 237

Autolycus, 44

Autonoe, 165

Aventine hill, 298

Babylon, 117–118

Bacchae, 56, 57

Bacchus (see Dionysus)

Baucis, 128–130, 312

Bear Mountain, 183, 184

Bebryces, 186

Bellerophon, 102–104, 312

Bias, 104–107

Black Sea, 97, 152, 179, 183, 184, 186–189

Boeotia, 207

Boreas, 181

Bosporus straits, 186–188, 195

Briareus, 29, 312

Brutus, 290, 305, 312

Burphagus, 72

Busiris, King, 157

Cacus, 154–155, 312

Cadmus, King of Thebes, 20, 22, 53, 58, 66, 71, 164–165, 178, 186, 192, 312

Calais, 181, 185, 187, 312

Calchas, 209–211, 213, 227, 312

Calliope, 75, 80, 81, 135, 312

Callisto, 20–22, 26, 65, 71, 312

Calydonian boar, 82, 107, 219, 312

Calypso, 246, 247, 250, 266, 312

Camilla, 294

Camillus, 290

Capaneus, 173, 175

Caria, 134

Carthage, 275–277, 286

Cassandra, 42, 205, 229, 237, 238, 277, 282, 312

Cassiopeia, Queen, 88–90, 312

Castor, 27, 99, 139, 181, 186, 192, 205, 263, 313

Caucasus Mountains, 17, 157, 179, 191

Cecrops, 29–30, 313

Celaeno, 282–283, 291

Celeus, King, 69

Celts, land of the, 195

Centaurs, 146, 148, 162, 180, 208, 313

Cephalus, 79–80, 313

Cepheus, King of Ethiopia, 89, 90, 313

Cephisus, 29

Cerberus, 33, 64, 76, 135, 158, 159, 313

Cercopes, the, 161

Ceyx, King of Trachis, 119–121, 313

Chaos, 3, 59, 313

Charon, 33, 64, 135, 136, 289, 313

Charybdis, 197, 265, 284, 313

Chimaera, 103, 313

Chione, 44–45, 313

Chiron, 180, 208, 313

Chryses, 213

Cicones, 251

Cinyras, King of Assyria, 75

Circe, 122, 195–196, 258–260, 264, 266, 313

Clashing Rocks, 187–189

Cleopatra, 219

Clio, 81, 313

Cloelia, 303–304, 313

Clotho, 81, 313

Clymene, 52

Clytemnestra, 27, 211, 214, 237–240, 242, 263, 313

Clytie, 51, 52

Cocalus, King of Sicily, 101

Coeus, 35, 313

Colchis, kingdom of, 179, 181, 183, 187, 189–191

Collatinus, 304–305

Colonus, 173, 174

Copreus, 144, 146, 149, 153

Corinth, 29, 102, 166, 170, 171, 199, 200

Corinthian Gulf, 24

Cottus, 6–7, 313

Creon, King of Corinth, 200

Creon, King of Thebes, 137, 140, 141, 166, 168–170, 172, 174–177, 314

Crete, 5, 6, 20, 69, 80, 94, 96, 97, 100–101, 149, 198, 271, 281, 282

Cretheus, 179, 180

Creusa, 43–44, 278–280, 314

Crommyonian sow, 92

Cronus, 3–8, 66, 77, 291, 314

Cumae, 284, 288

Cupid, 39–40, 47, 59–64, 191, 192, 277, 286, 314

Curiatii triplets, 300–301

Cybele, 56, 82–83, 314

Cyclopes, the, 3, 6, 7, 150, 253–256, 285, 314

Cycnus, 212

Cyparissus, 43, 314

Cyprus, island of, 5, 73, 74

Cyzicus, King, 183–184

Daedalus, 95–96, 99–101, 314

Danae, 84–85, 89, 90, 314

Danaus, 126–128

Danube River, 195

Daphne, 39–41, 314

Dardanus, 26, 281, 293, 314

Death, 33, 150–151, 289

Deianira, 162, 163, 181, 314

Deimos (Fear), 47, 98, 289

Deiphobus, 204, 225, 227, 230

Delos, island of, 36, 37, 281

Delphi, oracle at, 16, 37, 43–44, 90, 119, 143, 147, 160, 164, 166–170, 172, 173, 178, 235, 236

Delphi, valley of, 7, 12, 36

Delphinus, 30

Demeter, 5, 8, 18, 30, 66–67, 69–71, 76, 159, 175, 232, 314

Demodocus, 250

Despoina, 30

Deucalion, 12–13, 178, 314

Dexamenus, King, 148

Diana (see Artemis)

Dictys, 85, 89

Dido, Queen of Carthage, 275–277, 286–288, 289, 314

Diomedes, King of Argos, 209, 215–217, 220, 228, 315

Diomedes, King of Thrace, 149

Dionysus, 46, 53–59, 102, 107, 112, 136, 315

Dirce, 23, 24

Disease, 289

Dodona, oracle at, 16

Doliones people, 183–184
Dryope, 50

Earth, 3–6, 8, 13, 153, 240, 315
Earthmen, the, 183
Echidna, 144, 167, 315
Echo, 114–115, 117, 130, 315
Egypt, 127, 157
Egyptus, 126–127
Eileithyia, 8, 36, 138, 315
Eioneus, 15
Electra (daughter of Agamemnon), 237–239, 315
Electra (daughter of Atlas), 25–26, 315
Electryon, 137
Eleusis, town of, 69–70, 159
Elis, kingdom of, 134
Elpenor, 260, 261, 264
Elysium, fields of, 34, 289
Endymion, King of Elis, 134, 315
Enipeus, 179
Eos, 72, 79–80, 315
Epaphus, 18
Epeius, 228
Ephialtes, 31
Epidaurus, 92
Epimetheus, 11, 315
Er, 34, 35
Erato, 80, 315
Erebus, 3, 315
Erginus, King of the Minyans, 140–141
Erineus, village of, 93
Eriphyle, 173
Eris (see Strife)
Eros, 3, 59, 315
Erysichthon, 67
Eteocles, 172, 174–176, 315
Ethiopia, 88, 89

Etruscans, 154, 195, 293, 300–304
Eumaeus, 268–270, 315
Europa, 18–20, 94, 149, 164, 198, 221, 315
Europe, 20
Eurotas River, 245
Euryalus, 293
Euryclea, 271
Eurydice, 135–136, 315
Eurylochus, 258
Eurynome, 8, 45, 315
Eurystheus, King of Argos, 139, 141–144, 146–149, 152, 153, 156, 159, 234, 315
Eurytion, 148
Eurytus, King of Oechalia, 139, 160, 162
Euterpe, 81, 316
Evander, King, 292–295, 297, 316
Evanus River, 162

Fabius Maximus, 290
Fates, the, 8, 34, 81–82, 119, 208, 316
Fear (see Deimos)
Field of Mars, 299
Furies, the, 112, 136, 173, 196, 240, 242, 292, 316

Gaia (see Earth)
Galli, the, 83
Ganymede, 27, 203, 316
Garden of the Hesperides, 198
Gaul, 195
Gauls, 290
Gemini constellation, 27
Geryon, 153, 154, 316
Glauce, 200, 201
Glaucus, 121–124, 185, 316

Golden Bough, 288–289, 316

Golden Fleece, 135, 179, 181–183, 187–188, 191–193, 195, 196, 199, 200, 316

Gorgons, the, 15, 17, 30, 44, 85, 86, 316

Graces, the, 8, 10, 221, 316

Graeae, the, 17, 85–86, 316

Great Mother, 56

Hades (god of the underworld), 5, 8, 31–32, 46, 67, 70, 76, 98, 154, 159, 316

Hades (land of the dead), 25, 27, 31–34, 59, 63–64, 66, 117, 128, 135–136, 150, 159, 189, 222, 232, 260–264, 289, 316

Haemon, 176, 177

Hannibal, 290

Happiness, 64

Harmonia, 47, 58, 66, 165, 172, 173, 316

Harpalycus, 139

Harpies, the, 186–187, 282–283, 291, 316

Hebe, 8, 163, 316

Hecate, 67, 76, 122, 289, 316

Hector, 204, 212, 215, 217–218, 220–223, 225–226, 276, 278, 283, 316

Hecuba, 204, 217, 229

Helen, Queen of Sparta, 27, 98, 99, 124, 139, 181, 205–206, 209, 215, 228, 230, 245, 278, 316

Helenus, 227–228, 283–284, 291, 317

Helios, 29, 46, 51–53, 67, 69, 122, 147, 154, 179, 196, 262, 266, 317

Helle, 178–179

Hellespont, 124, 125, 156, 179, 183, 204, 209

Hephaestus (Vulcan), 8, 10, 27, 45–46, 51, 191, 223, 225, 232, 250, 317

Hera (Juno), 5, 8, 15–18, 21–22, 25, 26, 29, 32, 35, 36, 45–47, 54, 56, 65–66, 77, 84, 114, 120, 126, 138, 139, 141, 152, 156, 163, 174, 180, 191, 197, 200, 204, 205, 214, 221–222, 274, 276, 279, 286, 292, 294, 317

Heracles (see Hercules)

Hercules, 26, 32, 99, 119, 138–164, 181–185, 188, 190, 198, 204, 209, 229, 234, 261, 293, 317

Hermes (Mercury), 11, 17, 27, 33, 43, 44, 47–50, 54, 64, 70, 73, 86, 90, 128, 129, 139, 155, 182, 205, 225, 232, 234, 247, 258, 286, 317

Hermione, 206

Hero, 124–126, 183, 317

Hesione, 161

Hesperides, the, 156, 157, 159, 317

Hestia, 5, 77, 296, 317

Hippodamia, 85, 233–234

Hippolyte, 152, 153, 317

Hippolytus, 98, 317

Hippomedon, 173, 175

Hope, 11

Horatii brothers, 300–301, 317

Horatius Cocles, 302, 317

Hunger, 289

Hyacinth, 42–43, 81, 317

Hydra, the, 144–145, 146

Hylaeus, 107

Hylas, 184–185, 317

Hyperion, 51, 79, 317

Hypermnestra, 127–128, 317

Hypsipyle, 182

Iasion, 26, 67

Iasus, 107–109

Iberian peninsula, 154

Icarus, 100, 101, 317

Idas, 42

Idmon, 181, 189–190

Idomeneus, King of Crete, 209

Illyria, 165

Inachus, 29, 318

Ino, 54, 165, 178, 248, 318

Io, 15–18, 65, 84, 126, 318

Iobates, King of Lycia, 102–104

Iolaus, 144, 145

Iolcus, 180, 182, 199

Iole, 160, 162, 163

Ion, 43–44, 318

Ionian Sea, 17

Ionian tribe, 44

Iphicles, 138, 139, 318

Iphiclus, 106

Iphigenia, 211, 237, 238, 318

Iphimedia, 31

Iphis, 133

Iphitus, 160

Iris, 36, 70, 318

Isis, 18

Ismene, 172–174, 176, 318

Isthmus of Corinth, 233

Ithaca, island of, 206, 207, 242, 244, 247–248, 250, 257, 260, 262, 267, 268, 283

Itys, 110, 112

Iulus, 276, 277, 279, 280, 284, 286, 290, 296, 318

Ixion, King of Thessaly, 15, 318

Jason, 27, 31, 47, 107, 180–184, 186, 188–202, 208, 219, 318

Jocasta, Queen, 166, 168, 170–172, 263, 318

Jove (see Zeus)

Julius Caesar, 290

Juno (see Hera)

Jupiter (see Zeus)

Labdacus, 165

Labyrinth, the, 96–97

Lacedaemon, 26

Lachesis, 81, 318

Ladon, 156

Laertes, 219, 220, 242, 247, 251, 263

Laestrygonians, 257

Laius, King of Thebes, 165–167, 169, 171, 318

Lake Tritonis, 198

Laocoon, 229, 277, 318

Laomedon, King of Troy, 32, 161, 318

Lapiths, 98, 318, 327

Larentia, 297

Larissa, town of, 90

Lars Porsenna, 301–304, 318

Latinus, King, 291–292, 318

Lavinia, 291, 295, 296, 318

Lavinium, 296

Leander, 124–126, 183, 318

Leda, 26–27, 205, 263, 318

Lemnos, island of, 46, 182, 211, 227

Lethe River, 35

Leto, 8, 35–38, 49, 65, 71, 221, 318

Leucothoe, 51–52

Libya, 127
Liguria, land of, 154, 195
Lindos, island of, 157
Linus, 140
Liriope, 114
Little Ajax, 209, 229
Lotus Eaters, 252
Lucifer, 119
Lucretia, 304–305, 319
Lycaon, 11–12
Lycia, 36, 104
Lycians, 104
Lycomedes, 99
Lycus, King, 23, 189
Lydia, 38, 232, 233
Lygurgus, King of Thrace, 57
Lynceus, 127–128

Maia, 47, 49, 319
Marathon, battle of, 99
Marathon, plain of, 149
Mariandynians, land of the, 189
Marpessa, 42
Mars (see Ares)
Marsyas, 38–39, 319
Medea, 93–94, 191–201, 319
Mediterranean Sea, 153, 195, 197
Medus, 93–94
Medusa, 30, 85–87, 89, 90, 319
Megapenthes, 90
Megara, 141, 142, 160, 209, 319
Melampus, 104–107, 319
Melanion, 108–109
Melanippus, 175
Meleager, 82, 107, 181, 219, 319
Melpomene, 81, 319
Memnon, King of the Ethiopians, 226

Menelaus, King of Sparta, 205–207, 209, 215–216, 222–223, 227, 228, 230, 236, 244–246, 319
Menetheus, 209
Menoeceus, 165, 175
Mentes, 244
Mentor, 245
Mercury (see Hermes)
Merope, 166, 171
Metharme, 75
Metis, 6, 8, 77, 319
Mezentius, 293, 294, 319
Midas, King of Phrygia, 38, 39, 56–57, 319
Milky Way, 139
Minerva (see Athena)
Minos, King of Crete, 80, 94–96, 99–102, 149, 152, 319
Minotaur, the, 94–97, 149, 319
Minyans, the, 140–141
Minyas, King of Greece, 57
Mnemosyne, 81, 319
Morpheus, 120
Mount Atlas, 88
Mount Cithaeron, 23, 140, 143, 166
Mount Erymanthus, 146
Mount Etna, 285
Mount Helicon, 81
Mount Ida, 27, 73, 204, 227, 280
Mount Olympus, 6–8, 11, 15, 25, 27, 36, 40, 45, 46, 49, 50, 59, 67, 69, 83, 104, 115, 139, 152, 163, 213, 214, 216, 220, 233, 320
Mount Parnassus, 7, 12, 26, 36–37, 45, 143
Mount Pelion, 180, 192, 199, 203, 208

Mount Vesuvius, 288
Muses, the, 64, 80–81, 135, 203, 319
Mycenae, city of, 90, 137, 138, 141, 143–146, 148, 156, 160, 209, 234–237, 246
Myrrha, 75
Myrtilus, 233–234
Mysia, land of, 184, 185, 209

Nana, 83
Narcissus, 114–117, 130, 320
Nausicaa, 248–249, 320
Naxos, island of, 55, 97
Neleus, King of Pylos, 105–106, 160, 179–180
Nemea, 143
Nemesis, 115, 320
Neoptolemus, 227–228
Nephele, 178
Neptune (see Poseidon)
Nereus, 156, 320
Nessus, 162, 163, 320
Nestor, Old King, 209, 219, 220, 244–246, 320
Night, 3, 81, 320
Niobe, 37–38, 320
Nisus, 293
North Star, 22
North Wind, 185, 187
Numa Pompilius, 300
Numitor, 296, 298, 320
Nycteus, 22, 23
Nysa, 54–55

Ocean, 6, 8, 22, 30, 52, 153, 223, 320
Oceanus, 121, 122
Odysseus, 35, 44, 81, 206–208, 210, 215, 219, 220, 226–228, 243–273, 277, 283, 285, 320

Oedipus, 166, 168–174, 176, 177, 263, 320
Oeneus, King of Calydon, 172
Oenomaus, King of Pisa, 233
Oileus, 209
Olympia, town of, 162, 320
Omphale, Queen of Lydia, 161
Orchomenus, 178
Orestes, 237–240, 242, 320
Orion, 66, 72, 79, 320
Orpheus, 81, 135–136, 140, 181, 186, 197, 261, 320
Orthus, 154, 321
Ortygia, island of, 79
Ostia, 301
Otreus, King of Phrygia, 73
Otus, 31

Palamedes, 207
Palatine hill, 298
Palinurus, 282, 288
Palladium, 25, 228
Pallanteum, 292
Pallas, 94, 293–295, 321
Pan, 50–51, 61, 321
Pandarus, 216
Pandion, King of Athens, 109–110
Pandora, 11, 12, 321
Panic (see Phobus)
Paris, 27, 204–206, 215–217, 226, 227, 274, 278, 321
Parthenon, 78
Parthenopaeus, 173, 175
Pasiphae, Queen, 95, 149, 321
Patroclus, 208, 209, 220–223, 225–226, 321
Pegasus, 103, 104, 321
Peirithous, 98–99, 159, 321
Peleus, 107, 119, 181, 198, 203, 207–209, 220, 226, 321

Pelias, King, 179–182, 199–200, 321

Pelopia, 235, 236

Peloponnesus, 197, 234, 235, 252, 282

Pelops, 227–228, 232–234, 240, 321

Penelope, 206, 207, 232, 243, 244, 247, 249, 262, 267, 269–273, 321

Penthesileia, 47, 226

Pentheus, King of Thrace, 57–58, 321

Perdix, 100

Periphetes (Clubman), 92

Pero, 105–106

Persephone, 8, 63, 64, 67–71, 75, 76, 98, 136, 159, 321

Perses, 76, 89

Perseus, 84–86, 88–90, 101, 137, 321

Persians, 99

Phaeacians, 197, 249–251, 267

Phaethon, 52–53, 321

Phasis River, 191, 194

Pheres, 180

Philammon, 44

Philemon, 128–130, 321

Philoctetes, 163, 209, 211, 227, 321–322

Philomela, 109–113, 322

Philomelus, 67

Philonoe, 104

Phineus, 89, 186–188, 190, 282, 322

Phobus (Panic), 47, 174

Phoebe, 35, 322

Phoenix, 208, 219, 223, 322

Pholus, 146, 162

Phrixus, 178–179, 190

Phrygia, 38, 56, 82, 128

Phylacus, King of Thessaly, 106

Phyleus, 147, 148

Pierus, 81

Pillars of Hercules, 153

Pisa, 233, 234

Pisistratus, 245

Pittheus, King, 91

Pleiades, the, 25, 26, 322

Pluto (see Hades)

Plutus, 67

Po River, 154

Podarces, 161

Pollux, 27, 99, 181, 186, 192, 205, 263, 322

Polybus, King of Corinth, 166, 170, 171

Polydectes, King of Seriphus, 85, 89, 322

Polydorus, 165, 281

Polyhymnia, 80, 322

Polynices, 172–176, 322

Polyphemus, 185, 253–256, 285, 322

Polyxena, 230

Pomona, 132–134, 322

Poseidon (Neptune), 5, 8, 12, 28–32, 37, 46, 77, 89, 91, 94–95, 149, 152–154, 175, 179, 180, 197, 198, 199, 212, 229, 233, 245, 247, 254, 256, 260, 262, 274, 279, 288, 322

Power, 10

Priam, King of Troy, 42, 161, 204, 212, 217, 225–226, 229, 237, 278, 283, 293, 322

Proca, 296

Procne, 109–113, 322

Procris, 79–80, 322

Procrustes, 93

Proetus, 102–104, 107

Prometheus, 8–10, 12, 17, 157, 322

Propontis Sea, 183, 185

Protesilaus, King of Phylace, 212

Proteus, 246, 322

Psyche, 59–64, 322

Pygmalion, 74–75, 322

Pygmies, queen of the, 66

Pylades, 238, 239

Pylos, town of, 104–106, 160, 180, 209, 244, 268, 282

Pyramus, 117–119, 322–323

Pyrenees Mountains, 154

Pyrrha, 12–13, 178, 323

Pythia, the, 44, 323

Python, 35, 37, 323

Remus, 290, 297, 298, 323

Rhea, 6, 66, 77, 323

Rhea Silvia, 296–298, 323

Rhodes, island of, 51

Rhoecus, 107

Rome, 195, 290, 295, 298–300, 302, 303, 305

Romulus, 290, 297–300, 323

Rubicon, 290

Sabine women, 298–299, 323

Sahara Desert, 53

Salmoneus, 14–15, 323

Samothrace, 25, 26

Sarpedon, 152, 323

Saturn (see Cronus)

Satyrs, 64, 323

Scaevola, Gaius Mucius, 302–303, 323

Scamander River, 212, 225

Sciron, 93

Scylla, 121–122, 124, 197, 265, 284, 323

Scyros, island of, 99, 208

Sea, 20, 32, 121, 323

Selene, 134, 323

Semele, 53–54, 58–59, 165, 221, 323

Seriphus, island of, 85, 89

Sestus, city of, 124

Sextus Tarquinius, 304–305

Sibyl, 41–42, 80, 284, 288–289, 323

Sicily, 101, 132, 156, 197, 284, 285, 288

Sicyon, 23, 24, 235, 236

Side, 66

Sidon, 275

Silvius, 290

Sinis (Pine Bender), 92

Sinon, 229, 323

Sinope, 42, 190

Sirens, the, 34, 81, 197, 264–265, 323

Sirius, 72

Sisyphus, King of Corinth, 24–25, 102, 136, 323

Sky, 3–6, 8, 324

Sleep, 33, 120, 221, 222

Solymi people, 103–104, 324

Sparta, 26, 42, 63, 98, 99, 124, 159, 209, 230, 244, 245, 268

Sphinx, the, 167–168, 169, 324

Stheneboea, 102, 104

Sthenelus, 137, 138, 141, 190, 324

Strength, 10

Strife, 203–204, 220, 289, 324

Strophades islands, 282

Stymphalus, town of, 148

Styx (goddess), 10

Styx River, 33, 36, 52, 54, 63, 64, 117, 135, 136, 176, 208,

(*continued*) 289, 324
Syrinx, 50, 324

Taenarum, cave of, 159
Talus, 198–199, 324
Tantalus, 232–233, 242, 324
Taphians, 244
Tarpeia, 299, 324
Tarpeian Rock, 299
Tarquin the Elder, 301
Tarquin the Proud, 304
Tartarus, 3, 6, 7, 29, 49, 76, 289, 324
Taurus, 96
Taygete, 26
Telamon, 25, 181, 209, 218
Telemachus, 207, 243–246, 262, 268–269, 271, 272, 324
Telephus, 209–210
Tenedos, island of, 212, 228
Tereus, King of Thrace, 109–113, 324
Terpsichore, 81, 324
Tethys (see Sea)
Teucer, 281
Thalia, 81, 324
Thamyris, 81
Thasos, island of, 152
Thebes, city of, 20, 22–24, 38, 53, 57–58, 137, 140–142, 164–175, 192
Theia, 51, 79, 324
Themis, 8, 12–13, 37, 240, 324
Theophrane, 31, 324
Theseus, King of Athens, 27, 90–99, 149, 159, 173, 174, 181, 324
Thespius, King, 140
Thessaly, 98, 149, 180, 199
Thetis, 29, 45, 65, 96, 197, 203,

(*continued*) 207–208, 214, 220, 223, 225, 324
Thisbe, 117–119, 325
Thrace, 57, 109, 110, 149, 152, 156, 280–281
Thyestes, 234–237, 325
Thynians, land of the, 186
Tiber River, 154, 155, 284, 288, 290–294, 301–303, 325
Tiphys, 181, 189, 190
Tiresias, 57–58, 66, 114, 138, 169–170, 175, 177, 260, 262, 325
Tiryns, town of, 90, 102, 104, 160
Titans, 5–7, 14, 25, 30, 35, 51, 76, 79, 86, 88, 250, 325
Tithonus, 80, 325
Tityus, 36, 325
Trachis, kingdom of, 119, 162, 163
Triton, 198, 325
Troezen, city of, 91, 92
Trojan War, 27, 47, 161, 208–230, 237, 238, 243, 250–251, 274–280, 292, 293, 305
Tros, 27
Troy, 26, 27, 32, 73, 74, 152, 161, 179, 204–206, 208–230, 237, 274
Tullus Hostilius, 300
Turnus, 291–295, 325
Tydeus, 172, 173, 175
Tyndareus, King of Sparta, 26–27, 206, 209, 237, 325
Typhon, 7, 14, 82, 144, 167, 285, 325
Typhoons, 7
Tyro, 179–180
Tyrrhenian Sea, 154

Ulysses (see Odysseus)
Urania, 81, 325

Venus (see Aphrodite)
Vertumnus, 133–134, 325
Vesta (see Hestia)
Vestal Virgins, 296–297, 325
Vulcan (see Hephaestus)

Wandering Rocks, 197
War, 289

Xanthus River, 283
Xuthus, 43, 44

Zephyrus, 42, 325
Zetes, 181, 185, 187, 325
Zethus, 23–24
Zeus (Jupiter, Jove), 5–12,
    14–27, 29–32, 35, 42, 45–47,
    49, 51, 53–54, 59, 60, 63–67,
    69–71, 73, 75–77, 80–82, 84,
    85, 94, 102–104, 109, 114,
    128–130, 134, 138, 141, 149,
    150, 156, 157, 160, 161, 163,
    164, 175, 176, 178, 181, 185,
    186, 190, 196, 198, 202, 203,
    205, 214, 216, 218, 220–222,
    225, 232, 234, 242, 246, 247,
    254, 258, 266, 268–270, 274,
    279, 282, 286, 292, 294, 325